Letters of George Ade

Edited by Terence Tobin

Purdue University Press
West Lafayette, Indiana

For Shermans

God bless Mommy and Daddy, Missy, Jackie, Jimmy, Tina, Mathew, David and Andrew, Bubby and Papa, Nanie, Grandpa G. G., all my aunts and uncles. And thank you God for letting me have a good day.

First paperback edition, 1998
Published in the United States by Purdue University Press
cover design by David Black

Library of Congress Catalog Number 72-619681
International Standard Book Number 1-55753-147-1
Printed in the United States of America

Letters of George Ade

Acknowledgments

To piece together the mosaic of George Ade through a selection of his letters compares with the happy difficulty of expressing gratitude to all of those who have contributed much to the completion of this edition. I am indebted to Nadine Combs who granted permission to publish the George Ade materials. I wish to thank the libraries and institutions listed in the source section for permission to print Ade correspondence in their collections. The staffs of libraries throughout the country who sent materials to be considered for inclusion have been most helpful. It is, as Ahasuerus noted, inadequate but nevertheless a delight to try to honor particular individuals: special thanks to Olive Cooper; John Funk, president, George Ade Memorial Association; Mary Gibbs, librarian, Purdue University; William Kurfess; John McCutcheon, Jr.; Dr. John Martin, director, Union League Archives; the late Franklin J. Meine; Ruth Reeve; Helen Schroyer, Purdue University Special Collections; Professor Paul Fatout; and Diane Dubiel, assistant university editor, Purdue.

I am grateful to the American Philosophical Society for providing a grant-in-aid which facilitated the completion of this project. For kindnesses, interest, and encouragement, thanks to Professor Jacob Adler, Gladys Allanson, the Harry Lawrences, the Thomas Ohlgrens, Henry Rinehart, the Lloyd Taits, and Professor John S. Tuckey.

To Barbara Mathews, who typed the manuscript, corrected many editorial inconsistencies, and labored cheerfully and efficiently, a special thank you.

Foreword

by Paul Fatout, professor emeritus of English, Purdue University

I remember an occasion more than forty years ago when the guest speaker at a Purdue literary dinner was Elmer Davis, then coming into prominence as a capable writer and reporter. The man who introduced the speaker was George Ade. Although he was on record as saying "I do not choose to make speeches or listen to speeches," he was called upon, as a celebrated citizen, to make and listen to a good many speeches at testimonial dinners and convivial get-togethers.

On the evening I remember he looked the part of the assured performer. Iron-grey hair, still plentiful at sixty-odd, a countenance serious yet benign, distinguished bearing complemented by resplendent dinner jacket, immaculate shirt front and black tie—all gave the impression of a seasoned diner-out accustomed to delivering entertaining sentiments without a qualm. Notwithstanding many public appearances, however, he may have found such assignments irksome, for a slight suggestion of tension implied that he was not entirely at ease.

Evidently uncertain of his ability to extemporize, he read from a manuscript. The voice was the familiar twang of the midwest, flat, without resonance, faintly nasal, though never harsh or loud. The conversational tone was so subdued that the unobtrusive touches of Ade humor, which emerged like casual afterthoughts, took the audience by surprise, delaying the ripple of laughter. In his autobiography he says, "I never wanted to be a comic or tried to be one," but he did not have to try hard to be amusing because the wryly humorous observation came as naturally to him as it did to Kin Hubbard or James Whitcomb Riley or Mark Twain.

The offhand witticisms I have forgotten, but I recall the change in the manner of George Ade when he identified the man he was introducing. His whole attitude quickened into life, and his voice became animated as he made capital of the name "Elmer." Ade was delighted with it, remarked upon the fitness of such a name for a country boy born and bred down there in Dearborn County, Indiana, and rolled the syllables around his tongue like rare old brandy. "Ell-mer," he said slowly, "Ell-mer," and paused to savor the fine homely sound.

The name was in congenial company among the gallery of bucolic characters who populate the Ade stories and fables. On the roster are Jethro, Clarence, Ezry, Bert and Willie, Lutie, Mabel, Effie, Aunt Mehely, Flora and Myrtle, Lem and Minnie, Arvy Harriman, best horseshoe pitcher at the state fair, and Jasper Wilkins, champion checker player of the seventh congressional district. All of them are as indigenous to Indiana as the popping noises of growing corn on hot summer nights, as native as succotash, giblet gravy, and young cabbage slaw smothered in sharp cream dressing.

The brief dinner episode illuminated what seems to me the most engaging Hoosier attribute of George Ade: his lifelong alliance with the mid-country small town and surrounding farmland. In spirit he remained a countryman, no matter how far afield he traveled or to what great metropolis. Of Chicago he says, via Artie

Jethro and Lutie, courtesy of Dover Publications, Inc.

Blanchard, "When you come to know the town it's as common as plowed ground." He was acting in character when, at the age of thirty-eight, famous as the author of stories and plays, he bought property fifteen miles from his Kentland, Indiana, birthplace and built the big house he called Hazelden, which became a home base. He was an intermittent rural squire, still wandering over the world but always returning to be a good neighbor to the entire populace of Newton County, as well as to all others who enjoyed his open-handed hospitality.

In picturing life in the cornbelt of the last century, Ade is superb, none better. We see the village, bogged down in half-frozen winter mud, deep in summer dust, wooden sidewalks, coal-oil lamps, lace curtains and marble-topped parlor tables, high-crowned derby hats, and the feminine bustle, an extraordinary rear extension that looked, he says, "like an aft-deck or rumble seat . . . the most unbelievable item in human history."

We hear of stereopticon lectures, medicine shows, Swiss bell ringers, barnstorming troupes staging "East Lynne," "Lady Audley's Secret," "Ten Nights in a Bar-Room." Elocutionists were in vogue, "tall, brunette ladies of intense personality," who would "collect their victims into halls and goose-pimple them with 'Rum's Maniac' or 'Curfew Shall Not Ring Tonight.'" Popular preachers were "those who could make the most noise while picturing hell-fire. A really successful funeral could be heard a mile away." Among inhabitants are "the elderly man whose side whiskers were a tower of strength in the community," the citizen who was "a marked man because it was rumored that he kept bottled beer on ice," the four Saxby boys, "all of whom can move their ears," and the fellow who wrote to Sears, Roebuck for a package of macaroni seed.

Measured by the computerized frenzy of the late twentieth century, fraught with neuroses and coronaries, the sedate tempo of two or three generations ago may seem to have been sleepy and dull. George Ade did not find it so. "Was existence drab or the hours empty?" he asks. "No indeed! Life was one grand, sweet song."

The remark accurately defines his attitude toward all experience, which he accepted with a tolerance shaded by satirical reflections, more kindly than vicious, on the foibles of mankind. At the age of 73 he said: "It's a great world and most of the people are worth knowing. I am glad to have been among those present."

He knew a large number of the world's people, as this collection of letters attests. Still, as a discriminating man, somewhat reserved, he surely concluded that some were more worth knowing than others.

He was not a joiner, a professional booster, or an uncritical champion of his society. Nevertheless, keen observation, tempered by humor, allowed him to relish the human circus without being depressed by its stupidities or moved to carry the torch of the fanatical reformer. He said he wanted to be known as "a realist with a compact style . . . and the courage to observe human virtues and frailties as they showed on the lens."

He succeeded admirably in achieving these objectives. The charm of George Ade lies in his good-natured contemplation of our species, which he delineates, not with malice or with condescension, but with the gusty enjoyment of a spectator entertained by a continuous variety show.

The compact style—simple, unadorned, often relying on understatement—is capable of telling effects. Consider the quiet deflation of pretense in such remarks as "He traveled with a cowhide bag that must have used up at least one cow," or "He was so democratic he was ready to borrow from the humblest." Of an actor, down on his luck and down-at-heel, the description is: "His attire and bearing suggested the pathos of a summer pavilion with snow on the roof." A comment startlingly appropriate to our troubled times is this one: "The cardboard motto in the dining room said 'Love One Another,' but they were too busy to read."

This Foreword may indicate my admiration for the man as a writer and as a human being thoughtful and generous. The tribute he paid his father and mother by saying that they were "plenty good enough for this speckled world" may be said of him as well. I cherish the memory of that long-ago evening when I saw and heard George Ade.

Contents

Introduction

I GOT THE BREAKS. STARTING FROM NOWHERE IN THE CORN BELT, I HELPED EDIT A COUNTRY WEEKLY, THEN WAS JACK-OF-ALL-DEPARTMENTS ON AN OBSCURE DAILY, SO THAT WHEN I ARRIVED IN A BIG CITY EVERYTHING I TACKLED IN THE LINE OF COLUMN CONDUCTING AND SYNDICATE PEDDLING AND PLAYWRITING HAD TO BRING PROMOTION, BECAUSE I HAD NO SOCIAL STANDING WHICH COULD BE ENDANGERED, NO REPUTATION TO TOSS AWAY AND NO PRIDE WHICH MIGHT SUFFER A SETBACK. EVERYTHING I ACQUIRED HAD TO BE VELVET. YOU CANNOT LOSE YOUR SILVER SPOON IF YOU ARE BROUGHT UP ON PEWTER.

George Ade sent the above night letter to Ashton Stevens in reply to the drama critic's request for an autobiographical sketch to insert in his *Chicago Herald and Examiner* column, April 30, 1930. The night letter to Stevens illustrates the image Ade manifested throughout his career—the down-to-earth, common-sense, breezy character who remains unaffected even after achieving tremendous success. The image made this satirist a most palatable American figure. When a writer points up the foibles of his contemporaries and maintains the doctrine of rugged individualism, and if his observations possess pungency, he often makes enemies. Ade's writing made him more friends than foes, because his satire was general rather than personal and his humanity softened his criticism, making his audience feel he was laughing with them.

Ade's mirth-provoking topics were frequently classic: the city versus the country, the battle of the sexes, pomposity, and materialism have ever been grist for humorists. Ade's manor of presentation of these subjects was particularly suited to him and to his audience. A specialist in irony, parody, and verbal pyrotechnics, he incorporated these devices into pieces which entertained a city and then a nation. Incisive treatment of familiar subjects expressed in natural-sounding language indicated that intelligence lurked ready to back up flippancy. This made his readers wish they had made the writer's suffering remarks, and they often paid him the compliment of appropriating his statements. Feeling "like thirty cents" and "the cold gray dawn of the morning after" became part of the American idiom. The public recognized Ade's objective presentations of the ordinary as true, but his genial irreverence economically expressed was new. Ade was a blend of satirist and philosopher, who could entertain and enlighten in a few words which often unveiled pretense but never denuded the reader.

Ade frequently denied that he was a humorist; during his most productive years he considered himself a realist. While a journalist in Chicago, Ade became one of the more astute chroniclers of the daily preoccupations of ordinary people who were living through the "watershed period." In his column, "Stories of the Streets and of the Town," he produced daily reportage and *feuilletons* of a caliber which warranted Edmund Wilson's ranking him with Henry Mayhew. *Chicago Record* columns such as "The Junk-Shops of Canal Street," July 6, 1894, are vivid bits of city history. Ade varied his "Stories of the Streets" with sketches such as "Effie Whittlesy," March 13, 1896. This short story, which William Dean Howells included in his anthology, *The Great Modern American Stories,* 1920, recounts the plight of a hired girl who loses her job because she knew her employer before he could afford servants. This piece encapsules Ade's sentiments about origins:

> ". . . I'd hate to have her go back to Brainerd and report that she met me here in Chicago and I was too stuck up to remember old times and requested her to address me as 'Mister Wallace.' Now, you never lived in a small town."
>
> "No, I never enjoyed that privilege," said Mrs. Wallace dryly.
>
> "Well, it is a privilege in some respects, but it carries certain penalties with it, too. It's very poor schooling for a fellow who wants to be a snob."

As a recorder of the post-fire generation of Chicago, Ade was without peer. He prowled the bustling city, which was comprised of numerous rural transplants too busy with the business of living to establish traditions. Having come from a small town himself, Ade understood his fellow citizens and recorded fragments of their lives with perception bred of fascination. The place he called his workshop was a sprawling town. Its constant change gave the writer ever-fresh concepts. Chicago had a number of other good writers who provided the interchange of ideas. In addition to Ade's "hall bedroom twin," John McCutcheon, his circle in the nineties included

Ray Stannard Baker, James O'Donnell Bennett, Finley Peter Dunne, Eugene Field, Kirk LaShelle, Amy Leslie, Frank Vanderlip, and Brand Whitlock. The period which would become known as the Chicago Renaissance had started, and Ade was a star in the midwest pleiad. As he accurately recorded the city's people and places, he developed a pared-down style suited to his material and his métier. Ade set down his observations simply and realistically. His prose seemed imitable, yet he adorned his sentences with aphoristic home truths which were fashioned with the same precision as the illustrations his closest friend, John McCutcheon, drew to accompany the "Stories of the Streets." In "Il Janitoro," April 2, 1896, Ade observed, "There is nothing so irritates a real enthusiasm as the presence of calm scorn." In *Single Blessedness and Other Observations,* 1922, the bachelor noted, "The more you camp by yourself the more you shrivel." In this book he included the essay, "Advice," which Ade defined as the "cream of all jobs . . . perching on the fence and telling the other fellow how to saw wood."

Ade was influenced by the genteel realism advocated by William Dean Howells; McCutcheon was influenced by the crisp drawings of Charles Dana Gibson. Both Ade and McCutcheon simplified their models and developed styles sufficiently distinctive to be recognizable without signature. Writer and artist collaborated with such skill that selections from the column comprised eight paperback collections of *Stories of the Streets and of the Town* between 1894 and 1900.

The columnist varied his daily output by creating characters who entertained readers because they felt acquainted with the types depicted. *Artie,* 1896, the portrait of a brash office boy, *Pink Marsh,* 1897, a pioneer drawing of an urban Negro, and *Doc' Horne*, 1899, a sensitive rendering of a middle-aged hotel raconteur, all grew out of "Stories of the Streets." Like the McCutcheon drawings which illustrated these books, the concept of profile is sure. There is relatively little shading, however, and the caricatures, while devoid of the grostesqueries of cartoon, fall short of the rounded characters found in novels. Although these gatherings from the columns between hard covers lack the architectonic skill of long fictional works, these near-novels of the nineties brought Ade to the notice of the literary world which recognized his potential as a novelist.

Ade's talent did not lie in the creation of the realistic novel; his forte was recounting the incident. Ade said that he hit upon the fable by accident, but his columns, which frequently consisted of commentary upon human foibles, pointed to his parables. The fable was suited to his temperament, talent, and training. The brief and simple form provided opportunity for satire. Relation of a common occurrence to convey a truth appealed to the journalist. The fable's limitations of probability encapsuled Ade's view of writing and life. Since college days Ade had been more adept at concentrated prose, which contained several memorable lines, than lengthy discourse. His Anglo-Saxon Protestant background of strictly observed rural Sabbaths, and his education, which included large doses of copying pious sayings in notebooks, bred a distaste for the traditional homily, but not for instructing by exposing hypocrisy and uncovering frailty. His agnostic reaction provided the impetus for viewing a near random universe with tragic proclivities. "We are all wisps," said Ade, "and the winds of chance blow in many directions." His shyness, which he masked with dry wit, gave the impulse for comic treatment.

On September 17, 1897, Ade published his first fable in the *Chicago Record.* He reworked this as "The Fable of Sister Mae, Who Did as Well as Could Be Expected." The tale of two sisters, the good, hardworking "Lumpy Dresser" Luella and the slothful, stupid, shapely Mae, possesses the irony of Ade's better parables. Mae's progress in society to "Vogner" concerts enables her to hire her sister as her assistant cook at a raise in pay. This development leads to the moral: "Industry and Perseverance bring a sure Reward." On December 9, 1899, *Fables in Slang* was announced for publication. The collection of secular sermons on the human condition in all its absurdity, each ending with an incongruous moral tag, captured a nation embarking on a new century, seeking different modes of expression, and willing to trade new morals for old. Unlike Ade's previous books, which possessed sufficient local color to puzzle some Eastern seaboard reviewers, *The Fables,* for all their provincialism and "barbarities of language," were immediately popular with a generation which had been nurtured on the fables of McGuffey's readers. The fables were often criticisms of tenets held by an America of small towns, made by a critic who held the village dear. "The Fable of the Unintentional Heroes of Centerville" gently gibes at the ceremonies held to welcome home veterans. "The Fable of How Uncle Brewster Was Too Shifty for the Tempter" recounts the penury responsible for a farmer's remaining virtuous on a trip to the big city. "The Fable of the Honest Money-Maker and the Partner of His Joys, Such As They Were" tells of a rural skinflint who worked his wife to her grave. "The Fable of

What Happened the Night the Men Came to the Women's Club" describes a group out "to cut a seven-foot Swath through English Literature from Beowulf to Bangs."

Ade had learned what made readers laugh during his decade on the Chicago newspapers. The prejudices and penchants of the writer seemed to be those of the nation. The country laughed with Ade at the host of people he invented. Readers knew neighbors just like the village belle, the sissy, the high falootin' preacher, the lady martyr, and the other characters whose likenesses accompanied Ade's sallies. The fine line of realism was supplanted by the heavier strokes of woodcut. The broader comic delineations were immediately recognizable because the writer included only what was necessary. By selection of detail, Ade showed his sensitivity. More important, his decorous fables boasted the magic element humorous writers seek—the common touch. The common touch devolves upon the ability to treat familiar subjects in a manner which elicits a similar response from the majority of the audience. For an America in rapid transit from rural to urban, Ade assumed the pose of the man who knows city and country and finds foolishness in both locales. His humorous skepticism which valued horse sense and distrusted intellectualism was healthy. At his best Ade manufactured types found in town and country. The social climber, the luckless suitor, the money grabber were sufficiently universal to be recognized by readers anywhere. If types such as the Bohemian or the phrenologist were outside the realm of the reader's experience, a picture abetted the fable. Illustration of fables had been common practice since the eighteenth century, but no previous fabulist had relied so heavily on graphics. In most of Ade's books pictures are an integral part of the text. His imagery is frequently visual, for the reader must *see* situations in which the characters are placed to relish the absurdity. The types are static but their predictable behavior produces unpredictable consequences. Because the reader does not learn enough about these caricatures to take them seriously, he laughs. Frequently the inability to change is of tragic dimension, but the manner of presentation is comic. Ade's fables illustrate Leontinus' principle that humor is the only test of gravity, and gravity of humor.

The popularity of the fables freed Ade from the grind of producing a daily column, and he began syndicating the short pieces. Between 1900 and 1939, when the last fable appeared, Ade produced over five hundred fables, about half of which were collected in book form. *More Fables,* 1900; *Forty Modern Fables,* 1901; *The*

Girl Proposition, 1902; *People You Know,* 1903; *Breaking Into Society,* 1904; *True Bills,* 1904; *Knocking the Neighbors,* 1912; *Ade's Fables,* 1914, and *Hand-made Fables,* 1920, attest to the viability of Ade's treatment of the form, although the later fables are strained and inferior to the spontaneous creations which first appeared in his *Chicago Record* column. By 1920, when the last collection appeared, Ade had entered the ranks of the select, whose writing the public is preconditioned to consider funny.

While the fabulist was at his zenith, he succeeded in a different branch of comic writing. Ade had been infatuated with the theater since childhood, and after several attempts at writing theatricals, succeeded with *The Sultan of Sulu* in 1902. Oriental fantasies were popular, and Ade's operetta in the Gilbert and Sullivan tradition was more proficient than most of the American offerings of similar inspiration. The satire of McKinley's policy of "benevolent assimilation of the little brown brother" nudged the audience to question the wisdom of imperialistic policies. The plot was no less probable than most operettas at the turn of the century, and Ade's lyrics were more articulate.

In less than a year after *Sultan* opened, Ade rushed another musical, *Peggy from Paris,* which was first performed in 1903. *Peggy,* a Pygmalion–Cinderella plot, contained ingredients such as yokel pageantry and clever vaudeville bits, which Ade did well, but the creation of incident was superior to the overall theatrical product.

The season after *Peggy from Paris* he gave Broadway *The County Chairman,* his first full length hit play without music. This political satire, softened by an 1880s setting, presented a parade of corn-fed citizens who sped through a number of bits which captivated an audience enamored of vaudeville. While theatergoers were applauding *The County Chairman,* Ade's second play of the 1904 season opened. *The College Widow,* which introduced football to the American theater, was the prototype of the Saturday's hero story. Ade's depiction of the campus crowd as fresh, clean-cut, wisecracking adolescents, delectably free of responsibilities, who are concerned with games rather than grades, established the pattern of collegiate comedies and musicals for two generations.

The Sho-Gun was Ade's third offering of the 1904 season. This satire of "benevolent association" derived inspiration not only from the British masters of light opera but from his previous Oriental operetta. The formulas which Ade devised for fabling were sufficiently adroit to admit variations; his prescription for theatricals was not. Authentic atmosphere, some scintillating lines, inspired comic moments, and insertion of variety turns at the expense of pervasive unity may entertain once, but a vaudevillesque formula does not produce lasting comic drama. Ade tried to write too much too fast. He was called the most successful American playwright in 1904. The following season Ade's comedy *The Bad Samaritan* failed dismally. The eye which had seen so accurately, and the ear which had heard the language as it was spoken, did not help *The Bad Samaritan,* for its basic premise was not comic.

Ade continued to turn out comedies for Broadway for the rest of the decade, but *Just Out of College,* 1905; *Artie,* 1907; *Father and the Boys,* 1908; *The Fair Co-Ed,* 1908; *The Old Town,* and *U.S. Minister Bedloe,* 1910, form a long and painful denouement. Ade did shows for the Harlequin Club of Purdue University; he also wrote one-act plays, such as *The Mayor and the Manicure,* 1913, and *Nettie,* 1914, which proved popular with little theater groups, but his career as a dramatist was over.

Theatrical failure was a great disappointment, for Ade loved the glamor of the stage, although his reserve seems to have prevented his full immersion in the Broadway scene. His commercial successes in the theater enabled him to become financially independent, and Ade chose the lifestyle with which he was most comfortable. He delighted in the color of the city, but he sent his money home to Indiana where he invested in land. With the royalties from his plays he built Hazelden Farm, and moved into his Tudor-style mansion in Brook. At the height of his dramatic career he went back to the region which had inspired much of his writing.

In 1903, the year before Ade returned to the village from which he had never really revolted, he published *In Babel,* an assortment of the better short stories which had appeared in his column. H. L. Mencken and other critics praised highly "Effie Whittlesy," "Mr. Payson's Satirical Christmas," and "Why 'Gondola' Was Put Away." Ade took greater than usual pains revising this collection. The result was spare and polished fiction. In 1906 he edited pieces written during several trips to Europe and Africa, and issued *In Pastures New,* a Twainian travel book. The following year *The Slim Princess,* a Graustarkian burlesque, appeared.

Ten books, nine full-length plays, assorted articles, and ephemeral publications constitute an impressive output for a decade. A number of Ade's collections, which came out during the 1900–1910 period, consisted of work which had appeared originally in the 1890s. Most of the stories and fables were published originally in newspapers or magazines; Ade made few changes for their republication in book form. He was a facile writer who seldom revised extensively. The man who frequently finished a fable at a sitting resented the rewrites required in comedy. Ade's bibliography during the first decade of the century is as extensive as the entire corpus of many other authors. His prolific output jeopardized his health on several occasions. His trips abroad during this period were necessary respites from feverish productivity. Ade's writing relied heavily on timing the topical, and he no doubt realized that he was drawing increasingly from the past, and wished to capitalize on his popularity which he knew to be a fickle commodity. He had set *The County Chairman* in the days of his youth. Ade required distance. The future, because it is unknown, did not lend itself to his brand of humor. Treating the present requires familiarity. The country squire became concerned with local affairs which ultimately limited his range, as his opportunities for observation and immediate contact with a variety of subjects lessened.

Ade certainly retained his interest in the national scene; America, however, continued to change at a breakneck pace which was to become a hallmark of the twentieth century. Yet Ade's writing during the second decade followed earlier-established patterns and focused on the past. Ade did become involved in a new medium. He devised captions and advised film makers on the adaptation of slang fables into one-reelers. In the history of film, Ade's early silents are considered more important contributions than his later feature-length talkies, because the fable films represent some of the better attempts to provide family entertainment to quell the reaction against suggestive episodes such as *How Bridget Served the Salad Undressed.* Although Ade was as attracted to the movies as he was to the stage, he became disenchanted with studio scenario changes and business methods.

During the twenties Ade concentrated on philosophical articles and recollections for magazines. In *Single Blessedness and Other Observations,* 1922; *Bang! Bang! A Collection of Stories Intended to Recall Memories of the Nickel Library Days When Boys Were Supermen and Murder a Fine Art,* 1928, and *The Old-time Saloon, Not Wet, Not Dry Just History,* 1931, Ade appealed to readers who had been gay blades rather than to the current crop of sheiks.

With the Depression, demand for Ade's contributions diminished. His primary interest had always been writing, and he satisfied this urge by increasing his correspondence. One of his admirers, Carl Sandburg, observed that writing letters is writing, too. Ade dictated or wrote as many as thirty missives a week, thus making correspondence an avocation which filled the mornings of his later years. He often disclaimed the notion that he was an entertainer, and throughout his life seems to have been uncomfortable on the lecture platform. He belonged to many clubs and organizations, but enjoyed the White Chapel Club, the Forty Club, the Committee of One Hundred and other groups as an observer rather than as a participant. He was interested in politics, and almost certainly could have won a state election during the pre-World War I era, but refused all suggestions that he run for office. Writing was Ade's business.

The author's voluminous correspondence fills some gaps found in his autobiographical articles. Ade's compliance to requests is legendary. Friends, writers, and curious strangers wrote the Hoosier sage, who responded promptly with answers which shed light on numerous subjects, and, at times, the writer himself. But the man who worked furiously to produce copy that conveys an insouciance associated with leisure frequently wore the same mask in letters which he donned for publication. The only satirist who ever founded a country club was a more complex personality than is generally supposed. He was gregarious—on his own terms. He entertained frequently, preferring the role of host to guest. Ade deplored sentimentalism, yet kept a vast amount of memorabilia. He neglected to preserve copies of all of his writings, yet carefully filed menus, souvenir booklets, and programs. During his heyday Ade saved the letters he received from prominent people, but unfortunately preserved few carbons of the missives he sent. He did keep a number of letters which outline ideas for publications which never appeared in print. The writer who put newspaper columns between book covers, then recast the pieces for the movies and even a comic strip, was loath to part with a conception. There are, in his extant letters, comparatively few indications of his more fruitful ideas.

Ade kept copies of letters which contain autobiographical reflections, although he discouraged a number of would-be biographers. He never collected his own series of autobiographical articles, presumably because he felt there would be little market for his memoirs, but more probably because he relished privacy, even as he enjoyed clipping his own press. The author's reactions to his career and his observations about people and events which shaped the twentieth century form a patchwork of popular history and autobiography. George Ade was sufficiently formal in the preponderance of his letters to warrant speculation that he envisioned their eventual publication. The formality, which manifested itself in complete signatures to members of his family and his addressing long-time acquaintances by title, indicates a reticence reminiscent of letter writers born earlier in the Victorian period. Ade's earliest-known quasi-epistolary expressions exemplify strains found in the man and the writer who had a high regard for nineteenth-century tradition, but possessed sufficient individuality to rebel against its more restraining precepts. On April 10, 1878, he inscribed the autograph book of Annie, the sister of his future brother-in-law, Warren T. McCray:

Friend Annie:
Bear in mind.
A little word in kindness spoken,
A motive or a tear,
Has often healed a heart that's broken,
And made a friend sincere
Yours truly

George Ade

On April 1, 1881, the sixteen-year old boy wrote a forthright yet reserved message in Ella Ade's memory book. His penmanship was much the same as that found in his literary manuscripts. The message expresses a viewpoint which would become customary.

Be true to yourself
is the wish of
Your brother
Geo. Ade

No letters have come to light which Ade wrote before his Chicago decade. His college publications, while not addicted to furbelow, do indicate that he went through a stylistic transition during the 1880s. There are other gaps in Ade's papers which point to the author's disposal of certain letters he did not wish to be published. In 1941, Franklin Meine, while editing *Stories of the Streets,* queried Ade about the publication of his letters. He complied by sending Meine a list of his most frequent correspondents, but with typical modesty doubted that many would wish to read his letters.

As with most inveterate letter writers Ade often wrote when he had little to say, and as with many who make their living by being funny, yet deplore the label humorist, he was remarkably serious in much of this writing. Ade used everyday people and events in his publications; his letters also reflect his interest in the commonplace. Often he discussed climate. In his cub reporter days he had written weather reports in sufficiently creative fashion to make Chicagoans read more than the temperature. Forty years later he could still come up with a striking figure on the subject. In a letter to Mildred Gilman, April 25, 1936 (InLP), Ade wrote that "winter continues to linger in the lap of spring until the scandal is really beginning to cause talk." Weather affected Ade's disposition. His dislike of the midwestern winter drove him to Florida to avoid the cold.

At home or away, Ade associated with a male circle which included journalists, politicians, writers, actors, athletes, and businessmen. Franklin P. Adams, Theodore Roosevelt, Grantland Rice, George M. Cohan, Chick Evans, John Hertz and other notables figured in Ade's life and letters. When he received a copy of Elmer Ellis' *Mr. Dooley's America A Life of Peter Finley Dunne,* 1941, Ade marked the names of people he had known or met. He checked 147 entries in the index. He was cordial, helpful, and generous to his many associates, but appears to have been intimate with very few. Reserve impeded relationships which would have given much pleasure to Ade. Detachment produced the laughter which gave much pleasure to the nation. The trait which gave him literary strength circumscribed his private life. Ade rarely expressed his sentiments in letters, and yet there is an underlying sadness, particularly in his wintry serenity, which gives the career of The Man on the Chicago Papers Who Got the Breaks and Made it Big a fabled quality. Ade, like his characters, has often been typed in a phrase—"slick slang slinger," "warmhearted satirist," "literary rotarian." No label can encompass this complex man. The letters trace a multi-faceted career of an uncommon writer interested in the common; they show a man who knew many but was known by few. Frequently his correspondence conceals more than it reveals. Moral: George Ade Wanted It That Way.

Note on the Text

George Ade bequeathed his correspondence to Purdue University. Most of the extant letters are carbon copies which were typed by private secretaries and public stenographers. Because the letters are products of a number of hands from a mechanical standpoint there are discrepancies, such as the method of indicating book titles. These contrarieties have been kept because in his manuscript letters Ade himself was inconsistent in the method of italics. Obvious typographical errors which appear on uncorrected carbons have been silently corrected. Ade was an excellent speller. His notebooks from Kentland grammar school days through college contain few orthographic errors. In manuscript drafts of letters, articles, and stories spelling mistakes are rarer still. Ade tended to underpunctuate. The punctuation of the letters and the capitalization which was a trademark remain as they appear in the copy texts. Ade used a variety of secretaries, private as well as public stenographers. He was not fastidious about typing; therefore, indentation of paragraphs which occurs in most of the letters has been followed throughout the text.

For purposes of unity, each letter written from Ade's country estate bears the heading Hazelden. Ade's printed letterhead read Hazelden Farm as well as Hazelden at various times. The date line appears under the return address throughout the edition for ease of reference.

Each numbered letter which appears in this edition is printed in full. Portions of correspondence are included as notes to illumine Ade's views on persons and events. In the selection of these letters from thousands of pieces of correspondence, the primary concern has been to include letters of biographical, literary, and historical interest. A number of the missives are alike in character and content. At the risk of apparent repetitiousness, some quite similar letters have been included because they indicate Ade's proclivities and point to a life pattern.

The abbreviations for the more frequently cited libraries and collections which contain Ade's letters are as follows:

CLU	University of California at Los Angeles
CLSU	University of Southern California at Los Angeles
CSmH	Henry E. Huntington Memorial Library
DLC	U.S. Library of Congress
IEN	Northwestern University Library
In	Indiana State Library
InLP	Purdue University
InK	George Ade Memorial Association, Kentland, Indiana
InU	Indiana University Library
K	William Fred Kurfess
NN	New York Public Library
NJP	Princeton University Library
VU	University of Virginia

Autobiography of George Ade

My father was John Ade, born at Lewes, England, and his mother's maiden name had been Hazleton. My mother's name was Adaline Bush and my maternal grandmother was an Adair. This wing of the tribe came to Ohio and Kentucky by way of the Carolinas. I am English on my father's side, American-Scotch-Irish on my mother's side and came on the scene youngest of seven children and the youngest of the boys. From the time I could read I had my nose in a book and I lacked enthusiasm for manual labor.

After high school I attended Purdue University, taking the scientific course because I had no ambition to be an engineer or an agriculturist. A star student as a Freshman but wobbly later on and a total loss in Mathematics. In 1887 I received my B.S. from Purdue and the same school gave me an L.H.D. in 1926. Indiana University made me an L.L.D. in 1927, but I am seldom addressed as "Doctor."

Between 1887 and 1890 I did all sorts of work for two LaFayette newspapers and rather enjoyed a brief experience with a company making patent medicines and developing a health resort. Went to Chicago in 1890 and found a job as a reporter on the staff of The Morning News, later known as The Record. By 1892 I was covering outside assignments, such as the Homestead strike in Pennsylvania and the Sullivan–Corbett fight at New Orleans. All during the Columbian Exposition of 1893 I wrote special "human interest" stories about the World's Fair. From the fall of 1893 until 1900 had charge of a two column story department, the illustrations provided by John T. McCutcheon, who had been my friend at Purdue and with whom I roomed for many years. In 1900 I did my last newspaper work and went out to China, Japan and the Phillipines on a visit. Before that I had been to Europe twice and published five books. My early story stuff was intended to be "realistic" and I believed firmly in short words and short sentences. By a queer twist of circumstances I have become known to the general public as a "humorist" and a writer of "slang." I never wanted to be a comic or tried to be one. The playful vernacular and idiomatic talk of the street and the fanciful figures of speech which came out for years under the heading of "Fables in Slang" had no relation whatever to the cryptic language of the underworld or the patois of the criminal element. Always I wrote for the "family trade" and I used no word or phrase which might give offense to mother and the girls or a professor of English.

Having been absurdly in line with the theater for years I found time, after I began syndicating my Fables in 1900, to make a shy attempt at writing for the stage. A talented young Englishman named Alfred Wathall induced me to write the book and verses for a musical satire to be called "The Sultan of Sulu" and produced by a club of aspiring amateurs, Wathall doing the music. Henry Savage, well-known as a manager, induced me to permit him to give our light opera a professional production. It was whipped into shape and made a success. Later on I wrote the dialogue and "lyrics" for musical pieces known as "Peggy from Paris," "The Sho Gun," "The Fair Co-Ed," and "The Old Town." The plays without music which might be worth remembering were "The County Chairman," "The College Widow," "Just Out of College," and "Father and the Boys." I had three failures.

In 1905 I took up a permanent residence at Hazelden Farm near Brook, Indiana, and within fifteen miles of my birth-place. I have been away from this place very few summers since that time but the wanderlust was upon me every autumn. On checking up I learn that I have been to Europe ten times, cruised through the West Indies eleven times, visited China and Japan four times and, also, I have looped the globe twice.

Ever since I settled down in the country I have been involved in activities which did not call my name to the attention of the general public but which have been an interesting part of my career. In 1908 I was a delegate to the Republican National Convention and a member of the Notification Committee. Mr. Taft opened his campaign on my home grounds at Hazelden. Four campaigns later (1924) Gen. Dawes closed his speaking tour at Hazelden.

In 1910 I was elected Grand Consul of the Sigma Chi college fraternity and gave most of my time for two years to an effort to arouse and organize the "brothers." During the World War I was a member of the Indiana State Council of Defense, directing publicity. From 1913 to the present time (1933) I have promoted the Hazelden Country Club which has attractive buildings and a good golf course adjoining my home. Ten years ago David Ross, a worthy graduate of Purdue and now President of the Board of Trustees, invited me to go with him on an enterprise which involved the purchase of sixty-five acres of land, the incorporating of the Ross-Ade stadium, high up on a majestic hill overlooking the campus and the Wabash Valley. It was not a million-dollar extravagance. A glacial drift, some time ago, did most of the excavating. It seats 25,000 people and is almost a replica of the stadium at Athens. Purdue began to climb toward Big Ten ascendancy on the day we dedicated the stadium.

For quite a number of years I paid more attention to Purdue and various activities in my home state than I did to writing for the magazines.

I have done a number of short plays which have been played many times: "Mrs. Peckham's Carouse," "Marse Covington," "The Mayor and the Manicure," and "Nettie." The moving pictures for which I wrote the stories include "Back Home and Broke" and "Our Leading Citizen." I wrote others, but by the time they arrived on the screen they bore no resemblance to what I had turned in at the studios.

I am a bachelor but I prefer to live in my own home. My enthusiasms include golf, travel, horse-racing and the spoken drama. My antipathies are social show-offs, bigots on religion, fanatics on total abstinence, and all persons who take themselves seriously. I read all the periodicals, sober and frivolous, sacred and profane, and try to know what is going on in the world. I have card-index memory for the words and music of old hymns, old popular songs and old "numbers" from the light operas of day before yesterday. I love to put on big parties or celebrations and see a throng of people having a good time.

As I have a certain rating as an author, perhaps I should mention that the books number twenty, not counting some eight or ten published plays. Those not containing Fables may be listed as follows: ARTIE, PINK MARSH, DOC HORNE, IN PASTURES NEW, THE SLIM PRINCESS, SINGLE BLESSEDNESS AND OTHER OBSERVATIONS, BANG! BANG!, and THE OLD-TIME SALOON.

I nearly forgot to say that I am a member of the National Institute of Arts and Letters and on the Executive Committee of the Authors Guild, and, under an alphabetical arrangement, my name was first on the list of those selected to direct the efforts of the Association for the Repeal of the Eighteenth Amendment. I belong to no secret orders and I do not choose to make speeches or listen to speeches.

Ade wrote Stanley J. Kunitz, March 30, 1933 (InLP); that this sketch was "the hardest writing job that I ever tackled and I am in great doubt what to say about myself."

Ade's autobiography appeared in abridged form in Authors Today and Yesterday. *ed. Stanley J. Kunitz (New York: 1933), pp. 8–9, and in* Twentieth Century Authors. *eds. Stanley J. Kunitz and Howard Haycraft (New York: 1942), pp. 8–9. Ade had the complete text privately printed:* Personal Recollections of John Ade Autobiography of George Ade *(n.p.: n.d.).*

FABLES IN SLANG

by

GEORGE ADE

ILLUSTRATED

by

CLYDE J. NEWMAN

PUBLISHED BY
HERBERT S. STONE
AND COMPANY
CHICAGO & NEW YORK
M D C C C C

Title page, first edition, 1899

1894-1910

This collection of George Ade's correspondence begins in the gay nineties, when the journalist was bustling around Chicago to garner copy for his column. As the twentieth century dawned with exuberance and big beginnings Ade was bringing out successful books. It was a decade of national optimism and self-confident innocence. Albert Beveridge remarked that Americans were "trustees of the world's progress." Ade as a popular author and playwright reflects this spirit. He had progressed from a reporter to the toast of Broadway. While enjoying the limelight Ade returned to his native soil to follow the rhythm of planting and harvesting. His letters indicate that he was interested not only in accruing royalties but in helping the local postmaster. The tall, spare, dapper writer who was in great demand chose the life of a gentleman farmer. After sojourns in London, Pasadena, or Benares, he returned to the land which continually provided him with inspiration—Indiana.

1 TO JAMES WHITCOMB RILEY

Chicago [Illinois]
Sept. 20, 1894

Dear Sir:

The inclosed explains itself and in extenuation I would say:

In August 1893 I made my first and only attempt at dialect stanzas. The thing was done anonymously and the *Chicago Record*, with which I have been connected for several years, assumed the responsibility. A year later the lines re-appeared in various eastern publications, with the dialect altered to suit the New York conception. Proper credit was, in each case, given to the *Chicago Record*. Now comes the St. Louis Republic and prints the stuff, omitting one line, reading proof on "Peru" and otherwise embellishing to the extent of printing your name at the bottom. I have written the *Republic* requesting that a correction be made and that the *Chicago Record* be forced to acknowledge the parental relation.

It has been ten years since I met you. I was then attending Purdue University at La Fayette and the ambition to do something in dialect, which ambition has destroyed some of the best schoolteachers in my native state, had not come to me. When it did come, it remained but a day. I was delivered of the "brakeman" stuff and went back to writing world's fair specials. Charles E. Wilson, Booth Tarkington, Maurice Butler and some other good people whom I know will testify that I meant no harm to you when I wrote those rhymeless verses and then hid behind the name of the *Chicago Record*. I cast all blame on the exchange editor in St. Louis.

If you have found occasion to deny the authorship of the lines, or if you now choose to do them the honor of casting them off, my request is that you do not incidentally criticize. They have suffered enough already and the author is not in the business. He is writing "Stories of the Streets and of the Town" in the *Record* and there is testimony to the effect that they are altogether prosy.

Believe me to be your sincere admirer.

Truly &c.
George Ade

InU

An altered version of Ade's poem, "Wayside Ambition," appeared as the work of James Whitcomb Riley under the title "To be a Brakeman," in the St. Louis Republic, September 20, 1894.

Ade included "Wayside Ambition" in his Verses and Jingles, 1911.

2 ☙ TO JOHN T. MC CUTCHEON

Chicago, [Illinois]
Jan—1898

My Dear Mac—

Your letter of this morning was a surprise, as we had supposed that you were out on the bounding billows by this time. Hope you will get away next week. There is a report here that you were seen at Indianapolis last Monday. How about it?

Your mother and Jessie [McCutcheon] left on Tuesday. On Wednesday I moved to 113 Cass St. and took up with Drury Underwood. The place is a quiet and imminently respectable boarding house, although it has the size & the conveniences of a hotel. I like it very much. Ben [McCutcheon] is at the Grenada [Hotel] and I am inclined to believe he will remain there.

The stories & cartoons provide the same old grind. [Carl] Saska is doing quite well, especially with the cartoons. He is not a good illustrator, principally regarding house interiors and women's clothes.

This evening I am going to [Roswell] Field's. They have their 12th night celebration rather early this year. I hope to get away without breaking any furniture. Have not seen the [William] Camps or [Orson C.] Wells since you left—Was at home for Christmas.

I have a horrible confession to make on the McCrea testimonial. Could not get the doggerel to suit me in time to get it to them for Christmas so I have been compelled to make it a New Year gift.

No mail for you that I can find. Everybody has given you up for gone. Wire me just before you sail. Also, when you send back letters to your mother or someone else, cant you have them forwarded so I can answer questions?

My regards to [Edward] Harden.

Wish you a pleasant voyage.

Truly &c.
George Ade

Courtesy John T. McCutcheon, Jr.

Ade and John McCutcheon shared a hall bedroom in a rooming house in Peck Court, 1890–c.1893. McCutcheon describes this lodging in Notes and Reminiscences, *(Chicago: 1940), pp. 39–44. They then shared a room on LaSalle Avenue with newspaperman Charles Rhodes. From here the team moved, c.1895, to "The Commune," a Chestnut Street boarding-house where other journalists lived. Ade and McCutcheon moved from Chestnut Street to the Grenada Hotel on Ohio Street. When McCutcheon left with Ed Harden to cover the Battle of Manila, Ade shared expenses with another newspaper man, Drury Underwood, in the Cass Street boardinghouse. By the time McCutcheon returned home from the Philippines in 1900, Ade was living at the Chicago Athletic Club, where he stayed until he moved to Brook in 1904.*

Ade wrote Mildred Ryan Beatty, July 18, 1931 (InLP), that he lived in the Shoemaker house in Highland Park, Illinois, during the summer of 1903. There he wrote The County Chairman.

Carl Saska was assigned to illustrate Ade's column when McCutcheon went on his assignment abroad.

John McCutcheon, Drawn From Memory *(Indianapolis: 1940), p. 81, contains a photo of a Twelfth Night party at the home of Roswell Field, Eugene Field's brother.*

3 TO JESSIE MC CUTCHEON

Chicago [Illinois]
Nov. 16–1899.

My Dear Jessie:

Your letter came to me while I was in the sunny south. When I came home and walked into my transformed apartment I understood your reference to decorating. Certainly the room has been greatly improved. I walk softly across the floor now for fear that I will "joggle" down one of the canes and not be able to hang it up again—Ben [McCutcheon] and Mr. Casey of the Record will be in La Fayette on Saturday to see the football game and I should like very much to accompany them but I am due to attend a dinner at the Athletic Club. You may be aware that Grand Opera is now raging in Chicago. The engagement will continue for two weeks after this and if you find it possible to come up during the season I will promise you a couple nights of it. That is about as much as I can stand at one time. John [McCutcheon] wrote a long letter from Yokohama, which came last week. He was about to start for Manila. Trumbull White of the Record, who has just returned from a trip around the world, saw John in Japan and spent an afternoon with him. He said John was well and quite contented to remain in the Philippines until the close of the war. On Monday I forwarded a Christmas present of an ascot tie and a scarf pin. The tie was the best to be had in Chicago and the pin was of solid gold, a sort of unicorn design with pearls in it. I know that John has a weakness for swell cravats and [illegible] scarf pins. You may be interested to know that the "Fables in Slang" has proved a success beyond all reasonable expectations. It promises to outsell "Artie" three to one. [Herbert S.] Stone [and Co.] cannot get them out rapidly enough to fill the orders. All of which is very satisfying. Remember me to your mother and to George [Barr McCutcheon] and let me thank you for your valuable services as a house decorator.

Very sincerely,
George Ade

InLP

John McCutcheon was one of three reporters on location for the battle of Manila. See McCutcheon, Drawn from Memory, *p. 104–16.*

Trumbull (Butch) White was a reporter and later editor of the Chicago Record.

4 TO FRANK HOLME

Chicago [Illinois]
May 11, 1901.

My Dear Frank:—

The Fable for next week will be about the four Men who sit down to play Poker for just one Hour. You can imagine the rest. One gets behind and doesn't want to quit. Another is way ahead of the game and does not dare to pull out so they prolong the game and double up on the Jack-pots and every one gets sore and tired and the Man that was ahead gets bumped &c—a typical poker game, that is all. You could make three pictures of characteristic attitudes in poker-playing—say one of the offensive winner, another of the man who is down to his last chip and sore and another of old crafty that plays his hands close to his Bosom. It is probable that I will not get the Fable to you before I send it to [R. H.] Russell. If not you can send the Pictures the latter part of next week. I had a letter from Mac [John McCutcheon] this morning. Russell says he is going to get out a limited edition of the Fables next fall—5 a throw with an autograph and a picture thrown in. We will declare ourselves in and get a copy. Next week I am going down to my old home at Kentland, Indiana to attend my parents' golden wedding celebration so if you want to get any word to me you had better write so that I will receive it by Wednesday of next week. Remember me to the comrades.

With best wishes, Yours very truly,
George Ade

CLU

1901

R. H. Russell published Forty Modern Fables, *1901.*

Ade wrote Vause W. Marshall, a rare book collector, June 3, 1939 (West Virginia State Library):

> Early in 1891, I escorted John McCutcheon to Asheville, North Carolina to enable him to recover from pneumonia. While I was in Asheville, Frank Holme came there to remain for a while, hoping that the altitude might help him to fight a tubercular condition. At that time, I was syndicating my Fables and I made an arrangement with the agency handling my stuff to use one of Frank's pictures with every release. He received rather good pay for his pictures and I was glad to help him. He was full of courage and as happy-go-lucky as ever, although evidently a sick man. Later he went to Arizona and it was out there that he produced the crude copies of the Strenuous Lad's Library, printed in a country print shop with old type and the wood engravings carved out by himself.

5 ❧ TO ROBERT UNDERWOOD JOHNSON

Chicago [Illinois]
Nov. 21, 1901

Dear Mr. Johnson:

I have been casting about for some material that will prove a pleasing substitute for the stuff which you have in your office. I am thoroughly tired of the fable style of narrative and shall do my best to get up something entirely different and possibly little more worthy. What do you think of the idea of a story dealing with the experiences of the Homely Politician of some inland State who is plucked out of his backwoods home and made a consul in some town where he is compelled to mingle with the artificial society of the old world and what this society thinks of him and what he thinks of it? While on a business trip to Europe, three years ago, I visited about 30 of our consuls and of course I know the small town life of the middle West and so I think I can bring some knowledge to the subject. It will be a story necessarily humorous because of the facts of the situation and it might be an indirect criticism of our consular system but it would be particularly an effort to show that the man who is absolutely good and first-class in a country town is a very sad misfit in the consular service. If this brief suggestion of an outline appeals to you I shall go ahead and work on a story of three thousand words or more and submit it to you.

I am, with best wishes,

Dictated Yours truly,
InU George Ade

Ade used this idea, which he submitted to Robert Underwood Johnson, associate editor of Century Magazine, *in "The Story of What Happened to an American Consul,"* Chicago Sunday Tribune, *May 13, 1906, which became Chapter IX of his travel book,* In Pastures New, *1906.*

6 TO FRANK HOLME

Chicago [Illinois]
June 25 [1902]

My Dear Frank:

I am afraid that I have been insisting too strenuously on the wood-cut style. [R. H.] Russell wants a change by way of experiment and to satisfy a request from the Boston Globe so I am going to ask you this week to make three with a black border and a bold heavy style. Make them slightly old-fashioned and not too comic. I shall still insist on the wood-cut pictures going into the book, particularly if we can get the same effects that we got in some of the first you made.

This week, however, change your style and make something more modern and catchy and we will see what Russell thinks of them.

The Fable is to be about the family that tackles the Dollar Excursion given by the Steam Fitters' Union. A man and his wife and two children go on one of these humble railroad trips out to a country grove where they have the usual picnic experiences, a chestnut topic but perhaps I may be able to dress it up in a new way. I want one picture of the family with baskets &c on the way to the train. Another picture may show the Working Lad doing a dreamy waltz with his Girl, heads together and clinched &c. There may be a picnic background. A third picture may represent the "grove," a few lonesome trees, a pavilion, a hot sun overhead and one or two buildings. Use your judgment on this and if you happen to think of some other characteristic feature of the Sunday picnic that will fit in make it. If you can mail these by Saturday or Sunday it will be time enough. When you mail them request Russell to let you know whether or not he likes them better than the wood-cuts.

Mac [John McCutcheon] is here, as well as ever. Remember me to the colony.

Sincerely,
George Ade

CSmH

7 TO FRED HILD

Chicago [Illinois]
8th August, 1902

My dear Fred:—

Perhaps you have heard something of the scheme originated by Kirke Le Shelle, of New York, to organize the Bandar-Log Press, which Frank Holme has been running in a small way on his own account.

Holme's friends have agreed to subscribe for shares of stock and send Frank to Arizona, where he may get out his little books and at the same time recover his health. The shares of stock cost $25.00 each, and we want you to take one share if you can do so. We want Holme to start to Arizona right away, as the doctors advise him that it is necessary. We are going to put the Bandar-Log Press on a business basis and every stock holder will get a copy of the books, which are to be issued four (4) a year, and also will get his share of any profit that may accrue. John McCutcheon and I have charge of the Chicago subscription list, and we shall have prospectuses out in a few days. In the meantime, if you are disposed to take a share of stock, please send a cheque for $25.00 to Kirke Le Shelle, Knickerbocker Theatre Building, New York City.

Very truly yours,
George Ade

CLU

Fred Hild was the city librarian of the Chicago Public Library. Ade wrote Frank C. Lockwood, May 25, 1927 (CSmH):

> Frank Holme was a very good black and white artist who had done both newspaper and magazine work. Along about 1902 he was in Arizona trying to save his lungs. While out there he issued the little books of the Bandar Log Press, carving the wood cut illustrations himself and borrowing the type from a local newspaper office. The name "Bandar Log" was borrowed from [Rudyard] Kipling. I [illegible]

> a few copies of my own stories done by Frank in Arizona. Since starting to dictate this letter I have dug up these little books and find that they were printed at the office of "El Progresso," Phoenix during the summer and autumn of 1903.

See Edwin B. Hill, More Than a Memory *(Ysleta, Texas: 1936). This pamphlet contains a memoir of Frank Holme and the Bandar Log Press.*

8 TO R. H. RUSSELL

Chicago, Illinois
[Spring? 1903]

Dear Mr. Russell:

I am sending the Sultan half-tone proofs to you direct because I want to make a request or two in connection with illustrating of the book. I notice that Miss [Gertrude] Quinlan (Chiquita) does not figure in any of the pictures. As you know she is the manager's pet. I have protested against her appearance in the piece and [Henry] Savage knows that I do not like her work. If her picture is omitted from the book, he will think that I am deliberately trying to slight her and get back at him. We must put her in, whether she ornaments the work or not. Also I wish you would get in the soldiers somewhere, either as volunteers or Imperial Guards. If possible use three or four additional pictures and bring in the other principals. These actors are given to small jealousies and if any are left out, there will be weeping, wailing and gnashing of teeth. Rush the proofs.

Sincerely,
George Ade

VU

Colonel Henry Savage produced The Sultan of Sulu. *Ade and Savage were at odds over script revisions. Ade revised the operetta several times. He reduced the script from three acts to two, kept twenty-two of forty-six songs at the insistence of Savage. Later Ade and Savage quarreled over royalties. Ade wrote L. C. Wiswell of the Savage organization, November 30, 1915 (InLP), indicating that Savage was unfair in his royalty demands. Ade wrote Daniel L. Brown, September 15, 1930 (InLP):*

> Mr. Savage showed a disposition to claim one-half of all royalties which might come to me from any source on account of the old plays, I indicated a willingness to establish a flat rate of one-third to him for all of the old plays but that was based upon the assump-

tion that he was going to do some business with the old plays but he never turned up any business. Every one of the old pictures ever sold was sold by me or through my agents and Mr. Savage or the Savage office turned up to claim a percentage without even turning over a hand. I have read the contracts carefully and I am convinced, and my opinion is backed up by legal authorities, that I absolutely own all of the rights in all of the old plays except possibly THE SULTAN OF SULU and PEGGY FROM PARIS.

The College Widow *advertising card*

9 TO JAN WHEELOCK

Chicago, [Illinois]
February 26, 1904

My dear Wheelock:—

As I wired you last night, I cannot give any definite assurances as to the time when I can have the piece finished until I know how much re-writing will have to be done on the musical piece we are bringing out; we never can tell until after the first performance.

I have a letter from Miss [Elisabeth] Marbury in which she says she has been talking with you in regard to getting an offer from a manager. I suggest that we do not become involved in any misunderstanding regarding Miss Marbury. I have no doubt that she is a very clever woman and that her services would be of great value to an author seeking to establish connections with managers but I cannot see that her services would be of any value to one who is seeking to avoid connections with managers; in other words, I have had more offers than I wish to entertain and have had several offers for the piece which I mentioned to you, the terms being fully as liberal as those suggested by Miss Marbury. There was nothing in my conversation with her which would justify her in believing that I wished her to approach any managers in my behalf and I have written Mr. Charles Frohman to that effect. As I told you, I am not at all over-anxious to do any play writing for a long time to come and it would be nonsense for me to give Miss Marbury 10% of my royalties in order to induce her to make contracts for me when I don't want the contracts made. All that I want is to be let alone. You are the only man on earth that I have promised to talk business with at all for the next year. Because of my personal esteem for you and my faith in your abilities, I did tell you that I would take up with your manager a proposition in regard to the piece we have discussed.

Candidly, and without any reflection on our very clever friend I don't think we need the intervention of Miss Marbury. She would claim 10% of all the royalties that may ever come to me and I cannot figure out how she would be entitled to them since I already have two or three offers for the piece, some of them being much more liberal than those she mentioned in her letter. It is not so much a matter of terms with me as being associated with people in whom I have confidence and with whom I can work in sympathy.

There is no need of having any smash-up with Miss Marbury;

simply let her know that I will be very busy on other matters for a time and then later on, if we decide to come down to cases with Mr. Frohman or any one else, we can do so without referring the matter to her.

With best wishes,
George Ade

InLP

While Ade was working on The Sho-Gun *Elizabeth Marbury, the theatrical agent, wrote him about handling* The College Widow *and* The County Chairman. *Ade wrote Miss Marbury, February 25 and 29, 1904 (InLP), emphatically stating his unwillingness to employ an agent. He wrote Charles Dillingham, the theatrical manager, February 25, 1904 (InLP), explaining his agreement with Jan Wheelock and asked Dillingham to inform Charles Frohman, the producer, of the "little three-act piece"* (The Bad Samaritan) *he had outlined and intended as a vehicle for Wheelock.*

10 TO HERBERT S. STONE & CO.

Hazelden
Brook, Indiana
October 1, 1904.

Gentlemen:—

I am informed that a literary agent in New York has been recently offering to various publishers all the publication rights in the five books of mine that you have got out. I have not my contract at hand, but I thought we had in our revised contract covering all of the books a clause concerning the transfer of publication rights.

I judge from your recent reports that all of these books have had their day but I should not like to see the publication rights hawked about, and if you are anxious to dispose of them I am willing to talk business with you, not because I expect to go into the publishing business myself but because I should like to protect the future of these books in case I should ever want to revise the stuff and bring a number of my books out in uniform edition.

I shall be glad to hear from you at once concerning your intentions in regard to the books and I will entertain any reasonable proposition, but I do not think that under our present contract you have a right to transfer these books to publishers who will get them out in cheap form and from whom I may possibly have no guarantee of protection. I most certainly will not consent to any reduction of the royalties and I suggest that in fairness to all persons concerned you do not transfer these publication rights until you are sure that you have the legal right under our present contract.

For instance we have in our contract a clause declaring that the agreement shall be null and void if payments are not made at the time specified. This clause has been violated by you but I have not taken advantage of it to nullify the contract but shall do so if necessary to protect my rights.

Under the circumstances I think the reasonable thing to do would be to compromise and allow me to take back these books since you no longer find them salable. I shall be glad to hear from you regarding your views of the matter.

Yours truly,
George Ade

InLP

Herbert S. Stone and Co. had published Artie, Pink Marsh, Doc' Horne, Fables in Slang, *and* More Fables.

11 ❧ TO JOHN ADE

Hazelden
Brook, Indiana
May 17, 1905.

Dear Father:—

I am enclosing a letter from Mr. Hotchkiss of Chicago in regard to the naming of the new station on the railroad. If you don't wish to be immortalized now is your time to object.

I heard that he was going to glorify me by giving my name to the station, so I wrote to him and begged him not to do so. I suggested, also, the name of Bluford. I did not request him to name the station Ade, but I did say that if any one in our family was to get any credit here in Newton County it should be you on account of your long association with Newton County affairs.

If, for any reason, you prefer not to have this name used perhaps you had better communicate with Mr. Hotchkiss. Personally I don't see why you should object.

Am coming over to see you in a day or two,—as soon as the weather and the roads will permit.

Give my love to all.

Enc. Sincerely,
InLP George Ade

12 ❧ TO ALICE FISCHER HARCOURT

[New York, New York]
November 4, 1905

My Dear Mrs. Harcourt:

I have received your very kind invitation and am wondering if I could muster the courage to attend your Club Meeting and be publically unveiled. The fact is I am heading for Indiana on Monday, so that I may help save the country on Tuesday. For a Hoosier not to vote is almost a crime. So I am going back to retain my standing.

I shall be in N. Y. occasionally during the winter, and hope that some day we shall meet.

Thank you very much for remembering me, with such a cordial invitation.

I am, with best wishes,

Sincerely yours,
Museum of City of New York George Ade

Alice Fischer (Mrs. William Harcourt) was born in Indiana. During the 1890s this actress did melodramatic parts. By the 1900s she was playing comic roles.

13 ❧ TO E. A. BRADEN

Brook, Ind.
Nov. 7, 1905

THE TITLE: I quite agree with Mr. [Henry] Savage, from whom I had a letter yesterday, that it will be advisable to change the name and have in mind several titles which I will put down here for your consideration:

Fifty-two years young.
The Old Boy.
The Unhappy Millionaire.
Uncle Ike.
Uncle Ben.
Uncle Ben's Money.
Second Time on Earth. (A musical piece by this title has been produced.)
The Elderly Boy.

Of these titles I rather fancy either one of the first two. I believe it has been the rule that the plays with money mentioned in the title have never appealed strongly to the public whereas the idea of the old fellow becoming a boy again is always popular. THE OLD BOY would be a very short, simple and catchy title; probably it has been registered but I don't think it has been used. Whichever title you decide to use I would announce that the play will be "A Farcical Play with Music."

MUSIC: My principal idea in suggesting the use of music was to permit [Raymond] Hitch[cock] to retain the songs which, I understand, went exceeding well in DAWSON. So far as I have outlined the stuff in my mind I have made no provision for any elaborate or conventional musical numbers. My idea was to open the piece with a number of young people playing country games on the lawn in front of the hotel and to have incidental music continue throughout these games and perhaps have them introduce one or two of the old-fashioned singing games which went so well in the SHO-GUN, but of course not repeating anything that we have done before. Incidental to the first act I want UNCLE IKE to have an old fashioned singing school in which he lines off the songs to the young people and they sing it after him. This is the old fashioned way of singing, and I never have seen it done on the stage. Also he may have organized a very bad male quartette which attempts a selection and breaks down. I don't want any trained voices or any serious vocal treatment, but just a little incident. I think his best song should be introduced in the first act also so that the second act will be given over to rapid, farcical complications. I think I have a scheme now for leading up to an effective climax. In brief, let us not struggle to find places for the introduction of music and let us not use any unless we are sure that it will be effective. I think that Hitch wants to retain some of the music that he used in DAWSON and there will be no difficulty in finding spots for it.

THE CAST: This will be radically changed and our effort will be to eliminate as many of the elderly characters as possible and try to pervade the whole piece with the spirit of youth the same as in THE WIDOW. We will retain some of the characters that we used before but they will not be of the same relative importance. For instance, the young fellow who loves JESSIE will now be the lawyer employed by UNCLE IKE to fight the nephew for possession of the property, thus giving the part a dramatic interest that it did not have before. I will enumerate the principal parts as I now have them in mind with various suggestions concerning them and I hope you can get enough of an idea to permit you to cast the piece. Some of these names may be changed, but I will give you merely a suggestion of characters.

UNCLE IKE (or UNCLE BEN): This will be Hitchcock's part and we will try to give him most of the fat.

ALONZE, [Alonzo?] the nephew: This part will be much the same in character as it was before although possibly not of so much relative importance.

HIGGINS: Proprietor of the hotel—very much the same as before, as I think it is a good part if we elaborate the interest in the struggle between HIGGINS and UNCLE IKE to capture the housekeeper. The rivalry between them should be more probable and interesting as Hitchcock will play UNCLE IKE as a younger man.

JACK WESTON, returned from the Golden West. This is a young mining expert who owns a gold mine out west and is trying to raise money to work it. UNCLE IKE backs the scheme heavily thinking it is a good way in which to squander the money before the nephew can get hold of it. At the end of the second act when all of Uncle Ike's reckless speculation suddenly turns in his favor and make[s] him twice as rich as he was before the young miner returns from the west with a barrel of money and in the last act captures one of the village girls who has been waiting for him.

(The parts of GALLOWAY, McGEE, JONES and GARGELINI will be cut out absolutely.)

SPILLERS: This part will be retained much the same as before except that the love interest between him and the village belle will be elaborated and as a greater period of time elapses between the first and last acts his slangy scene in the last act will be more consistent and probable.

THOMAS GILROY WEBB, the young lawyer in love with JESSIE GRIDLEY: This part will be entirely rebuilt and will be an energetic and oratorical young lawyer who is striving to capture

JESSIE and at the same time is compelled to turn her parents out of doors.

PURKEY, the Notary Public. I think we can retain this part and perhaps make a little something out of it. The same is true of HENRY, the boy who works in the livery barn.

MR. FOX, of the detective agency. I believe his pantomime bit in the second act can be made very effective with Hitchcock and it will be retained.

THE CHAUFFEUR: I have been told by Mr. [Charles] Frohman and others who saw the piece that this is the best bit in the piece and it will be retained.

The Waiter, Bell-Boy and other small bits can be easily handled.

THE WOMEN.

MISS WHEATLEY, housekeeper. I have great faith in this part if it is played as a strong-minded character woman. It will be entirely changed and must be played as a vigorous matronly woman of thirty-five or so. I believe it is possible to have a very effective comedy love interest between Hitchcock and this woman, whose principal reason for refusing to marry him is the fact that he has money and she is afraid that people will say that she married for money. This will give IKE an excuse for blowing in his capital.

MRS. ALONZO: I think it will be necessary to retain this part although it was not very effective before. It will not be an important part but will help to give variety to the characterization.

JESSIE: This part should be improved by the development of a dramatic interest in her love affair with young WEBB.

BELLE HINKLE: This part will be of much the same character as before but probably can be made more effective by making it more positively a low comedy character.

BESSIE PUTNAM: This will be the girl with whom the young miner is in love and to whom he becomes reconciled after his return from the west.

BITS: About a half dozen attractive girls who in the first act are at the village lawn party. At the end of the first act UNCLE IKE takes them under his wing to give them a seminary education in the city. In the second act (three months later) they have blossomed out as seaside belles with city manners and in the last act they are back at the old town dazzling the natives.

(NOTE: I am in doubt regarding the part of LAURA who becomes the French Maid. The part was played in such an exaggerated and grotesque manner that it was absolutely impossible so I think I will play safe and cut it out entirely.)

GENERAL SUGGESTIONS REGARDING CAST AND EXTRA PEOPLE

So far as I am concerned I want no large crowd, no varigated costumes and no attempt at spectacular effects. Even in the second act where we will have all of our people at the seashore I want simply light colored summery costumes. I want the piece to depend upon the new situations which we introduce, upon the lines and upon character drawings, and not to attempt anything suggestive of spectacle or extravaganza. In other words, if we haven't got the goods we cannot help it a particle by making it a cumbersome or expensive production.

THE SCENERY: There will be three sets. The first scene will be laid at New Boston in the spring, the second scene will be laid at the seashore three months later and the third will be back at New Boston in the autumn. For the first scene we can use the present set, except that I would like more stage room, take out the pumpkin patch and the corn fields up stage and give us more elbow-room. Make it more wide and free and open the same as the first act of THE WIDOW or the second act of THE CHAIRMAN. I think this can be done with very little trouble. Put some rustic benches at stage L built around the trees or put under the trees so that UNCLE IKE can group the young people in front of him when he is conducting his old-fashioned singing-school. For the second act I want a semi-interior at the seashore. At R and L are the entrances to the seaside hotel which may be in light colors and not fancy. Overhead, sheltering this half-enclosed court, a striped awning. At the rear opening out from this semi-interior is the long promenade or board walk leading off right and left and beyond that the open sea. I don't want anything gorgeous or spectacular about the set, but would like to have it in good taste suggestive of first class establishments and harmonizing in tone and decorative effect with the simple summery costumes that will be worn in this act. The third scene will be once more in New Boston. I thought that in THE SAMARITAN we could get a finer result by showing the first scene with autumn effects in the trees and the vegetation. For some reason we failed to get this effect; there seemed to be no striking contrast between the first set and the last and therefore if it is possible I should like to vary the last act set showing the autumn effects and also the country hotel, but looking at the whole picture from another point of view. If possible move the hotel building over to stage L so that if we were looking at it from the north in the first act we are now looking at it from the south. This will necessitate changing the panorama drop at the rear but it will vary the pictures and I believe that in a three-act piece of this kind it would not be safe to duplicate two of our sets. On the other hand I think that the three sets as I have indicated them herewith will make effective stage pictures, answer all of our purposes and will not make a cumbersome production requiring long time for setting.

I am sending herewith some simple ground plans of the sets as I have them in mind. Inasmuch as the second and third act have now been welded into one act I believe that our only safe plan to head off criticisms of the kind we received in New York is to make our second act set comparatively simple. I don't see how we can modify the big third act set so as to make it answer our purposes and besides it is the safe rule in playwriting to always use an interior for a semi-interior for scenes depending upon lines or comedy situations rather than upon crowds or spectacular effects. Inasmuch as this is a farcical play and not a big musical comedy it will be a great mistake to strain for big scenic effects. In other words make each of the three sets modern and realistic and not fancy.

I hope I make myself clear on this point.

x x x

As I said before the only assurance I can give you is that I will go right to work and prepare the stuff as rapidly as possible. You can help me if you will let me know which of the parts [Flora] ZABELLE will probably play and I will build it up accordingly. Also indicate to me just what songs or musical numbers you have on hand and wish to interpolate and I will find the spots for them. It will be better to wire me suggestions you have to make except those regarding the songs; this will probably require written explanations.

With best wishes,

Sincerely,

InK George Ade

The Bad Samaritan an Informal Comedy in Four Acts *had opened at the Garden Theater in New York, September 12, 1905. The play failed. The Joseph Reeve papers (InK) contain a manuscript of* Fifty-two Years Young. A Three-Act Farcical Play with Music. *There is no record of this revised version of* The Bad Samaritan *ever having been performed.*

Raymond Hitchcock, a comedian under the management of Henry Savage when he starred in Easy Dawson, *had recently married Flora Zabelle, an actress.*

14 ☙ TO ADALINE WARDELL BUSH ADE

London [England]
Feb. 2, 1906

Dear Mother:

I suppose you received the cable announcing our safe arrival in London. We had pleasant weather nearly all the way—only one bad day and on deck it was so warm that we seldom wore our overcoats. As this is my fourth visit to London, I feel at home here, I have done but little sight-seeing, although Will Kent and Will Esten have been going around every day with a guide. We expect to leave here next week and after a few days in Paris, sail from Marseilles for Alexandria, Egypt on Feb. 14. We do not know how long we shall remain in Cairo—it depends on how we like it. All of us are feeling pretty well and enjoying our trip. Give my love to all.

Sincerely,
George

InK

Will Kent, the son of the founder of Kentland, Indiana, Ade's birthplace, was a childhood friend, as was Will Esten.

15 ☙ TO CHARLES BELMONT DAVIS

Hazelden
Brook, Indiana
June 20, 1906.

My dear Davis:—

I am sending you herewith a number of clippings to show you the kind of "overheard conversations" I used to do for the daily papers. Some of them are pretty crude but they will give you the idea. There are specimens of boy-talk, chappy-talk, girl-talk, street-car-conversations, etc. You can run them over and indicate which you like the best. Also I have sent several monologues or "thoughts spoken aloud." I have thought that "innermost thoughts" would be a good heading for a series of this kind. For instance you will find one on the innermost thoughts of the hobo. This was done hastily for the newspaper years ago; it could now be rewritten and greatly improved. Would the fact that I used this stuff in the newspapers years ago make it unsaleable now provided the stuff is entirely reconstructed? Or would you want me to get up something entirely new following the lines of some of the stuff I sent you?

After you have looked over this stuff please pin to the various clippings any comments or suggestions you wish to make and return them all to me.

I am, with best wishes,

Sincerely,
George Ade

VU

Charles Belmont Davis of Collier's *did not publish any articles based on the clippings Ade describes.*

16 TO CHARLES W. FAIRBANKS

Hazelden
Brook, Indiana
January 10, 1907

My dear Mr. Fairbanks:

We have as postmaster at Brook, Indiana, a very capable, courteous and efficient man named Morris A. Jones. He is an old soldier, a good Republican and I don't know why any one should want to see him put out, but I have heard that complaints are being lodged against him and that somebody here, I don't know just who, is trying to get his job.

I trust that he will be retained and I give you my assurance that he has conducted the office in a manner highly satisfactory to this community.

Mr. Jones has not asked me to intercede in his behalf, and I am not sure that there is any immediate danger of his removal, but I have learned that an effort is being made to remove him and if you are at liberty to make any suggestions in the matter of his retention and feel disposed to do so, I want to assure you that you will make no mistake.

Largely through his efforts the business of the local office has been developed until, on January 1st, it was advanced to the third class and now that the office pays a fixed salary of attractive dimensions somebody else wants it.

I regret to say that I am detained at home by the very critical illness of my mother. We are much alarmed regarding her condition.

Remember me to Mrs. Fairbanks and permit me to thank you again for your extreme kindness to me while I was in Washington.

With best wishes,

Sincerely,
George Ade

InU

Charles W. Fairbanks was vice-president of the United States 1905–1909.

Morris A. Jones retained his position as postmaster.

Adeline Ade died January 26, 1907.

17 ❧ TO JOHN M. STUDEBAKER

May 10, 1907

UNDERSTAND YOU ARE NEGOTIATING WITH CHARLES DILLINGHAM REGARDING LEASE OF STUDEBAKER THEATRE. SINCERELY TRUST YOU MAY COME TO AGREEMENT WITH HIM AS I BELIEVE HE IS MOST ENTERPRISING AND RELIABLE OF THE MANAGERS. AM WRITING MY NEW PLAY FOR HIM AND HOPE IT CAN BE PUT ON AT STUDEBAKER THIS FALL. BELIEVE WE CAN DUPLICATE SUCCESS OF CHAIRMAN AND WIDOW.

GEORGE ADE

InLP

Artie *advertising postcard*

John M. Studebaker and his brothers owned the largest vehicle works in the world. J. M. Studebaker also owned the Studebaker Theater, Chicago, Illinois. He was a friend of Ade's father.

Ade was adapting Artie *for the stage.*

18 ❧ TO JOHN M. DICKEY

Hazelden
Brook, Indiana
June 3, 1907

My dear Mr. Dickey:

I am grateful to you for your cordial letter but I am still unconvinced regarding any "call" to the rostrum. I do know, however, that I can do much better than I did at La Fayette. I have no hankering to undertake any platform engagements as long as I can get money doing something else, but as I wrote you once before, if I decide to tackle this form of graft I will communicate with you.

I am with best wishes,

Sincerely,
George Ade

InU

Ade wrote Robert Mountsier, June 30, 1908, and Aug. 24, 1908 (NJP), refusing to speak at the University of Michigan.

19 ❧ TO LA TOUCHA HANCOCK

Hazelden
Brook, Indiana
July 16, 1907.

Dear Mr. Hancock:

I don't know that I have any definite opinion as to the wisdom of keeping up a course of reading while doing a protracted job of writing. When a man gets to working on a job under pressure, he doesn't want to read anything except ball scores. I think a little reading on the side would not hurt under any conditions, and when a man is writing plays it will help him to read from the good modern plays every day in order to remind himself of the importance of keeping dialogue boiled down.

Yours truly,
George Ade

VU

(Ernest) La Toucha Hancock contributed verse and humor to magazines and newspapers. Desultory Verse, *1913, is representative of his work.*

20 ❧ TO B. F. LAWRENCE

Hazelden
Brook, Indiana
November 26, 1907

My dear Sir:

Pardon my delay in acknowledging receipt of your letter. I cannot recall that I did anything in the dramatic line until about ten years ago, when I submitted to May Irwin a little one-act play entitled "Mrs. Peckham's Carouse." Much to my surprise she accepted the play and sent me a check for $200. It seemed wrong to accept such a large sum of money for such a small manuscript but I needed the two hundred and I kept it. Miss Irwin put the manuscript into her trunk and forgot about it.

Occasionally during the last ten years I have been tempted to return the money to her feeling that I had obtained it under false pretenses. Last winter she was in violent need of a one-act play to fill out an evening's entertainment, so she fished out my first effort and played it. Much to her surprise and much to mine, the little play was highly successful. I had always regarded it as the crude and amateurish attempt of a beginner, but the critics, who supposed that it had been written the week before, recognized in it a ripening improvement in technique, construction, sub-plot, etc., (which are understood only by critics) over certain other plays.

"Mrs. Peckham's Carouse" seemed to excite so little enthusiasm on the part of Miss Irwin that it was five years before I had the courage to take a second dip into the troubled waters of dramatic authorship with The Sultan of Sulu.

Yours truly,
In George Ade

B. F. Lawrence was the managing editor of the Indianapolis Star.

According to Irving Lewis, "Written Hurriedly on a Pullman Car and Produced Therein, etc." New York Telegraph, *Sept. 25, 1904, Ade created his first dramatic effort "Conquered in the F.[irst] R.[ound]: or Woo by Force," in 1894. The reporter concocted this farce while traveling by train to cover the Midwinter Fair in San Francisco. John McCutcheon made handbills which the journalists-turned-actors passed throughout the train. No women responded to the invitation, but the "Pullman Car Monadnock Theatorium" was packed with male passengers who witnessed two Chicagoans, Hogan (The West Side Chicken) and Tandy (The North Side Nobby One), stage a fight in McCaffrey's Gymnasium to decide who would win the girl both loved. After the slapstick pugilism, Ade and McCutcheon, dressed in formal attire, traded jokes in "Sidewalk Conversation," and finished with a song.*

In 1897 Ade wrote "The Back-Stair Investigation," which he labeled "a satirical take-off on the attempt to discover wickedness in our beloved city." This spoof of the Baxter Investigation, which poked fun at the political chicanery rife in Chicago politics, was written for the team of Hap Ward and Harry Vokes while they were playing at the Great Northern Theater.

Amy Leslie had suggested that Mae Irwin contact Ade to write her a comedy. Ade wrote Mrs. Peckham's Carouse *in 1898. Miss Irwin incorporated the skit into her vaudeville act in 1905. See* Mrs. Peckham's Carouse, *ed. Richard Cordell (Press of the Indiana Kid: Pawnee, Indiana, 1963).*

21 ❧ TO WILLIAM HOWARD TAFT

New York, New York
June 20, 1908

ACCEPT MOST CORDIAL CONGRATULATIONS YOURS FOR GOD FOR COUNTRY AND FOR YOU.

DLC GEO ADE

22 ❧ TO FRED SIMS

[Hazelden]
[Brook, Indiana]
August 26, 1908.

My dear Mr. Sims:

I write you in regard to our rally here on September 30th. Please regard what I say about Charley Hernly as confidential. I don't want to hurt his feelings and I am not making any complaint against him, but he, meaning well, has put me into an embarrassing position.

When he was up here last summer he proposed to some of the republicans here that we should have a big rally here this fall. We were heartily in favor of it, so he went back to Indianapolis and gave out an interview announcing a barbecue here at the Farm, and saying that thirty steers would be slaughtered to feed the multitude. I regarded this announcement as one of Charley's jokes until the other day I found a big first-page article in the Star to the effect that this rally would be the most stupendous affair ever pulled off in northwestern Indiana, and that I would kill forty steers in order that the republican host might be fed.

Since this second publication I find that all the people in this part of the state are considerably worked up. They have taken Mr. Hernly seriously. Aside from the fact that forty good steers would cost at least $4,000, the republican [*carbon incomplete*]
InLP

Ade refers to the rally held for William Howard Taft who opened his Indiana campaign for the presidency at Hazelden, September 23, 1908.

23 TO WARREN T. MC CRAY

Benares [India]
Mch 11, [1909]

At last we have struck a country in which the cow is respected according to her real merits.

InK G. A.

This postcard depicting Anapurna Cow Temple, Benares, was sent to Ade's brother-in-law, who raised prize Herefords. Ade sent many postcards to his sister's family, most of which he addressed to his niece, Marian McCray. Since Marian collected postcards, Ade usually just dated and signed his contributions to her album.

24 ☙ TO W. M. TAYLOR

[Algiers]
[March 24, 1909]

I have just had a rye & soda but this is all I could see of her face.
InK G Ade

Ade refers to the photo of a veiled Moorish woman on the postcard. It was his custom to write a "one-liner" referring to the picture.

Drawn by H. T. Webster

1910-1920

The second decade of this century was perplexing. There was ferment as new ideas clashed with old traditions. The avant garde expressed itself in publications such as *The Masses,* and clamored for social and political reform. In addition to publishing books and articles at which America chuckled, Ade was also interested in improving conditions, but his middle-brow approach was to work within the framework of existing institutions. Although Ade was vitally interested in the man who thought the White House a bully pulpit as well as in Theodore Roosevelt's Progressive Party, his political concerns were centered on the state rather than on the national level. His country club, activities as a board member and benefactor of Purdue University, and work for the State Council of Defense all point to a localizing of interests during the World War era when everyone pitched in to make the world safe for democracy.

25 ✤ TO JOHN BARRETT

Hazelden
Brook, Indiana
August 13, 1910.

My dear Mr. Barrett:

I am in need of information, and I believe you are the man best qualified to give it to me, although I do not want to draw too heavily upon your time and patience. I am undertaking a play dealing incidentally with some experiences of an American Minister in an imaginary Republic somewhat on the order of the smaller republics of Central and South America.

In the case of a minister to one of the smaller and less important republics, what would be his official family?

What would be the name of his official residence? The consul's home is a consulate, and an embassador lives at the embassy; but where does the ordinary medium kind of minister live?

Would his secretary and confidential man for dealing with the general public probably be an American or a resident of the country?

Would there be a military attache?

How far would his authority go, unaided by instructions from Washington, in preventing local authorities from dealing with American citizens who have become involved in a local revolutionary movement? This covers a lot of ground, and you need not bother to go into any discourse on the powers and limitations of a minister, but I thought possibly you could give me an idea in a few words.

I want very much to conform to the possibilities if not the probabilities in my comedy. It is being written for William H. Crane, and he will play the self-made, homely, rather unpolished type of American who is not well acquainted with the rules of diplomacy, but manages to acquit himself with credit because he is a man of action and possessed of rugged common sense.

If there is any printed document laying down rules for the guidance of American ministers of course it might be a big help to me.

I have visited American ministers and consuls in all parts of the world, have been through the West Indies a couple of times and to South America once, and I know something of the general atmosphere of these Caribbean countries and the social customs, but of course I am not familiar with the rules of the state department. If you can help me in getting a line on the exact scope of the duties of an American minister to one of these smaller republics I will be exceedingly grateful.

I see [John] McCutcheon once in a while. He is well and happy.

Sincerely,
George Ade

DLC

In response to Ade's request for information pertinent to his writing U. S. Minister Bedloe, *John Barrett, director general of the Pan-American Union, urged the playwright to insert favorable comments about stable South American governments, then answered each question in detail.*

26 ❧ TO HELEN HERRON TAFT

Hazelden
Brook, Indiana
June 21—1911.

My Dear Mrs. Taft:

I was happy to find myself invited to your anniversary festivities and I am sending—even though a day or two late—a little piece of silver that may possess the merit of being different. I found it in *Java,* and it is a good specimen of native workmanship.

You and Judge [William Howard] Taft, as we still feel impelled to call him, have our neighborhood best wishes for many pleasant years.

Sincerely,
George Ade

DLC

27 ❧ TO MC CLURE NEWSPAPER SYNDICATE

October 21, 1911.

Gentlemen:

I am sending this in care of the McClure Company as I have a notion that you have moved since I had any correspondence with you. I write to ask you to tell me whatever you are at liberty to tell regarding the present syndicating of fables. Perhaps you know that they are being syndicated without my authority and in opposition to my wishes.

The facts in the case are as follows. About a year ago I undertook a series of twelve sketches of 1500 words each for Mr. Norman Mack of Buffalo. The stuff was to be printed in his Sunday Magazine which is circulated as a supplement to certain Sunday newspapers. After I had written seven of the stories I became involved in other work, and also desired to take a trip to the West Indies, so I expressed a desire to discontinue the series. Mr. Mack asked me to complete it. I told him that if he would permit me to stop the series for a while I would break my solemn vow not to write any more fables, and would write him five installments of fables, of 1500 words for each for the same price that I had been receiving for the sketches, namely, $150.00 each.

I explained to him that I could get much more for the fables by syndicating them in the Sunday newspapers, but I did not care to assume the perils and responsibilities of a new series, but would have no objection to writing just a few for his magazine. I did not make any legal stipulation that he should not syndicate the stuff but I most certainly indicated my wishes in the matter, and besides we had a very definite understanding that the stuff I was writing for him would appear in the Sunday Magazine and then revert to me if I wished to put it in a book later.

After I wrote the first fable he asked me to split the stuff up into short ones. I did so. He took the five installments for which I received a grand total of $750.00 and syndicated them through your agency, as I have since learned. I had no indication of his plans until I saw myself billed like a circus all over Chicago.

Now, if I am not breaking into your confidential arrangements with Mr. Mack, I would like to know what success you have had in handling the present series. Whether or not they have been favorably received and whether or not it might be advisable for me to write a few more. I am back in the game against my own will but since I am once more being syndicated, I might as well get something out of it.

You will understand of course, that Mr. Mack will not figure in any future arrangements regarding the fables.

I am, with best wishes,

Sincerely,

InLP George Ade

The fables to which Ade refers ran from September through December, 1911, in the Chicago Daily News *and other papers. Dorothy Ritter Russo,* A Bibliography of George Ade 1866–1944 *(Indianapolis: 1947), pp. 180–81. A number of these fables appeared in* Knocking the Neighbors, *1912.*

28 TO HAMLIN GARLAND

French Lick, Indiana
Nov. 15, 1911.

Dear Mr. Garland:—

Your letter has been forwarded to me.

I regret to say that I have not on hand any one-act plays except some old ones that have been used a great deal. You may remember the rather serious little play, for men characters only, which was done at the opening of the New Theater in Chicago. You are welcome to this if you care to use it, but I dare say you would not care to repeat anything so familiar.

I have a few little plays in outline but I could not promise to get them ready very soon and I could not give any assurance as to the quality after they were finished. So I fear that I can not be of help to you.

Sincerely,
CLSU George Ade

Hamlin Garland, the novelist, had urged Ade in 1895 to write a novel. Garland and Ade corresponded on occasion, but they were antipodal personalities and remained distant.

Ade's only serious play, Marse Covington, *premiered at the New Theater, October 8, 1906.*

29 TO ROLLAND PHILLIPS

Chicago [Illinois]
February 27, 1912.

Dear Mr. Phillips:—

Pardon the delay in answering your letter. I wanted to give it my prayerful consideration.

In the first place, the compensation you offer is altogether satisfactory. It is extremely generous. The only doubt in my mind is whether or not I should attempt any more Fables. In one month the last Fable will be printed in the McClure Syndicate. My plan for fixing up the twelve for you, will be to go over all of those that I have written and check off the ones that have been most popular and talked about, so as to get a line on the topics that have the most general appeal. I will deliver the Fables as suggested to you, but I should like the privilege of sending on revised copies. If you will let me know the date on which each one will go to the printer, I could send on the first draft for the use of the artist and then after the stuff got cold, possibly I could go over it again and greatly improve it, for in this kind of stuff, the merit lies in the manner of telling and not in the subject matter, which is usually common-place.

Regarding the option on the twelve additional Fables I will agree to your suggestion, if it be understood that I am not under compulsion to deliver the extra twelve, in other words, there will be no additional series, except by mutual agreement, but if I do any more, certainly you shall have the option on them.

I shall be glad to submit to you any short story stuff I may do within the next year.

The only clause which needs explaining, is the one in regard to the option. I may be in your city at the end of this week, but probably you had better address your letter here. The first installment will be in your hands by April 1st.

Sincerely yours,
George Ade

InLP

Ade began publishing fables in Cosmopolitan, *August, 1912, and continued to contribute fables and other pieces until 1925 when* Hearst's International *combined with* Cosmopolitan. *Ade wrote regularly for* Hearst's International *until 1931. See Russo, pp. 232–36, and 239–40.*

Ade had other offers to syndicate his fables, but with characteristic loyalty he adhered to his original agreement. In a letter to William Gerard Chapman, head of the International Press Bureau, May 19, 1913 (VU), Ade stated that Rolland Phillips, the editor of Cosmopolitan, *had syndication rights.*

30 ☙ TO THOMAS R. MARSHALL

April 12, 1912

My dear Governor Marshall:—

I have a letter from your Secretary informing me that you have named me as one of 5 representatives from Indiana on the National Committee for the Celebration of the Hundredth Anniversary of Peace Among English Speaking People. I thank you for thus honoring me and I wish very much to act as a member of the Committee, but my acceptance will hinge somewhat upon the dates of the Committee Meetings. I am booked to sail for Europe early in July and will return early in September. My plans for going are quite definite and could not easily be cancelled. Perhaps your esteemed Secretary can tell me something about the plans of the National Committee, as I say I wish to accept this very flattering appointment, but I do not think it fair to accept, unless I can actually participate in the work of the Committee.

I am with best wishes,

Sincerely,
George Ade

InLP

Thomas Marshall was governor of Indiana, 1909–1913.

31 TO WINFIELD T. DURBIN

Hazelden
Brook, Indiana
[c.]Oct. [15, 1912]

My Dear Colonel:

Pardon the delay in answering your kind letter: I have been away from home most of the time for two weeks. What you have heard about me is true. I have enlisted with the Progressive party because, under the new alignment I wouldn't be satisfied anywhere else. The so-called progressive policies might have been made effective within the republican party and a split averted if the majority had not been overruled by the minority at the convention in June. I am heartily out of sympathy with men who dominated that convention. I dont believe I agree with them in any thing. If they constitute the authority of the party, I no longer wish to be known as a republican. But I will not quarrel with my good friends who remain with the organization.

Sincerely,
George Ade

InLP

Winfield T. Durbin, governor of Indiana, 1901–1905, had written Ade a lengthy personal plea to reconsider his decision to join the Progressive party because Durbin felt Ade would take other Republicans with him to the new faction.

32 TO WILLIAM FRED KURFESS

Brook–Ind.
Nov. 4–1912

My Dear Kurfess:

If you have won any large sums on the election, give us a lift on our house-furnishing fund. We don't like to nag the recent alumnus but if you *can* help us, we need the help and your example may induce some of the others to loosen up.

Sincerely,
George Ade

K

William Fred Kurfess married Ardis Ade, the author's niece, in 1921.

Ade contributed about $25,000 to the building of the Sigma Chi Fraternity House at Purdue University. He also donated truck loads of furnishings which he had gathered in this travels. He had been elected grand consul of the Sigma Chi Fraternity in 1910.

33 [HAZELDEN COUNTRY CLUB BULLETIN]

Hazelden
Brook, Indiana
4th October 1913.

The first tournament of the Hazelden Golf Club will be held during the week beginning October 13th.

On October 13th, 14th and 15th every member desiring to compete for the trophy must play 18 holes (twice around the course in continuous play) and turn in a carefully kept score of the total number of strokes required.

The eight contestants having the lowest scores shall be qualified to contest for the championship.

On October 16th the four pairs of contestants will be matched up by drawing the names from a hat. Each two shall play an 18-hole match. The four winners will then be matched for the semi-finals, to be placed on the afternoon of the 16th or the morning of the 17th.

The final round between the two remaining contestants will be played on the afternoon of Friday, October 17th. There will be an approaching and putting contest also, followed by the first annual dinner of the Club, at which time the prizes will be presented.

These contests are open to residents of Newton County. All

who have been invited to play on the links are considered members of the Club. Other candidates may now be admitted on the nomination of members.

Let every one take part in the preliminaries. The trophies will be on exhibition during the tournament.

InLP George Ade

Ade wrote innumerable bulletins to the members of the country club which he built on the grounds of his estate. He usually wrote these bulletins in epistolary form, had them mimeographed, and often signed each copy. In later years Ade had a secretary or members of the club copy his signature on mass produced communications.

34 ☙ TO WILLIAM C. BOBBS

Chicago [Illinois]
January 30, 1914.

My dear Colonel—

I was glad to have your letter because it contained the first real information as to what all this fuss was about. It is evident that when you are stalking a timid bird you want to be right up on him before he suspects anything.

I thought that long wire I sent you the other day would convince anybody that I am not a candidate. However, I shall try to make this letter more emphatic, if possible. When your wire came this week, I was at the hospital. That is why I did not write you on Tuesday. Perhaps you don't know that I have been pretty badly under the weather for many months. I have not been able to do any work since early last fall. I was booked to go on a cruise to South America, starting next week, but my doctor would not permit it. And yet you suggest that I now embark on the troubled sea of politics. I am still feeling a little weak, but I have to laugh when I think of it.

Why don't you make James Whitcomb Riley your candidate this year? He is a thousand times more popular in Indiana than I could hope to be. He would enjoy the publicity and the hand-shaking and the speech-making just as much as I would, and he is almost as well qualified physically as I have been for the last six months.

If I felt strong enough to fight Gunboat Smith tomorrow I would not even consider being a candidate for anything. I am not qualified by temperament or training to be a campaigner and I would as soon serve a term at Michigan City as sit in a legislative assembly. Furthermore, I do not propose to convert my peaceful country home into a bear pit. Also, as I have not done a stroke of remunerative work since last September and my chauffeur requires a new Packard, I am not in position at this moment to purchase immunity by financing somebody else's campaign.

Now then, why in the Lord's name, do you want to see me and talk to me? What is there to talk about? I am going to the country tomorrow to spend Sunday with my father. I am coming back here sometime Monday. On Tuesday I will be packing up; Wednesday morning I take a train to LaFayette, arriving there at one o'clock. We have a meeting of the trustees at two o'clock. I have planned to spend the evening quietly with some friends there and then take the night train to Florida.

I would gladly try to have an interview with you if there was any earthly reason for it; but why is it that you do not give me credit for knowing the state of my own mind? If [Albert] Beveridge and others are pestering you, refer them to me and I hope I can convince them that I am not a candidate for anything, although I may violate some of the U. S. Postal regulations in doing so. Just consider that we have had the interview and that it is all settled.

Sincerely,

InLP George Ade

Senator Albert J. Beveridge and William C. Bobbs, the publisher, were both anxious for Ade to run for the state legislature on the Progressive party ticket. Ade wrote G. R. Coffin, February 15, 1911 (InLP), reiterating his decision not to seek political office. Ade continually refused to participate actively in politics although he remained interested in government throughout his life.

35 ❧ TO THE *NEW YORK TIMES*

Hazelden
Brook, Ind.
[Autumn, 1914]

I suppose the best joke or anecdote a man ever hears is the latest new one. For some reason the joke that I seem to remember best of all is a very brief wheeze that I caught from the pages of a funny paper several years ago.

Two solemn-looking gentlemen are riding together in a railway carriage. One gentleman says to the other, "Is your wife entertaining this Summer?" Whereupon the second gentleman replies: "Not very."

I know it is a chestnut now, but it will always seem fresh and glistening to me.

New York Times George Ade

The Times *asked seventeen humorists to give their favorite joke. The letters of reply were published under the title "'What is Best Joke?' Answered by Humorists,"* New York Times, *November 1, 1914.*

36 ❧ TO WINTHROP ELLSWORTH STONE

Chicago, Illinois
4th January, 1915.

My dear Dr. Stone:

I have your letter, and before it came I had learned something about the scrapping between the coaches and the Athletic Director.

I hesitate to make any definite suggestion at this time. I believe that the final and proper solution of the problem of directing athletic contests will be to have the general control vested in a Board in which the faculty, the alumni and the undergraduates will be equally represented. I do not believe that the alumni representatives should be members of the faculty. They should be men of sufficient age and experience to permit them to stand as a kind of buffer between the intemperate zeal of the under-graduates and the restraining conservatism of the faculty. I believe you will find out that in colleges which have adopted this plan of control the faculty and alumni usually work together to correct and modify the too-ambitious projects of the students. I believe this Board should select a good coach for each department of sport and that it should have a capable business manager who has no connection with the work of coaching. The plan of having one Athletic Director and giving him supreme control might work out all right if you could accomplish the miracle of getting a man who would command the loyal affection of the students and win a large majority of his games. Chicago has [Alonzo] Stagg and for a long time Huff came very near being the boss of Illinois, but even Illinois has changed her plan and George Huff is very much in favor of giving the students a voice in the management.

I can well understand that faculty members often become discouraged when compelled to abide by student legislation, but we must remember that the men in college average more than 21 years of age and are supposed to be ready to go out and manage important business affairs, and I believe the modern policy will continue to be to give the under-graduates certain legislative powers, even if they do muss things up once in a while.

A Board, such as I have suggested, would control the general athletic policy of the University and select the coaches, but it would not undertake to deprive the faculty of the right to pass upon the eligibility of any athlete, supervise the financial management or reserve a final veto power if some action of the Board went squarely against the best traditions of the school. I think that even in Yale and other eastern schools, where student control is very strong, the faculty would always have the power of a kind of supreme court, if it cared to assert it.

I am, with best wishes,

Sincerely,

InLP George Ade

Winthrop Ellsworth Stone was president of Purdue University, 1900–1921.

Alonzo Stagg was director of athletics at the University of Chicago.

George Huff was director of athletics at the University of Illinois.

37 TO ELSIE JANIS

[Chicago, Illinois]
November 23, 1915

My dear Elsie Janis:—

Confirming my wire of last evening I am more than pleased to turn the play over to you if I receive the royalty usually paid for regular union author and can have some assurance that it will be prepared and produced by people who know their business. If you are on the job I think the piece will be protected. As I wired you, I could not undertake the immediate preparation of a scenario but

I will be glad to go over the book and make suggestions and possibly revise the dialogue and subtitles.

Remember me to your mother.

Sincerely,
George Ade

InLP

Elsie Janis, the actress-comedienne who had starred in the stage play, requested that Ade let her do a film version of The Fair Co-Ed.

Ade wrote Thomas Meighan, July 14, 1927 (InLP),

> Last year Mr. [William Randolph] Hearst bought for his Cosmopolitan picture outfit the old play which I did for Elsie Janis called THE FAIR CO-ED. It was understood that I would do nothing on the play. Mr. Hearst and Marian Davies have been looking over the play and they want to change the character of the star part. In doing so, they have wiped out the old play. Ray Long and Salisbury Field met me in Chicago about three weeks ago and explained the situation to me and asked me to submit an outline which would permit the star to play a yap country girl.

The Fair Co-Ed *was never filmed.*

38 ❧ TO CHARLES DENNIS

Belleair Heights, Fla.
March 12, 1916

Dear Mr. Dennis:

I am much pleased to have your letter and I wish I could get frolicsome and try to report a real fight once more. I remember that Mr. [Victor] Lawson, discovering that the lowbrow public was feverishly interested in these polite arguments, used to send me on every time when two of the champions got together. I rather enjoyed seeing them and I would not mind watching the big fellows in the approaching contest, but my plans are such that I cannot be in New York on the date of their controversy.

I trust you are well and happy.

Sincerely,
George Ade

Victor Lawson

This letter is printed in Charles Dennis, Victor Lawson *(Chicago: 1935), p. 165.*

Because Ade had given "remarkable service at pugilists' training camps and prize fights" in the 1890s, Charles Dennis had tried to get Ade to cover the Jess Willard–Frank Moran fight of March 25, 1916, for the Chicago Daily News.

39 ❧ TO WILLIAM ALLEN WHITE

Hazelden
Brook, Indiana
April 17, 1916.

My dear White:

I find awaiting me the book you were good enough to send and I sure thank you for remembering me, and for the pleasure I have found in the reading. No doubt you are enjoying the political spectacle just at present. Our old friends of the old party are in a bad way. One year ago, it seemed certain that all they had to do was name some dignified old party wearing a frock coat, and having a church connection, and land him right in the White House. It is now evident that the voters have no hankering for any old fluff who refuses to admit that there is a war in Europe. I don't know what is going to happen, but it looks as if the Colonel [Theodore Roosevelt] might be in evidence.

I am with best wishes,

Sincerely,
George Ade

DLC

William Allen White, the editor of the Emporia *[Kansas]* Gazette, *had sent Ade* God's Puppets *(New York: 1916).*

On May 25, 1916, Ade and other writers sent White the following wire (InLP): "WE A COMMITTEE REPRESENTING MANY AMERICAN AUTHORS HAVE SIGNED AN ADDRESS TO [THEODORE] ROOSEVELT EXPRESSING THE HOPE THAT HE WILL BE THE NEXT PRESIDENT MAY WE ADD YOUR NAME PLEASE WIRE ANSWER IMMEDIATELY TO HAMLIN GARLAND TWELVE VANDERBILT AVE NEW YORK CITY."

Ade wrote Hamlin Garland, September 17, 1916 (CLSR), endorsing Charles Evans Hughes for vice president.

40 ❧ TO MR. WENGLER

Hazelden
Brook, Indiana
6th August, 1916.

Dear Mr. Wengler:

I have your long and friendly letter.

Of course, I do not undertake to write plays of any sort on order. It takes just as much time and hard pumping to write a college play as any other kind of a play, and no college club could afford to pay what an author counts on receiving in the way of royalties from any sort of success. The work I have done for Purdue has been not only gratis, but I have followed it up with plenty of hard coin. Believe me, I am not looking for another job as private playwright for a college dramatic club. At the same time, I am always willing to help out, if I can do so without involving myself too deeply. If your club wished to take the Revue done at Purdue last winter and localize it for your own club, dividing up the authorship, I would be quite willing for you to use the manuscript and I think that you could get all the music and parts from the club managers at Purdue. I have nothing in manuscript form that would be of any use to you, and under no circumstances would I attempt the presentation of anything that would serve for a whole evening's entertainment.

I am, with best wishes,

Sincerely,
George Ade

VU

Ade had written Around the Campus *for presentation by the Harlequin Club of Purdue University April 24, 1916. Ade enlisted the help of Charles Dillingham and Irving Berlin on the revue which was elaborate, if* deja vu. Around the Campus *boasted a college widow, a fair co-ed, and a football cheering scene.*

41 ❧ TO THEODORE ROOSEVELT

Belleair Heights, Fla.
March 7th, 1917.

My dear Colonel:

Thank you very much for the book. I think I have read most of the articles as they came out but I shall read them again with satisfaction and profit.

During the past few months I have been with you more emphatically and more angrily than ever before. I am wondering now if, when the time comes for us to make a show of defending ourselves, the bewildered people will accept with confidence a leadership which never has had any confidence in itself. More power to you! You were on to him from the very start. He was re-elected by an incredible fluke and I really believe that he regards his re-election as a vindication of the policy of inaction. [Edgar G.] Sisson of the Metropolitan [Magazine] came down to see me the other day and he tells me what I never knew before—that Col. [Edward M.] House has been urging the Professor [Woodrow Wilson] for many months to arm this country and get it ready, but even his counsel is rejected. When Robinson Crusoe refuses to confer with his man Friday he surely does find himself on a desert island. I am with best wishes,

Sincerely,
George Ade

DLC

Theodore Roosevelt had sent Ade Americanism and Preparedness *(New York: 1917).*

Woodrow Wilson's special adviser, Colonel Edward M. House, even as Theodore Roosevelt, had been of the opinion since 1915 that the United States would go to war against Germany.

42 TO WILLIAM FRED KURFESS

Belleair Heights, Fla.
March 11th, 1917.

My dear Fred:

I am much interested to have your news from Lafayette, and to know that the boys are managing their affairs so well. Henry De Hart is undoubtedly a capable fellow and am mighty glad that Judge [Henry] Vinton and I went to the [Sigma Chi] house and compelled the boys to take him in. I have not been at Purdue for about a year. I left there disgusted with Doc [Winthrop] Stone and most of the Faculty and thoroughly discouraged because of the lack of any real spirit or enthusiasm among the students. After devoting many weeks of hard work and a considerable sum of money to putting on the annual show, it did not seem to me that the general body of students were grateful or even interested. A man's only reward when he tackles a college job is the knowledge that the boys are with him so I have been off of Purdue ever since. I have made no definite plans for returning at any time although I still have the kindliest feelings in the world for the Sigs. As for Doc Stone I wish him everything he wishes me and I could not say anything rougher than that. Remember me to John [Sayler].

Sincerely,
K George Ade

In a letter to Ade, May 9, 1916 (InLP), Dean Stanley Coulter of Purdue University apologized for the lukewarm reception of Around the Campus. *The Purdue annual Harlequin Club show of 1917,* One Moment Please *was written by Henry T. De Hart. There is no indication that Ade was connected with this Purdue production.*

John Sayler was William Kurfess' roomate at Purdue in 1912.

43 TO JAMES A. STUART

French Lick, Indiana
April 26th, 1917

Dear Mr. Stuart:

I shall try to enclose herewith a brief boost for the Penrod stories, which deserve all the praise that may be lavished upon them.

Sincerely,
Enc. George Ade

I hope you can read the copy. Better have it typewritten & checked up.

We Hoosiers may not be properly keyed up over our home attractions. I understand there is a man in South Bend who went to Luxor to see the Temple of Karnak but he has not been to Indianapolis to see the Soldiers' Monument. Our own majestic work of art lays it over the clumsy relics of Egypt. It is in a better state of preservation and has more late-model cars parked around it.

By the same token, the literary clubs that get the head-ache working on Bernard Shaw and [Edward Plunkett, Lord] Dunsany and Ipskovitch (there is no such person but he may appear at any moment) must not overlook the luminous fact that we have, right here in our own bailiwick, an expert literary craftsman who has taken the husk off of boyhood and shown us the entrancing processes of the most inward section of the juvenile soul.

In George Ade

James A. Stuart was the editor of the Indianapolis Star.

44 ❧ TO THEODORE ROOSEVELT

Hazelden
Brook, Indiana
June 12–1917

My Dear Colonel Roosevelt–

I thank you for your friendly letter. The other day a harelipped man working for me stopped me and said he wished to ask a question. I told him to shoot, so he said: "I want to find out who got us into this war. I know [Woodrow] Wilson kept us out, but I can't find out who the dickens got us in."

You are quite right. We cocained ourselves into believing that the war was no quarrel of ours and now, when asked to arouse ourselves, we are still a bit dopey and incredulous. A medley of mellifluous sounds is not always a battle hymn. Probably we will have to be kicked a couple of times in some vital spot before we get fighting mad.

I am on our State Council of Defense and trying to be of some help. We find it hard work to induce the farmers and other small investors to take the Liberty Loan bonds. They have been talked at so much from so many different angles that some of them seem to be in doubt as to the wisdom of taking advice from any one. The enlisting in this northern half of Indiana was active and continues so, I am happy to report.

We have a hefty job ahead of us but I suppose the only thing to do is go ahead and use the tools at hand. We must not even think out loud, but ever and anon give three silent cheers for some of the lawyer-politicians down at Washington.

I am, with best wishes,

Sincerely,
DLC George Ade

45 ❧ TO GEORGE M. COHAN

Hazelden
Brook, Indiana
July 8th, 1917.

My dear George:—

I am trying to be a retired and reformed playwright and I am not looking for extra work just now as I am a member of our State Council of Defense and busy with a lot of volunteer duties, but the suggestion for a play popped into my head the other day and it has stuck there ever since, so I am going to relieve myself by telling you about it. I select you as my victim because I think that you are an expert on the practical end of the show business and understand the value of any story which might combine comedy and melodrama.

Just now I suppose you managers are wondering what the public will go after during the war period and we certainly are in for a period of real war. A few months from now, with thousands of men embarking every week and with the advance guard fighting in the trenches, there will be a lot of interest and attention given to the real issues of the war. The whole fight on the part of the allies is to prevent Germany from enforcing her cold-blooded and deep-layed plans, with the rest of the world as victims. If some one could write a play taking off the German method and applying it to an individual and illustrating, in a dramatic way, how the German method works out, it seems to me that the public would be interested especially if the play is given the comedy treatment. It seems that during war times there is a special demand for plays that amuse.

Doubtless you will agree with me that Germany, in the present war, has out done all of the villains of melodrama that ever were put on the stage. Germany has frightened the weak, bribed the corrupt, tortured the virtuous, slandered the upright and pulled every other conventional trick of old time melodrama. Of course, we could not put a character into a play and call it Germany, but the idea that came to me and which I am putting up to you, is as follows:

The play would be called "Efficiency" or "The Efficient Man." At the beginning of the play a young man of large ambitions has returned to America after several years in Europe. He has large ambitions, he has become imbued with European notions and cannot help but show a certain contempt for the crude and simple-minded people of his own country. Although the word Germany need not be used in the play his plans, as outlined to a friend, will indicate that he is following the very policies which have governed Prussia. For instance, we find him at the beginning of the play desirous of marrying the girl of much wealth and personal attractiveness, of putting out of the way her dissolute brother so that she may inherit the whole fortune, of check-mating a rather easy going and not very intellectual rival for the girl, of causing dissention between the girl and her friends who oppose the match, in fact, working all of the opposing influences against each other. This ambitious central figure in the play, outlining his program, gives the whole key-note to the German method of procedure. He has become convinced, while living abroad, that a man has a right to anything he can take, that a man is a fool to be bound by any scruples or even written obligations, when his own interests are acutely involved. He believes that nearly all of the people in the world are simpletons, some to be won by flattery, some to be frightened into submission, some to be bribed by money and some possibly to be put out of the way altogether, but all to be controlled, absolutely by a man who is bold, resolute, systematic in his methods and with enough blood and iron in his system to go ahead and execute his plans without flinching.

The play would be the attempt of the young man, highly educated, perfectly groomed, with knowledge of the world, and perfect manners, starting out to use all the people about him for his own selfish purposes. All of the servants surrounding the people he wishes to handle and influence are either bribed or intimidated to take orders from him and make reports to him. All the time he is working on his devilish schemes he is smiling, polite and agreeable. You may recall that while Bernstoff plotted to kill the women and children on the Lusitania he continued to drink tea with the ladies in Washington and pay them courtly attentions and they will still tell you he was the nicest man in the world. It is admitted that Germany has the most wonderful spy system in the world and the cleverest method of getting information from one agent to another. It could be shown in the play that the gentlemanly villain upon entering a room where his agents were employed as servants could tell, by the arrangement of the furniture or the character of the books that had been placed on the reading table, just what had happened since his last visit and how his plans were progressing.

Without attempting to go into details, which I have not tried to work out, the development of the play should indicate that there is such a thing as a man being so clever that he gets in his own way and that the man who plays every other person for a fool or a crook, cannot hope to claim very many real friendships. Also, and this will be the important and valuable development of the play, it must be shown that a good many easy-going, patient and good-natured people in this world become exceedingly combative and fairly dangerous when they have been kicked too often in the same place, and that the smoothest con man that ever lived never fooled all of the people all of the time. For a time in the play it should appear that the plans of the smooth citizen are working out perfectly. He becomes confident and over reaches himself, "tips his hands," so to speak, and before he gets through all of the people he has tried to control and influence and use to his own selfish purposes are lined up against him and he is in the discard.

From the above outline, it would be very easy to construct an old-fashioned melodrama of the Al Woods variety, but any play written this year with the German idea of efficiency as a central theme, should be given the comedy treatment I believe.

I have given you only the barest outline of what might be put into the play and possibly the fool thing will sound idiotic to you, and yet I have a feeling that a good saterial [*sic*] comedy with the Prussian modern military religion of efficiency as the central theme, would appeal to the public at this time. I have no plans for writing such a play and don't know how far I could go on a scenario. What I want to know now is, does the suggestion strike you as having any merit?

I am spending most of my time in the country and feeling much better than I did a few years ago. About the only work I do is an occasional story for the magazines, I mean by that the only writing work. I am busy enough with forty things that do not get my name into the papers.

Remember me to Sam Harris, Bert Feibleman, Eddie Dunn and all the other comrades.

Sincerely,

InLP George Ade

Ade served as publicity committee chairman of the Indiana State Council of Defense, 1917–1918. During his term of office he wrote a number of patriotic articles. See Russo, p. 116.

Since Ade had not written a highly successful play for more than a decade, he was wary of becoming directly involved in theatricals.

George M. Cohan had written Ade, May 3, 1906 (InLP), suggesting that his partner Sam Harris travel to Indiana to discuss the possibility of

1917

Ade's doing a play for the actor-playwright noted for his patriotic musicals.
When Ade sent his suggestion for "Efficiency" eleven years later Cohan insisted that Ade was the only playwright to tackle the story.

46 ❧ TO VICTOR BURBANK

Hazelden
Brook, Indiana
29th July, 1917.

My dear Mr. Burbank:

I have your letter.

You may go ahead and work up twelve (12) Fables from the list submitted, the price to be two hundred and fifty dollars a release. I shall not produce Fables with any other company while you are handling this series.

I think it is important that we should strike a happy medium in the matter of inserting sub-titles. The first Fables produced were shy of sub-titles. Toward the end, when the scenarios were returned to me for more text, possibly the sub-title thing was over done. These sub-titles must be crisp and concise and absolutely boiled down, so there will not be one superfluous word. There should be no straining for comedy effects. Mr. [Richard Foster] Baker tried to improve my text, and very often the sub-titles would become involved and altogether too long.

If you want me to pass upon the sub-titles, I shall be glad to do so and if I change them it will be to make them more compact and not more intricate.

I am, with best wishes,

Sincerely,
InLP George Ade

Victor Burbank was a representative of the Essanay Film Company.

Fifty-nine Ade fables were made into films by Essanay between 1915 and 1917. A number of these one-reel movies were directed by Richard Foster Baker.

Paul Terry wrote forty-seven fable films for Pathe Exchange, Inc., between 1922 and 1923, which further attests to the popularity of the fable picture. See Motion Pictures 1912–1939 *(Washington, D.C.: 1951), pp. 232–34.*

47 ❧ TO H. S. LATHAM

Hazelden
Brook, Indiana
30th September, 1917

Dear Mr. Latham:

I thank you very much for Hamlin Garland's new book "A Son of the Middle Border." He certainly knew the middle west when it was bleak and formative and he has told the uncharming facts in a very charming style. This part of the middle west has passed beyond the lonesome and unrewarded existence of the frontier farmer. The farmer who owns a Ford and Victrola and whose children play the ukeleles and go to the movies two or three times a week and have all their clothes made to measure—he is not the same fellow that Garland describes. But Garland told the truth about a very interesting period of middle west development.

I am, with best wishes,

Sincerely,
George Ade

CLSU

H. S. Latham of MacMillan Company forwarded Ade's endorsement to Hamlin Garland who wrote Ade the following commentary (InLP):

> Your letter endorsing my new book deeply interested and pleased me. I am the veteran—you can not rightly claim to be of my precise generation and yet the west you knew and in which you now live is essentially the same as that of which I have written. You could not have known the precise life and precise place of A SON OF THE MIDDLE BORDER for you are my junior but your quick imagination has more than made up your lack of experience in Iowa and for Dakota. It was, as you say, a bleak and formative period but the point is, no one considered it so in those days. As a nation we were in a vain and boastful mood and resented any criticism from idealistic folk whether of foreign or domestic derivation.—
>
> What a change is indicated in a few words. The motor car, the telephone, Free Delivery, two dollar wheat, thirty cent cotton and the Motion Picture Theater! and yet do you know there is still considerable drudgery on the farm? Of course it falls on the renter and the hired man but it is still there for I have seen it. I wonder who curries that herd of percherons at Hazelden farm? This is a poor time to express sympathy with the hired man (wages sixty dollars per month) but I find the taste of equine dandruff just as annoying to me now as it was in the days of the Middle Border. I'd hate to

curry a herd of shetland ponies "let alone" a herd of percherons.—Well, Well! We both belong to the "I Knew Him When Club" now and sometime I hope to drive out in my feeble flivver and congratulate you on your success as a Captain in the Live Stock Industry.

Courtesy Isabel Garland Lord and Constance Garland Doyle

48 ☙ TO THEODORE ROOSEVELT

Jacksonville, Fla.
March 27th 1918.

My dear Colonel:

The big drive on behalf of the third Liberty Loan is at hand and the State Council of Defense wishes to arouse a proper interest among the people of Indiana. The editors will be smothered with copy from various sources. We wish to send to the newspapers of Indiana some very short but very good appeals signed by well-known people. I am asking of you merely a paragraph on behalf of the good cause. Make it as compact as you choose and you need not use up more than one hundred words.

When you have the stuff ready, mail it to E. F. Warfel, State Council of Defense, State House, Indianapolis. The time is short and we must get the copy to the editors very soon. I know you are being hounded with requests, but so are all of us, and this time I am asking only a paragraph.

I am, with best wishes.

Sincerely,
George Ade

DLC

Theodore Roosevelt sent Ade a copy of the speech he made to the Liberty Loan group at Sagamore Hill, April 2, 1918, and promised to write something else if this did not prove satisfactory.

49 ☙ TO WILLIAM ALLEN WHITE

French Lick, Indiana
22nd April, 1918.

Dear Mr. White:

I have two letters from you, one in regard to the book, which probably will be waiting for me at the farm, and which I know I will enjoy ever so much. The other letter, which I should have answered a day or two ago, is in regard to Will Hays. Mr. Hays is all right. He isn't much to look at, being frail and skinny and having ears that stand out from the head, and, for a long time, I had a poor opinion of him, probably because he was at the head of the regular stand-pat organization in this state. In the last two years I have come to know him well and we have been together on the State Council of Defense for about a year. I have learned that he is personally on the square. He is a fellow of ideals, inspired by genuine patriotic motives. The worst you can say about him is that he is a strong organization man, but I believe he recognizes the value and the necessity of the recent progressive movements, and believes in giving the fullest recognition to the progressive elements in the future organization of the Republican party. Probably he does not endorse now all the planks in our platform, but I really believe he would welcome the nomination of the Colonel and be glad to support him. He is a sincere little cuss and a hard worker, and I think you will like him after you get next to him. Sam Blythe reports that out in California he has made a great hit, and that all of the factions out there have taken him to their various bosoms.

I am with best wishes,

Sincerely,
George Ade

DLC

William Allen White had sent Ade a copy of The Martial Adventure of Henry and Me *(New York: 1918) with an accompanying letter, April 16, 1918 (InLP). In a letter of April 30, 1918 (InLP), White advised Ade to read Chapters 7 and 8 "because it was for those two chapters the book was written."*

In a second letter dated April 16, 1918 (InLP), White had requested information about Will Hays because the Republican chairman had invited the editor on a trip.

50 TO SAMUEL M. RALSTON

Hazelden
Brook, Indiana
May 20th, 1919.

My dear Governor Ralston:

I am taking courage to write you because I learn that you are on very good terms with Mr. [John] Hillenbrand, one of the trustees of Purdue University. I am taking an awful chance in writing this letter because I don't know what you think about Doctor [Winthrop] Stone of Purdue. What I think about him cannot be set forth in this letter as I do not wish to violate the federal statute against sending profane matter through the mail.

Without pestering you too much, I may explain that there may soon be a crisis at Purdue and the re-election of a new president. The trustees are now about equally divided. I rather suspect that Mr. Hillenbrand may have a deciding vote some time or other when it comes to electing a president. A great many of the alumni believe that Doctor Stone by his hard and dictatorial methods, his lack of tact and friendliness, his failure to establish any sympathetic relations with the students and his vindictive attitude toward all those who do not fully agree with him, has been a blighting influence at Purdue instead of a help. A lot of the alumni are hoping to see a regular human being at the head of the school. Probably you are in a position to learn from Purdue men something about the Doctor's attitude toward the students and alumni of recent years. He has banked on a very foxy control over the trustees and a sort of business and political alliance with Henry Marshall, editor of the La Fayette Journal. He and the alumni have been carrying on a running fight and it seems to me significant that his allies in this fight are outsiders who never attended Purdue and who cannot have the sentimental regard for the school felt by the older alumni. If any private inquiries you choose to make lead you to believe that it would be better for Purdue to have a president who can establish a morale and work in harmony with students and alumni I hope you will not hesitate to have a little talk with Mr. Hillenbrand some time and sort of brace him up to vote right when the time comes. He is a bully good fellow and I like him very much.

If you want to ask any further questions regarding the Purdue situation, I shall be only too glad to tell you everything I know. I am so absolutely convinced that the future development and influence of the school will be enhanced by a change of administration that I write you this very candid letter. Of course the letter is not for publication, but it is not so blamed confidential either because it contains nothing which I am not ready to say to anybody at any time.

I am, with best wishes,

Sincerely,
George Ade

InU

Samuel M. Ralston was governor of Indiana, 1913–1917.

In 1921 the Purdue alumni managed to have a law passed which stipulated that three of the governor's appointments to the university's board of trustees should be based on the recommendation of the alumni.

Ade favored liberal, student-oriented policies. Winthrop Stone held a conservative and at times autocratic course during his term as president of the university. For a consideration of Ade's conflict as a trustee, see H. B. Knoll, The Story of Purdue Engineering *(Lafayette: 1963), pp. 50–52+.*

In addition to his duties as a member of the board of trustees Ade edited the Purdue Alumnus. *The first issue which he brought out appeared in November 1918. At that time he changed the format from a magazine to a newspaper of eight pages entitled* Purdue Alumnus Newspaper and War Bulletin. *In June 1919, the publication reverted to the* Purdue Alumnus. *The last issue Ade edited appeared July 1921. From October 1921 until his death in 1944 he was listed as a member of the editorial board or as contributing editor.*

51 ❧ TO WILLIAM DUDLEY FOULKE

Hazelden
Brook, Indiana
June 24th, 1919.

My dear Mr. Foulke:

I am wondering if you would find it possible to visit my farm here on the Fourth of July and make a little speech to all the soldiers and sailors of Newton County. I am speaking for our county committee. You would get away from the city and out into the country and I believe you would have a good time and you would not be expected to make a real long speech. How about it?

I enclose a folder which will indicate how you can get here if you decide to come and, of course, we will meet you at any station you may select within reach of here.

I am, with best wishes,

Sincerely,
George Ade

In

The homecoming for returning military was held July 4, 1919. Fred C. Kelly, George Ade: Warmhearted Satirist *(Indianapolis: 1947), p. 221, describes it as one of Ade's largest parties, "with thousands of cars parked in his nearest pasture."*

William Dudley Foulke (Robert Barclay Dillingham, pseud.) a distinguished political reformer, was at this time devoting most of his time to creative writing. Foulke did not attend Ade's party.

See Arthur W. Shumaker, A History of Indiana Literature *(Indianapolis: 1962), pp. 234–38.*

52 ❧ TO DAVID E. ROSS

Hazelden
Brook, Indiana
October 17, 1919.

My dear Dave:

I think it highly advisable that the Purdue alumni who are opposed to the [Winthrop] Stone administration at Purdue should begin to take counsel among themselves regarding the election of a Governor next year. I have been approached by a local committee and asked to sign a letter of endorsement for Warren McCray. There are certain reasons why I should sign such a letter. Mr. McCray is my brother-in-law. He is a Republican and so am I. He is the only candidate from this part of the state. We have not been in political accord at all times in recent years and there has been a degree of coolness between us and if I refuse to endorse him, my refusal will be attributed to petty reasons and small local jealousies. I want you to know that my refusal to endorse him is based upon the fact that when he became a trustee at Purdue he was an ardent supporter of Dr. Stone and his policies, without giving the alumni a chance to state their case. He declared emphatically to friends of mine in Kentland that Dr. Stone was altogether in the right and that I was altogether in the wrong regarding the investigation ordered by the State Council of Defense as to the treatment of soldiers at Purdue. Mr. McCray is on very close terms with Henry Marshall, of La Fayette, and I have a feeling that he is virtually committed to whatever policy Marshall may suggest in regard to Purdue. Also I understand that Dr. Stone has been compelled to support Ed Jackson for Governor and that gives us some hope of a division in the opposition.

Several weeks ago Mr. McCray called on me and asked me to give him my support. I told him that I would not make any attempt to prevent his nomination but I also told him that it would be impossible to line up the Purdue alumni in his support since it was believed that he was outspoken in his support of Dr. Stone and in his opposition to the alumni. He replied that he was not committed to any support of Dr. Stone and would be glad to get further information in regard to the Purdue matter and would be guided more or less by my judgment in the matter. I do not attach much importance to those vague promises because he put himself on record long ago regarding the Stone issue. Now I am coming to the point. I am told that Mr. McCray is going to be nominated and that probably he will be elected. Is it worth while for the Purdue alumni to try to get to him and show him the facts in the case? The alumni cannot master any terrific vote. If the alumni openly oppose him and he is elected, of course, we will have no standing. If we support him, will we have any standing?

Shall we attempt to get the new bill through the legislature before a new Governor is elected? I am informed by an Indianapolis man who claims to be posted, that John Isenbarger is going to be nominated by the Democrats. If so, I will be in a devil of a fix. If I support McCray, I will have to throw down our best friend on the Board and I am more interested in Purdue University than anything else in Indiana. If I support Isenbarger, I will have to desert my party and oppose the man who married my sister and I will be given credit for being actuated by small and selfish motives. If the Purdue issue were out of the way, I would be willing to line up for Mr. McCray. I don't see how I can declare for him, however, without throwing down all of my Purdue friends who have been with me in the long fight against Dr. Stone.

What shall we do in the premises? What is the wise and politic thing to do in order to help our case?

I am sending duplicates to [Franklin] Chandler and [Henry] Vinton and I will ask them to give me a private opinion.

I am, with best wishes,

Sincerely,
George Ade

InLP

Warren T. McCray lost the gubernatorial primary in 1916, when James P. Goodrich became the Republican candidate and subsequently governor. In 1919 the party machine backed McCray, who won the governorship by a vast majority in 1920.

Edward L. Jackson ran against McCray in the primary of 1920; he became McCray's secretary of state.

John Isenbarger was a candidate in the Democratic primary. See Thomas R. Johnston and Helen Rand, The Trustees and the Officers of Purdue University 1865–1940 *(Lafayette: 1940).*

George Ade by Robert Grafton

1920-1930

The Great War ended and America devoted itself to having fun. During this period of national adolescence Hollywood became the glamor capital. Ade devoted much energy to writing movie scenarios, but he did not succeed in devising a film formula palatable to the lost generation. The author blocked out a number of story lines. Numerous submissions were rejected. In the Tea Pot Dome era political scandal touched Ade's family. There were compensations, however. People continually sought his advice. There were reunions and trips with old friends. It was the past rather than the present that concerned Ade as the decade crashed to a finish.

53 ❧ TO JAMES D. RATHBUN

Belleair Heights, Florida
6 February, 1922.

My dear Jim:

Glad to have your letter of the 1st. Probably you have received a box of grape-fruit from here. I sent it rather soon after the first shipment because my friends who run the packing-house here were about to make the final shipment of the season. A hurricane swept over this region in October and blew nearly all the fruit off the trees, but I was assured that the stuff they sent you would be very good.

I note what you say about the political situation. So far as I am concerned, I will have to climb a tree. I have known [Albert] Beveridge for years and of course we were together in the Progressive movement and I could not very well oppose him, but it happens that Harry New, with whom I have not always been in political sympathy, is a very good personal friend of mine, and incidentally a fraternity brother. Over a year ago, before there was any intimation that he would be opposed by any one, he wrote me a letter of inquiry and, although I have no copy of my reply, I think I told him that I had heard of no opposition to his re-election and that I would be friendly to him. So you see I am in somewhat of a hole. I learn on good authority that the administration has offered Beveridge all sorts of important posts but he has refused all of them and is evidently determined to make a fight for the Senate. I hear the President is willing to make Harry New Postmaster-General but New would rather go back to the Senate. I wish you would let me know the date of the primary so that I can arrange to hide somewhere until it is over. I don't mean this literally, but I am really in a predicament as to what I should do if I am called upon to commit myself.

Glad to get the news from home at any time. Joe and Otto showed up the other day for a visit and both are enjoying good health and having the usual number of arguments. Best wishes to all.

Sincerely,
InLP George Ade

James D. Rathbun married Nellie Ade, the author's niece. Rathbun managed Ade's property.

Albert Beveridge was a senator from Indiana, 1900–1910. The Old Guard never accepted him completely. He was defeated for a third term in 1911. Beveridge went with Theodore Roosevelt in the Republican split of 1912, and became temporary chairman of the Progressive National Convention. He lost the senatorial race of 1922 to Samuel Ralston. After this defeat he resumed his career as a historical biographer, working on the first volumes of Abraham Lincoln.

For a consideration of Beveridge's campaign and his difficulties with Harry New see Claude G. Bowers, Beveridge and the Progressive Era *(New York: 1932), pp. 530–35.*

54 ❧ TO JESSE L. LASKY

[Florida]
8 March, 1922

My dear Mr. Lasky:

Thank you for your telegram and for your very kind offer to assist the Indiana Society. The date for the dinner has not been set and it probably will depend upon the time when the picture can be secured. The whole idea is being worked up by the officers of the club in Chicago. I would much prefer to find out what we have in the way of a picture before we try to make a splurge with it. If you have any inside information as to how the darned thing is working out, I wish you would let me know and, if you can now make a guess as to when the picture might be secured for a private showing before the Indiana Society, I will be very much obliged.

Now, in regard to "Back Home and Broke": The treatment accorded me by you and all of your associates has been such that I am extremely prejudiced in your favor. I would rather do a picture for you than anybody else. As I wired you, I have been disposed to wait and see what we had accomplished with "Our Leading Citizen" before I tackled another continuity. I have been connected with the show business long enough to find out that nothing must be taken for granted and that no play is a success until the returns are in. Also, I have always hoped that sometime or other authors writing for the screen might be paid on a royalty basis. I never have made important money selling stuff outright. Each successful play which I did for the stage brought me in a great deal more than the sum you are now offering. The two failures which I had out of a total of fourteen plays on which I drew royalties brought me practically nothing, as I never in my life asked or accepted an advance payment until I signed the contract with you for "Our Leading Citizen." Two or three pieces that were moderately successful brought as much, or more than I am able to get for a screen play, and the real winners such as "The College Widow," "The County Chairman" and "Father and the Boys" ran as high as a hundred thousand dollars for a single play before the piece was finally sent to the stock companies. Always in writing for the stage I had a chance to get some real money provided the producer got his. Of course I am not pretending that I know anything about the details of your business. Under present conditions and when you are compelled to take a gamble on an untried story, I can understand that you would not feel disposed to offer large money, but on the other hand the author who has only a few stories ready to market can see no prospect of juicy returns so long as he sells his stuff outright. I am convinced that sooner or later the plays for the screen will be produced on a percentage basis. The percentage would not have to be high. At present undoubtedly a good many writers would possibly be skeptical as to the bookkeeping methods of some of the companies, but I would not be afraid to trust your organization.

I am trying to come to a decision regarding "Back Home and Broke." I could use the fifteen thousand dollars but I don't want to sign unless I feel that I could deliver a good continuity on the date you set and that the play would not infringe upon anybody else's story. What would be your idea as to the date of delivery? I expect to go north about the middle of April, or sooner, and I would much prefer to do the work at the Farm as I believe that I could turn out a continuity which would include everything we might want to use and then be subject to cuts, the same as the other play. I believe in letting the first draft run very full and not attempt any editing too soon because one can never tell in advance which part of the story will develop the best. After a script gets cold it is very easy to work the blue pencil, and Mr. [Frank] Woods and Mr. [James] Young will tell you that I am just as much in favor of cutting as they are. The only time I might put up a kick is when the changes have a tendency to alter the whole intent of the story.

I shall be very glad to hear from you at your leisure. Perhaps Mr. Woods has told you that the American Magazine has accepted a story for the May number, to be out April 15th, which I believe will be welcome reading to you and your associates. I am still considering a proposition from the Bell Syndicate to do eight or ten articles for a whole string of newspapers. I want to be sure that I have the proper material in sight before I promise delivery. Mr.

[Seymour] Eyton promised to send me some photographs and data, and I suppose they are on the way. This is a good time to pull some sensible propaganda and offset the vicious and inexcusable stuff being written by Doherty, of the Chicago Tribune, and others.

I shall be at this hotel until March 18th, and then for a couple of weeks I will be at the Hotel Alcazar, St. Augustine, Florida. I will notify the studio as to my movements after that time.

I am, with best wishes,

Sincerely,
George Ade

InLP

On February 17, 1923, Jesse L. Lasky, the head of Famous Players Corp., had sent Ade a contract and had enclosed a $5,000 advance. Ade was holding out for a percentage of the gross.

Frank Woods was a scenario writer.

James Young was a director.

The propaganda to which Ade refers is his "Answering Wild Eyed Questions about the Movie Stars at Hollywood," American Magazine *(May 1922).*

55 ❧ TO THE *NEW YORK AMERICAN*

Hazelden
Brook, Indiana
June 16th, 1922

Gentlemen:

I have your request that I shall name the greatest woman in the United States and give my reasons for the choice. I submit the following:

To attempt to elect the "greatest" woman in the United States, at a time when talented women are in evidence before the public, is a difficult and dangerous task but after considering the claims of several candidates, I shall vote for Mary Roberts Rinehart. Mrs. Rinehart is a highly successful novelist, a playwright of marked ability, an essayist with a real sense of humor, a traveler and explorer and a student of all present day problems. As a young woman she qualified as a nurse and because of her early training she was enabled to render war work of unusual value. She went to the front and flew in airplanes and put herself strenuously into the big activities of the war. She is a good mother. She never has sacrificed any of the distinctive charms of her sex. She is well-groomed and companionable and interesting. I know of no other woman in this country who has shown so many unusual qualities and retained at the same time all the desirable qualities of womanhood.

Yours very truly,
George Ade

InLP

Ade wrote Mary Roberts Rinehart, August 19, 1927 (InLP), and reiterated his high opinion of her.

56 ☙ TO WILL HAYS

Hazelden
Brook, Indiana
29th June, 1922.

My dear Will Hays:

Just for your information and so that you may keep track of some of the absurdities of the present methods of censorship, I want to tell you what happened to OUR LEADING CITIZEN in Pennsylvania. I would have sworn that this picture was fumigated, deodorized and scrubbed up until even the most finicky censor in all the world could not find a scene or a word of text which might not properly have been shown in any church on a Sabbath evening. It remained for one of the wise birds in Pennsylvania to detect in a sub-title a phrase which he must have regarded as unpatriotic to the point of treason, for he had the words cut out.

You will remember in the picture that after Dan Bentley meets the girl in France, she comes home and talks to the women's club as to her experiences at the front. This scene is preceded by the following text:

> After the Great Disturbance had ended, and people were trying to find out what it had all been about. Katherine Fendle was telling them—back in Wing-field—that Foch and Pershing and Major Dan Bentley really won the war.

The Board of Censors in Pennsylvania cut out:

> and people were trying to find out what it had all been about.

Why? Of course the phrase was put in as a mere pleasantry, but also it was meant to suggest the fact that everywhere, since the war, people have been discussing the issues involved and trying to discover the hidden causes of the great conflict. I don't think the censors meant to dispute the suggestion that people have been talking about the real causes of the war. It is pretty hard to fathom the mental operations of the feeble-minded, but I suppose these censors figured that I was trying to put over an implication that there was really some doubt as to the righteousness of America's participation in the war. Of course we meant nothing of the sort and I can't imagine any one detecting dangerous propaganda in such a harmless little paragraph.

All of which is submitted merely for your information. I don't know that we can do anything in the premises.

I am, with best wishes,

Sincerely,
George Ade

InLP

Will H. Hays served as president of the Motion Picture Producers and Distributors of America, Inc., 1922–1945. The Hays office was the censor librorum *of films. This incident inspired Ade to write "Censorship in America,"* Indianapolis Star, *January 14, 1923.*

57 TO WILLIAM FRED KURFESS

Hazelden
Brook, Indiana
11 October, 1922.

My dear Fred:

Whatever Miss [Grace] Smith's scenario may be, I have no doubt it will look like a D. W. Griffith script compared with the one which came in the mail with your letter last night. It was from Mrs. Fowler, of Watseka, Illinois, and the title was THE GYPSY'S WARNING. She had condensed a six-reel feature into two hundred words and, as nearly as I could make out, the plot of the piece was that George and Frank both loved the same girl and Frank pulled a lot of dirty stuff and deceived the girl for a while but eventually virtue triumphed and the girl threw herself into the arms of the true-hearted, faithful and honest George. After reading Mrs. Fowler's scenario, I am convinced that she has a great name for her hero. These people who have an itch to write for the movies little know about the drudgery connected with the preparation of a real working script. Our final revise of BACK HOME AND BROKE consisted of ninety-five long typewritten pages, about four hundred and fifty separate photographic "shots" and three hundred and fifty inserts of text. Of course we will cut out possibly one-third of this stuff on the final editing but, at that, we will do much less photographing than usual. Many of the plays which are finally exhibited in six thousand feet, or so, are cut down from twenty to thirty thousand feet.

When Miss Smith sends me her manuscript I shall try to break some of the horrible truth to her.

I count upon visiting you in your new apartment. Before I close the house next month you and Ardis [Ade Kurfess] must come down here and load up on honey. We took a hundred and fifty pounds away from the bees yesterday. Also, we have a large crop of hickory nuts. If there is no chance of your being here within the next three or four weeks, I will ask Jim Rathbun to take charge of your share and see that it is delivered. Remember me to Ardis.

Sincerely,
George Ade

K

58 ☙ TO L. W. BOYNTON

Hazelden
Brook, Indiana
7 November, 1922.

Dear Mr. Boynton:
I have your letter asking for an expression of opinion as to what Mr. [Will] Hays and his associates may accomplish in the way of regulating and improving the output of motion pictures.

I believe that Mr. Hays is sincere and has a very definite program in mind and will be of immense help to the makers of motion pictures. Also I believe that the public, which is paying to see plays on the screen, will gradually decide upon the kind of plays it wants and that these plays will be somewhat different from most of the picture plays which have been released up to date. I think that the screen drama probably will go through the same periods of evolution and change as those which have marked the development of the spoken drama in America. All of us can remember when every native play was a melodrama, packed full of sensational incidents and leading up to highly theatrical climaxes. Gradually we got away from the "thrillers" and the intelligent theatre-going public became interested in plays in which the story moved deliberately and in which characterization was just as important as plot. Up to the present time the average producer of motion pictures has felt that he must put into his picture, all of the time, swift action and intense melodrama. He has piled one sensational episode on top of another. I think we are due now for a reaction against this feverish type of picture play. The same public which reacted against the lurid melodrama of years ago is now getting tired of the play which is merely a series of death-beds and crimes. Of course, love interest will always be sure-fire but I am convinced that the public is ready to accept and support picture plays which tell a simple story in a pleasant way without making any attempt to be bloodcurdling.

I am, with best wishes,

Sincerely,
George Ade

InLP

L. W. Boynton, editor of the Exhibitors Trade Review, *had asked Ade for his opinion of the Motion Picture Producers and Distributors of America, Inc.*

59 TO WILLIAM FRED KURFESS

French Lick, Ind.
22 November, 1922.

Dear Fred:

I am glad to know that the tickets turned out all right. Tomorrow I go up to LaFayette to pull for Purdue against Indiana and I hope we may win at least one game.

You ask me about [Albert] Beveridge: He was defeated by

the Republicans. The old stand-pat crowd organized very carefully against him, picked out a certain number of men in each precinct and pledged them to vote for [Samuel] Ralston. It was all done very systematically—not only to punish Beveridge for supporting [Theodore] Roosevelt in 1912 but also to prevent him from becoming a Presidential possibility. The old organization men knew they could not control him, and so they formed a secret organization which was a darned sight more effective than their regular organization and deliberately knifed him. For instance, in one strong Republican district in Indianapolis, Merrill Moores, a Sigma Chi and a stand-pat Congressman, was elected by six thousand majority and Beveridge, in the same district, was defeated by six thousand. This made a difference of twelve thousand votes in one district. The regular Republicans in this district voted against him, not because he was against union labor or they doubted his war record, but simply because they were good organization men and did whatever the party leaders told them to do. They were lined up and pledged and the work was done so thoroughly that Beveridge never had a chance. Undoubtedly he got a great many women votes from the Democrats and a lot of independents favored him, and yet he was defeated by about 34,000, while the Republican State ticket made up of nobodies and claiming only the regular party support went through by about 24,000. When all of the facts become known, I think we will have civil war in Indiana. The stand-patters have told us all the time that we should vote for the party nominee, no matter what our personal preferences might be. They voted for Ralston this time in order to remove Beveridge from public life, and I have a notion that the old Progressives all over the State will be fighting mad.

I arrive back in Chicago Sunday but I count on leaving for White Sulphur Springs on Monday to meet Tom Meighan and discuss plans for another picture and at the end of next week I go on to New York to help edit and cut BACK HOME AND BROKE. I will be back in Chicago shortly before the Indiana dinner, which falls on December 9th.

Remember me to Ardis [Ade Kurfess]. I am, with best wishes,

Sincerely,

K George Ade

60 ⁂ TO ARTHUR S. BOWES

January 9, 1923.

Dear Mr. Bowes:

I have postponed answering your letter of the 4th because I have been laid up with the grippe.

I shall now attempt to include in one letter all the advice and tips that I can give you. I thought it was understood from the beginning that I would not attempt to write anything for this review and it must be understood that my name is not to be used in any way. I have a great amount of work which must be done and I simply can't assume the responsibility for a show which is being put on far away and beyond any possible supervision. I will go through your letters and take up various points which have been suggested by you and try to make a clean up.

1—When you lay out the show be sure that you know what scenes are to be used and what settings and fix up your scenes so that all the changes can be made promptly and without holding up the show. Do not postpone your set rehearsals too long. Get the mechanical end of the show organized and let the boys run through the changes repeatedly so that they understand the order in which everything comes.

2—It will be necessary to alternate front scenes in one with deeper sets and, of course, finishing Act I—with a big full stage scene and many people.

3—In putting your show together remember Act II—shall be shorter than Act I—and should contain your best material. The stuff that you are confident will get over big. Do not rehearse acts in the order in which they come on the bill. Put in more time on numbers coming late on bill than on the early features. Whatever you do keep the show moving. Cut out the two verse songs with long waits between verses. I know you won't do this but if you don't your show will suffer. Every author thinks that his song will not get over and get a fair show unless two verses are sung. This is all nonsense. Have some pity on the people in front. Sing one verse and then go to your chorus and dances. Do not permit encores unless actually demanded. This is most important and is the secret of the success of a good Ziegfield show. The curse of amateur performances is that every author wants two or three verses of his song done and every singer wants to respond to encores. Keep the performance speeded up. Go from one scene to another without delay. Have your people come on promptly, deliver the goods and then get out of the way for the next feature.

4–Do not attempt to carry any story through a review. Make your entertainment a series of singing and dancing and a dramatic feature. Make these various numbers as short as possible and avoid the type of number for which college clubs seem to have a special fondness. That is, all the lights down and somebody in evening clothes with a spot light on him singing a long dragging sentimental song to some beautiful goddess. It is all right to have two or three numbers in which light effects are employed but most of the time keep your stage lighted and shoot your stuff promptly and don't over play the sentimental stuff.

5–You should have at least one or possibly two features where no music is used. If you want the very catchy little song entitled "Words Mean Nothing To Me" now being done in the "Music Review" and recently seen in Chicago, I can get the manuscript from Sam Harris. Also I think that out on the farm I have a sort of burlesque play using the radio called "Old New Stuff." Your one act program stuff should come in the first part of the show.

I wrote Mr. [O. K.] Quivey approving his general suggestion but I wish to say now that his proposed number in front of the new Union Building should not run eighteen or twenty minutes. It should be kept down to six or eight minutes and consist of songs only. No talk. The idea of showing the old couples on the side is very good. But this kind of an act with only a few people employed and no chorus and with the lights down would die a terrible death if strung out for twenty minutes. It could be made a good feature, snappy and not too serious.

He makes another suggestion in regard to [Purdue] "Blues." The song would have to be a corker to stand for twelve or fourteen verses. A safer plan would be to have some boy on the Harry Clark corner come out with a big book and do a series of parodies. Take all the popular songs of the last year and write a parody for the refrain of each and let him do them one after the other, saving three or four of his best one[s] for encores. In my opinion the "blues" stuff has been over done and is a little out of date.

In regard to the "Conference Medley." It is good and the scenes are all fine for a college farce. This feature has been done before but it is always safe.

I note his fourth suggestion, the number called the "Butterfly and the Rose." In a review of this kind it is always advisable to open Act II, with a full stage setting and have some kind of allegorical dance number. This would be a good feature for the setting he proposes but would not make it a song number. I would make it a dance number.

The great thing to remember in connection with numbers of this kind is that they must not be too long. The only possible exception might be a big dance number beginning Act II. This can be made a little longer if you have several principals to draw on. I think for a college show a safer plan would be to have a ball room setting introducing different kinds of ball room dancing. I have seen very few amateurs who can get away with the "allegorical" stuff. When they try that Isadore Duncan acting, they [act] as if they were trying to pick grapes. Put in lots of dancing. You can't have too many good dance numbers and you need a good teacher who knows stage dancing. You can also stand for at least two big musical numbers keeping the larger act for the latter part of the show.

I note that some of the boys have been writing sentimental songs. They are all right if you get them in and get them over with but—don't try to string them out with a repetition of voices.

The trouble with the suggestions you are sending on is that they do not make any provision for comedy. They all deal with moonlight and love and the other old ingredients. You might do this year a number which I suggested once before. Show a football coach talking to a bunch of candidates in playing costume. Pad the costumes out and make them look like giants. He is predicting a successful season. Have a messenger from the faculty come in and take out some man who is behind in his work and offer as a substitute some man who is absolutely tough in everything and weighs about ninety pounds. As the practice progresses and the conversation goes on various professors come in and black list players and substitute others, until the team consists of a bunch of misfits. The finish being someone representing Dr. [Edward] Elliott coming out and telling the coach to go ahead and beat Chicago.

I note that Miss [Katherine] Kennedy favors the song entitled "The Little Red School House." The suggestion sounds promising, but remember you must not make a mistake in getting all your songs alike. Don't get too many sentimental songs.

A feature easily worked up and one that is always good would be to produce a photographic album. Have a huge album built into the middle of the setting, someone to give a talk about the different students of the past and then open the album revealing one at a time some of the funny looking types of the past.

I note your suggestions in regard to style show scene. I have never thought that these could be done well enough in a college show to pay one for bothering with them. You can't expect to compete with the big producers so far as dresses are concerned. A college show should consist of wit, life and color and there is no need of struggling for a lot of elaborate costumes.

A good finish for Act I, would be "Memories of the Purdue Minstrel." Build up the setting so as to show off your people and make it a big singing finale, with a couple of jokes and possibly some brass on the elevated seats.

I wish I could undertake to assume the responsibility for this show but I cannot do so at long range and my time will be so taken up that I would not dare to undertake the job. I have simply tried to give you a few hints and also feel quite sure that you will find them available if you have the courage to put them into effect.

With best wishes,

Sincerely,

InLP George Ade

Arthur S. Bowes, the manager of the Harlequin Club of Purdue University, had written Ade for advice on a proposed revue. Bowes, Katherine Kennedy, the director, and O. K. Quivey, the composer, expected Ade to write the dialogue.

This revue was never staged. The Harlequins presented George M. Cohan's George Washington Junior, *April 26–28, 1923.*

61 ❧ TO ROBERT G. KANE

Miami Beach, Florida
January 26, 1923.

My dear Mr. Kane:

I am going to ask you to do me another favor and for the present you may regard this letter as confidential. Here is my tale of woe:

About a year ago Tom Meighan asked me to send to Dick Barthelemes the story which I had submitted to Tom called "The Melancholy Hoosier." I thought it would be good for Tom but Tom believed it would be better for a man of Barthelemes' type. I sent a very full outline of the story to Mr. Barthelemes and he kept it for several weeks and I gathered from the letter he wrote me that it was considered by his associates. He finally returned it saying that it was a good story but it was a comedy treatment and he thought he could do better in more serious parts. I did not urge him to consider the play any further and did not offer to change the outline so as to make it fit him, although, it would have been an easy matter to do so.

Two or three weeks ago I picked up a picture magazine and read the outline of the new picture play called "Fury" in which Barthelemes is starring and was considerably upset to find out that the outline of the story was in all instances practically the same as "The Melancholy Hoosier." I said nothing about my discovery. My secretary, Mr. Ray Rice, who is now in the North went to see the play in Chicago and immediately wrote me that the outline was exactly the same as our story. I had not asked him to look at the picture. He helped me in preparing the outline and was familiar with our story.

"Fury" was written by Mr. Gouldey or [Edmund] Goulding who does all the scenario work for Mr. Barthelemes. I do not want to do anything in haste but from the outline of the play sent to me by my secretary, we are put out of business so far as "The Melancholy Hoosier" is concerned. The back-grounds are changed, but what you might call the dramatic essentials are exactly the same in each story.

In each story the central character is a young man who makes a pledge to an older man to avenge a certain wrong. In my story he is an adopted son. In the other story he is a natural son.

In each story the older man knows he has but a short time to live. He has a "bad heart," and so he tells the young man the story of his ruined life. Of the man who came between him and the woman he loved and how this man wrecked not only his life but the woman's life. How he has brooded over the villiany of this man and therefore he pledges the young man to hunt up this man who has done the great injury to him and punish him. In other words, beat him up.

In each story the young man dare not tell the girl he wants to marry. In each story the young man dare not marry the girl until he carries out the promise.

In each story the girl misunderstands the situation and thinks that he is neglecting her or throwing her down.

In each story the young fellow hunts up the man he has promised to lick, never having seen him before he deliberately picks a quarrel with him and is therefore beaten up.

In each story the young man then makes a new vow that he will keep his promise. He carefully prepares himself for a second battle with the villian and this time he is successful and licks the man and is free to marry the girl.

Now that this story has been produced I feel that I would not dare go ahead with "The Melancholy Hoosier" for everyone would say that I was stealing the "original" story done by Mr. Gouldey or Goulding. I don't know what to do in the matter, but I am absolutely convinced that somebody in the office of the Company handling the play for Mr. Barthelemes did grab my story.

A few months ago Mr. Douglas McLean asked me to show him the manuscript of "The Melancholy Hoosier" and he has been after me ever since to give it to him for production, promising that he would get me a good production and a good price for the story.

I have heard very convincing reports regarding Mr. Duerr, the head of the Company, and I am reluctant to make trouble but I simply can't help but feel that somebody double crossed me.

When Tom Meighan gets back I will put the thing up to him. I am perfectly willing to employ a good lawyer to go to Mr. Duerr and lay all of the facts before him. I am quite sure that I have been badly treated. If the Company was getting ready to produce a play that resembled my play they should have said so. Instead of that they go ahead and produce a play that has exactly the same outline as mine without saying anything to me.

I hope that I am not bothering you too much but I surely want your advice.

I am with best wishes,

Sincerely,

InLP George Ade

Robert G. Kane was a representative of Famous Players Lasky Corporation.

Edmund Goulding published Fury *(New York: 1922).* Fury, *which was credited as "From a novel by Edmund Goulding," was released by Inspiration Pictures, Inc., 1922.*

In a letter to John N. Wheeler, July 2, 1926 (InLP), Ade described The Melancholy Hoosier, *a comedy version of* Hamlet, *as a "rip roaring farce, full of physical violence and melodrama." Famous Players rejected* The Melancholy Hoosier, *September 30, 1926.*

62 TO WARREN T. MC CRAY

Hazelden
Brook, Indiana
July 5th, 1923.

My dear Governor:

I have read over very carefully the document left here yesterday. It strikes me as very binding and obligatory and probably was framed by some enterprising attorney for the bank who wished to make everything air-tight. The sum of money involved is so large and the chances of marketing any kind of farm property within the next few years are so uncertain, not to say hazardous, that I cannot bring myself to the belief that the signing of this document will be a mere formality. If I have read the document in its true meaning I would be assuming an obligation equivalent to all of the assets that I could possibly command, even by a forced sale of all of my holdings. As I told you yesterday, I am operating in a small way now—I am not buying, selling, or speculating, but simply trying to live safely within my income and carry out some reasonable plans in connection with Purdue University and other institutions in which I am interested. I would not dare to guarantee any project of my own which involved the sale of large tracts of land within the next few years and I am just as reluctant to guarantee any projects for any one else.

In the matter of contracts I have found that the only safe plan is to submit all written instruments to my attorney, Mr. [Carl] Meyer, of the firm of Mayor, Meyer, Austrian & Platt, of Chicago. I have sent in to him a copy of the proposed guarantee or surety and I am asking him to what extent I would be obligated and bound in case I signed my name. I am awaiting an opinion from him, but I think it is only fair to let you know, in the meantime, that probably I will be compelled to say that I cannot sign any document which would put into jeopardy everything that I possess. I would not do it for my own benefit and I cannot convince myself that it is my duty to assume what might develope into a large risk, however much I am desirous of granting a favor.

I shall write you again when I hear from Mr. Meyer.

I am, with best wishes,

Sincerely,
George Ade

InLP

Warren T. McCray had asked Ade to sign a guaranty which would make him personally liable for $600,000 and any legal fees incurred in connection with the enforcement of the guaranty.

63 TO THOMAS MEIGHAN

[Hazelden]
[Brook, Indiana]
Sept. 7th, 1923.

My dear Tom:

As I wired you today I was very happy to get your letter written on Sunday, and to learn that the old play was going right through on schedule time. Unless I made some mistake on figuring our footage should be much less than it was in the other plays and unless a lot of new material has been put in the cutting should not be a hard job.

Regarding what I wrote you about love interest, I did not mean to compare you with some of the former stars and I quite agree with your point of view regarding the necessity of a good clean love story backing up the comedy and drama. What I have felt, in looking at a good many pictures, is that the studio methods of indicating that a young man is in love with a young woman are a little too emphatic. Somehow I don't like to have the hero take the girl in his arms until we know that he has a right to do so. Of course, we will all be interested in studying this new picture and I really believe people will like you in the part. You are not a woman-hater but a very busy man who hesitates to plunge into an affair with any woman until he knows what he is doing.

I note what you say about the possibility of another story. Let us wait and see how the present one turns out. I don't mind telling you that at times I have been very much afraid of it. If we do tackle another one I hope we can get all of the main points settled so far in advance that there will not have to be any mad house work on the script just before the shooting begins. In the case of the present picture there was a long delay because we were dickering over terms. When [Thomas] Geraghty and [Al] Green[e] came here we did not know what the construction project was to be and that held up the whole thing. Mr. [Jesse] Lasky insisted on my coming to Hollywood at once, so I could not talk with you and get your views. Consequently after you arrived and made your suggestions, which were all good, we had to take the whole thing to pieces and put it together again. Ray [Long] and I would get up at seven o'clock in the morning and go at that script. We made practically three different copies out there and revised as high as fifty pages of script a day. After working all day I tried to attend parties at night and the consequence was that when I arrived at San Francisco I keeled over. I had the doctor come in Tuesday morning and I did not get out of my room until Saturday afternoon and I sure was in a bad way. If I tackle another picture I want to get my program laid out in advance and have a thorough understanding with you and the director and every one else as to what we are trying to do, so that I will not be compelled to go through any such strenuous experience as I did this summer. Of course, I am not putting the blame on any one else but conditions were such that in a short time . . . and this fact, with other complications, put me on the hummer. After I got back to Chicago Doctor [Frank] Billings told me that I must never tackle another picture and I took a solemn vow that I never would although I am convinced that there is no need of all this strain and worry and anxiety if we all get together in plenty of time.

As I wired you this morning, I count on going to New York with you. Of course, I would be delighted to have all of you come to the farm, but Geraghty will be in New York and the facilities for editing and cutting will be much better at the studio. I have written [John] Jenks asking him to go along. If he cannot go I will gladly join your party and share a drawing room with anyone (male) who needs a roommate.

The idea of the preview is mighty good. I am just as sorry as you are about Larry [Wheat] not being in this picture. The part was written for him and I supposed he would be in it until I got word from you that he had signed with Miss [Norma] Talmage. When I arrived at Hollywood Mr. [George] Agnew had been practically signed up.

I have seen some of the advertisements and the new title looks good in print. I think we acted wisely in making a change.

Remember me to Mrs. Meighan, Al, and all the others. I am, with best wishes

Sincerely,

P.S. How about changing spoken title 175, in the revised text,—speech by Col. Lynwood, to read as follows:

"—the absolute finish! We sail tomorrow—on the Majestic. I'm going back to England—the home of the Scotch!"?

InLP G. A.

Ade had known Thomas Meighan since the actor played Billy Bolton in the New York production of The College Widow. *Frances Ring, who had appeared in* The County Chairman, *at Ade's behest, played Jane Witherspoon, the "Widow." Meighan married his leading lady and Ade considered himself "their matrimonial agent." George Ade, "Thomas Meighan,"* The Lambs Script, *3 (August 1936).*

Ade had recently returned from the West Coast where he had completed the scenario for Woman-Proof.

64 TO JAMES P. GOODRICH

Hazelden
Brook, Indiana
October 24th, 1923.

My dear Governor:

I have just arrived home after a busy month in New York City where I have been engaged in a moving picture project.

I find on my desk a note from you regarding that note of mine which we do not remember to have received here. I have no doubt it was merely lost some where but I was advised by a very good authority in Chicago yesterday that if the note every should turn up it might make trouble for me. I was advised to get an indemnifying bond which you very kindly offered to send me and I wish you would do so so that we could close the incident and know that there would be no chance of the darn thing showing up and making trouble. The note was dated August 22nd, the amount was ten thousand dollars, payable to you at the Continental & Commercial National Bank at Chicago on August 31st and the rate of interest I believe was seven per cent. The check to take up the note was dated August 24th and was received by you and acknowledged by your secretary on August 25th with the understanding that it was to be used on the 30th to take up the note. It was deposited in your bank on the 29th and was cleared in Chicago on the 30th.

I don't want to bother you by sending a lawyer over to have an indemnifying bond made out and I don't want this incident to annoy you, but I am simply making this suggestion on the advice of . . . [*carbon illegible*] friend who says I should protect myself against the remote chance of somebody getting hold of the note in some way and possibly using it as collateral or being led to believe that it was negotiable.

I have kept some track of developments while I was away and

have been rather interested to learn that the Governor did not show you any degree of gratitude for your work in organizing the jack-pot. It is certainly a terrible mixup and the passing out of the bank at Kentland has had a most depressing effect upon our whole community.

I will be here at the farm for the next ten days. With best wishes, I am

Sincerely,
George Ade

InLP

James P. Goodrich had been helping Warren T. McCray to avoid scandal by organizing a group of friends to raise $350,000 to aid Governor McCray pay his outstanding debts. The press referred to the fund raisers as the Goodrich Pool.

Earlier in October James Moorman, McCray's political adviser, accused Goodrich of instigating the Washington investigation of McCray's financial affairs for political advancement. Goodrich denied the charge. McCray in his holograph Memoirs *(InK), notes that Moorman was loyal but ill advised in his accusation.*

During the Marion County Grand Jury investigation, witnesses from McCray's hometown of Kentland testified that they knew nothing of the obligation of notes on their firms which their banker had negotiated. The repudiation of the governor's notes resulted in a run on the Discount and Deposit Bank of Kentland, and the institution was forced to close for reorganization.

The grand jury investigation was postponed in mid October when McCray was charged with forgery of a note signed "A. Messman and Co." in a suit filed by the Brownstown Loan and Trust Company against the Meyer-Kiser Bank. The Inter-Southern Life Insurance Company filed suit to foreclose on the mortgage of McCray's Orchard Lake Stock Farm. The grand jury then demanded McCray's records for the $155,000 loan from the State Board of Agriculture. Post office inspectors sent questionnaires to state banks inquiring about McCray's dealings with these institutions through the mails. As a result, McCray was accused of thefts which totalled $255,000 in eight indictments containing 192 counts.

He was convicted of using the mails to defraud, April 28, 1924, and was sentenced to the Federal Penitentiary in Atlanta, Georgia, for ten years.

Ade wrote John McCutcheon, Autumn 1923 (InLP):

> I was interested to know that W. T. [McCray] had written you. He is very firmly convinced that he never did anything wrong and from his point of view I dare say he didn't. Probably you will agree with me, after trying to borrow money from one bank, that anyone who

can borrow from 207 banks should be given the Nobel prize and a Carnegie medal instead of being incarcerated at Atlanta. We are trying to get him out but I don't know what he will do after he gets out because the last shred of his fortune has gone but he thinks that he is a financial wizard and can immediately make large sums of money by generous and judicious investments. I don't know where he expects to get his money. He told a visitor lately that I was going to provide it. If that is the way he is talking he should be in an asylum instead of a federal prison.

65 ❧ TO JAMES D. RATHBUN

French Lick, Indiana
November 11, 1923

My dear Jim;

Glad to have your letter. The dentist certainly did things to me. I was under the gas for half an hour and he busted a couple of teeth and mangled me more or less—my jaws are still aching.

Glad to know that everything has been attended to over at Hazelden.

I had an awful shock last night when I got the news from the Ohio game. It is not a very hopeful prelude to Home Coming.

All the later reports on the picture are most encouraging. I understand it went very well at Lafayette.

The news regarding the Governor [Warren T. McCray] does not surprise me. He has always regarded me as a criminal because I had a few amiable vices of which he sternly disapproved. His code seems to be that if you never drink a highball or play a game of poker, you have a dispensation to go out and rob the widows. Of course I talked about that letter from [James P.] Goodrich. It was not confidential and the facts reported in the letter were already known to the people with whom I talked. I am enclosing to you another letter from Goodrich which you may return to me in due time. Joe Kealing and Tom Taggart have given me some interesting dope down here. They are certainly off of the Governor for life.

I am sending you some hickory nuts, about the hardest thing in the world to get this year.

With best wishes to all

Sincerely,
George Ade

Note enclosures—Also, see if you can find in Mss. drawer—lower large drawer in large file, some type-written copies of "The Microbe's Serenade"—Send me a couple. Here until Friday morning.
InLP G. A.

Joseph B. Kealing, a prominent lawyer, had served as the United States district attorney for Indiana, 1891–99.

Thomas Taggart, former United States senator from Indiana, 1916, had been elected chairman of the board of directors of the Fletcher National Bank of Indianapolis. This institution figured in the Warren T. McCray case.

Ade had written "The Microbe's Serenade" as a lyric for The Sho-Gun. *This Gilbert and Sullivan imitation proved too difficult for the chorus, and was excluded from the libretto. It remained one of Ade's favorite verses, and he frequently recited it when called upon to speak and handed out printed and mimeographed copies to friends.*

66 ❧ TO CHARLES G. DAWES

Hazelden
Brook, Indiana
Sept. 24, 1924.

My dear General:

I want to explain somewhat in detail my reasons for sending the wire inviting you down here for a meeting. I am sending a copy of this letter to the Speakers Bureau at Western Headquarters of the National Committee.

The county chairmen of Newton and Jasper Counties joined with me in a suggestion for a meeting because my place out here in the country is much more suitable for a "rally" than the main street of a town. I have around my house many acres of shaded lawn and the place itself has an interest for visitors on account of the flower gardens and landscaping and whenever we open the place for a big meeting of any kind we always have a great crowd. We have good roads in all directions and our visitors come from Crown Point, Logansport, Monticello, LaFayette and a large number of smaller towns in Indiana and also from Kankakee, Watseka, Danville and many smaller towns in Illinois, as we are only ten miles from the state line. When motor cars were not very abundant Mr. [William Howard] Taft opened his campaign here at my place in 1908 and the crowd present was estimated at 20,000. In 1919 we had a home coming for soldiers which was intended to be a county affair although visitors from the outside were not barred and we had about 3,000 motor cars here that day. At the Red Cross golf tournament in 1918 we cleared over $5,000 which was about four times as much as was realized at any other match in Indiana. When we pull a big show we always have a crowd here. We are equipped with everything needed for pulling off a big meeting under pleasant conditions. We have shade and water and parking space and can arrange for all of the seating capacity needed. I am telling you all of these things so that you will understand that we are not planning any small front porch affair but would expect to have a whale of a meeting. I have no particular interest in dragging my old friend Charley Dawes down here except that I favor him very strongly and a large number of people down here have been urging me to invite him. So, if the meeting is arranged, it should be quite an affair. The visitors from Chicago could come down on the Monon or the Big Four in the morning and arrive here in time for luncheon and we could get fast trains back to Chicago during the afternoon. We have no particular dates to suggest. The farmers have their work well in hand and would turn out at almost any time.

I am, with best wishes

Sincerely,
George Ade

Copies S. C. Robinson, Rensselaer, Ind.
Kenneth McCain, Kentland, Ind.
Speakers Bureau, Western Headquarters,
National Republican Committee,
Conway Building, Chicago, Ill.

InLP

In a letter to John McCutcheon, September 28, 1924 (IEN), Ade expressed concern that Ku Klux Klan candidates would disrupt the Charles G. Dawes rally. The meeting took place November 1, 1924. In addition to the political speeches Ade arranged for a picnic, dancing, a horseshoe pitching tournament, band concert, and fireworks in honor of the vice presidential candidate.

67 TO JESSE L. LASKY

March 17, 1925.

Dear Mr. Lasky:

I have your letter of March 10th and also the scenario.

When you said that drastic changes would be made in the script, you did not over state the case. I discovered several commas which might have been in the original text.

I am glad that it will not be necessary for me to definitely express my wishes at this time. I want to read the script again. In the meantime if you have any proposition to make, feeling that it would be fair to all concerned, I should be very glad to hear from you, and I shall be at the Ponce de Leon, St. Augustine, from the twenty-second until about April first.

I am, with best wishes,

Sincerely,
George Ade

M.S. notation to Thomas Meighan: Copy Please return as it is all I have. I want it for the files. G.A.
InLP

Ade wrote to Thomas Meighan, December 20, 1924 (InLP), outlining the scenario of Old Home Week:

> Soon after your first visit home, you have the first test of the big Gun and then things blow up because of the bad construction, and you then start in and build a new one, watching every part of the construction yourself. Before starting the second one, you are in desperate need of funds, and you go back to the home town and plaster a big mortgage on your last piece of property which helps to convince the people there that you are no good. When the Gun is finally accepted by the Government, you are still under a pledge of secrecy, and the nominal sum you accept cannot be paid until after a lot of red tape proceedings, so you and Larry [Wheat] are absolutely down and out when you get word about the Circus. I think you will see that we are getting a condensed outline which will keep the Story going and give us a little comedy all the way through.
>
> When [Thomas] Geraghty came yesterday, both of us had thought of putting in another character, a young wise-crack small town loafer, who is no good and lazy, but who thinks he is very sly. He is a kind of a private detective for you and is your faithful friend

and admirer, and when you finally win out of course it is a big day for him, and he gets a job with the Circus.

Thomas Geraghty was the continuity writer for Back Home and Broke *and* Old Home Week.

Ade wrote John N. Wheeler, October 31, 1926 (InLP), of his general reaction to film writing:

> You cannot do business with a producing company unless you have ready at a certain time an outline story which seems to fit some star who is all ready to produce another play. Also, each studio has tucked away hundreds of magazine stories or books on which they have an option or the rights and the boys in the scenario department have to work these off or else they will be jacked up for buying stuff which is not good. The producers will fall for a successful play or a talked about novel or magazine story, but will turn down good picture material which has not yet been produced in any form. They have no faith in their own judgments.

68 ☙ TO THOMAS MEIGHAN

[St. Augustine, Florida]
March 28, 1925.

Dear Tom:

After I sent the wire yesterday I received your letter of the 25th. I can assure you there is no reason why you should feel embarrassed or annoyed because of the unfortunate complication.

I wish I could have explained to you my ideas in regard to the play. I deliberately tried to make the play different from those in which you had been playing. I did so because I had heard expressions of opinion from dozens and dozens of your admirers, and I thought I knew what kind of a play they wanted for you. I did not attempt to get in much melodrama, and I did not attempt to build up the love interest as much as some of the directors seem to demand.

I believed, and still believe, that we had the right outline to start with—a man goes back to his native town and finds that he has no standing with his relatives and old time friends. He finds that a lot of false alarms are regarded as great men. He is engaged in a big and honorable task which is greatly to his credit, but which is bringing him no immediate money or glory. In order to win the girl and rebuke the small town skeptics, and to square himself with everybody, he starts out to make good. Just when he has a chance to grab some money, he does the generous thing and gives his important discovery to the Government free of charge. As a result he has neither money nor glory.

He is still, so far as the old home town is concerned, an utter failure. He is a great man at Washington but he cannot tell of his big achievement. Then, by a curious turn of fate, he is pitched into the circus business by the death of an uncle who ran away and had been for years the black sheep of the family. In a spirit of fun, and realizing that, to a small town, the circus is the biggest thing in the world, he sails into his home town in triumph, as a gaudy showman and wins everybody except the girl, who is disappointed in him and does not yield until she learns, by accident, at the last moment of the really big thing he has accomplished.

That, boiled down, was the outline of the story I saw for you, and I still see it as the kind of story which I think you should do, in spite of the fact that I have been shot into the waste basket by Mr. [Victor] Heerman, Mr. [Edward] Sheldon and others. What I plan to do is to take this story and write a long serial for one of the good magazines, either Cosmopolitan or Liberty, and prove to some of our friends that the thing has story merit, whether they like it for a picture or not. The point is, that the stuff I put in, and which they took out, I deliberately put in and knowing that a good many people connected with the business would not class it as picture material. Of course, we had too much material, but we did not have nearly as much material either as to shots or titles as we had in "Back Home and Broke" when we started making that picture.

I am perfectly sincere in saying that I want to get out of the jam as gracefully as possible. I have taken on all of the work which I can handle for a long time to come. I enjoy doing it and the financial returns are very satisfactory and the people for whom I am working tell me that the stuff is running better than it has in years, and I don't believe they are kidding me because they have voluntarily raised prices.

Under all the circumstances, the sensible thing for me to do is to regard "Old Home Week" as a closed incident, so in any arrangement you make with Mr. [Jesse] Lasky I simply want you to suggest that I be given whatever is fair compensation for my work up to date, remembering always that I submitted my material well in advance and that it was approved, and that Mr. [Thomas] Geraghty, representing the company, approved the script and accepted it. Repeatedly, while I was at work on the stuff out in California, I suggested sending the script, a few pages at a time, by fast mail to make sure that we were not doing anything which would be disapproved later on by somebody at Long Island, but he always said that there was no need of sending any pages on as he had been given full authority to pass on the stuff. If, while he was putting his okeh on this material, he privately disapproved of it and was sending word back east that the material was not what you wanted, of course he was putting me in a tough position. He did not write a single word on the script, and he made no suggestions which I did not immediately try to carry out, and that is why I was led to believe that he favored the general outline and did not, after he arrived at Long Island, favor rejecting the whole story. That will be about all for the present.

Last evening I dined out on the "Claribel" with John and Clara [Brander] and John's sister. Mrs. Herb Jones went home yesterday. The Branders leave here Monday. I leave on April 2nd for Augusta, Ga., remaining at the Bon Air-Vanderbilt until about the 15th, and then I go to White Sulphur [Springs] for ten days or so. I am feeling fine and shooting pretty good golf.

With best wishes to Mrs. Meighan,

Sincerely,
George Ade

InLP

Ade was working on the scenario of Old Home Week, *which was to be directed by Victor Heerman. Eddie Lowe and Edward Sheldon had requested script changes. The Long Island studio of Famous Players Lasky rejected Ade's scenario.*

69 ❧ TO CHARLES T. NELLANS

[Miami Beach, Florida]
January 22, 1926.

Dear Doctor:

I am exceedingly interested to have your letter, and it confirms my own opinion as to a most unfortunate situation. Ever since some of us began making an effort to secure a pardon or a commutation, a lot of emotional friends and relatives have been telling Mr. [Warren T.] McCray and his relatives that our efforts were sure to succeed almost immediately, and the consequence has been that possibly false hopes have been raised.

I quite agree with you that he should not be constantly reminded of the present critical situation. I am wondering how I can be of some help.

I believe I will write a careful and confidential letter to my nephew [James D. Rathbun] at home, a very bright young man who handles all of my business affairs, and who is in close touch with all of the relatives and many of the friends, and let him, in a quiet and diplomatic manner, pass the word around as to the wise policy to be pursued.

I can well understand your situation in the matter. W. T. or Warnie as we always call him, had the misfortune to be convinced that he was a child of destiny and that all the influence in the world were co-operating to give him great political importance, tremendous influence, and unlimited wealth. He did things which got him into trouble while deluded by certain happy beliefs.

Knowing him as I do, I can understand why he now is unable to understand why all of the necessary influence are not working in his behalf.

You understand that this letter is for your perusal. I think he has been terribly punished, and that it would be an act of mercy and common justice to permit him to go to his family, and I am willing at any time to do what is needed in his behalf, but I agree with you that it will be most unwise to excite him with all kinds of promises and assurances until we know where we stand.

I shall be glad to hear from you at any time and possibly I may report to you later.

GA/F Sincerely,
InLP George Ade

Warren T. McCray had suffered a stroke and was hospitalized for three months. Dr. Charles T. Nellans, the prison physician, attended him at Atlanta Penitentiary.

McCray had sent Ade a copy of the nine-page resumé of his career, (c. March 23, 1925), which he sent to Will R. Wood and a number of other politicians (InLP). Wood was to present McCray's case to President Coolidge. Thirty-two governors and former governors and twenty senators interceded for McCray. A petition requesting his release circulated in the Indiana General Assembly contained 142 of a possible 150 members' signatures.

Ade wrote James D. Rathbun and Joseph Reeve, December 11, 1925 (InK), of his forthcoming visit with Calvin Coolidge:

I went up to the Capitol with Tom Shipp and met our new Senator.

As soon as I saw him I remembered him. He was out at the farm once with Henry Vinton. He certainly exerted himself to make everything pleasant for us, and I was very favorably impressed.

Will Wood is out of town, but will return tomorrow morning, and left word that he wanted to see me as soon as possible. I think he is planning to take me to see the President. I shall act on his advice, no matter what it is.

I have a letter from Everett Sanders, which arrived at the farm after I left home, and he indicated that the President would not discuss the case with anyone until a report had come from Mr. [John G.] Sargent, but possibly Will has arranged for an interview. Will Wood called on W. T. [McCray] the other day, and his report in regard to the general physical condition is not favorable. I will let you know regarding later developments.

Thomas R. Shipp was private secretary to Senator Arthur R. Robinson, who was appointed to fill the vacancy caused by the death of Samuel Ralston. Robinson took his seat December 7, 1925.

Everett Sanders was secretary to Calvin Coolidge.

John G. Sargent was attorney-general.

McCray was not pardoned until he was eligible for parole after forty months in the penitentiary. Paroled August 30, 1927, he did not receive a pardon until December 23, 1930, when Herbert Hoover restored the former governor's civil rights.

70 ☙ TO JOHN T. MC CUTCHEON

Hazelden
Brook, Indiana
May 6th, 1926.

Dear Mac:

I am interested to have your letter of the 4th and, of course, I am delighted to know that the copy of PINK MARSH was so welcome. If I were you I should not be discouraged over the fact that these illustrations seem so good that you have to wonder if you could turn out as good work now. Recently I sent in to the Cosmo an essay that I wrote when I was 13 years old and it was far more didactic and inspiring and uplifting and reformatory than anything that I could possibly compose at present.

You must remember that when you made these pictures for Pink Marsh you were simply a newspaper illustrator. Since then you have been a world traveler and a writer of books, a war correspondent, promoter of public enterprises, prominent citizen, and successful family man. Along in the 90's you were concentrating as a specialist along one line. Now you have become a citizen of the Universe and you need not be discouraged because you may have neglected your one-time specialty. All of which means something if you can discover what I am driving at.

I am, with best wishes

Sincerely,
George Ade

Courtesy John T. McCutcheon, Jr.

Ade's juvenile essay "A Basket of Potatoes," 1881, appeared in Cosmopolitan, *August, 1926.*

71 ☙ TO JOSEPHINE CROWDER

[Hazelden]
Brook, Indiana
Aug. 29th, 1926

Dear Miss Crowder:

I have been some what under the weather lately and my regular work has been so interrupted that I simply cannot undertake to dictate a long article for you this morning and it must be understood that I am not writing and signing any article for a syndicate. I have not your letter at hand but I think you wanted me to say something about the turning point in my career. I don't think that any man determines his whole career by any single performance. He is constantly changing the program. Of course, a very important day for me was the one on which my father told me that I might go to Purdue University. If I had not gone to Purdue it is probable that I would not have broken into the centers of population and had all the interesting experiences which came to me as a newspaper man and a playwright and a traveler.

In 1890 when I went up to Chicago and joined John McCutcheon I was simply carrying out a plan which had been in the back of my head all of the time. I became a newspaper worker. The day in 1894 when the editor put me in charge of a department was an important mile post because I was given a chance to write the kind of stuff which could be put into books and my long service as a story writer prepared me for writing dialogue and inventing situations and so in time I found myself writing for the stage. The money which permitted me to travel and sort of map out my own time-table every year came from the theater. So I suppose the day on which Henry Savage induced me to submit a play to him was another turning point. Going back to that, the day on which John McCutcheon and I decided to go to Europe, even if we had to swim, was another turning point.

I think the important moves I made were those which put me in the way of seeing the world and which led to independence. I don't believe that a man who writes for a living should sacrifice everything in order to get the money. I think it important and highly convenient for him to direct his efforts so that he will get some money which will enable him to take orders from himself instead of all the time being a creature of circumstances.

I am sending you some material which may give you some ideas but which, of course, you do not wish to copy verbatum. Also, I am sending you under separate cover a photograph.

I am, with best wishes

Sincerely,
George Ade

InLP

72 ❧ TO THE EDITOR, *HERALD TRIBUNE*

Hazelden
Brook, Indiana
Sept. 8, 1926

My dear Sir:

Yesterday I found on my desk a wire reading as follows:

NEW YORK CITY
SEPT. 7, 1926.

JOHN H. RAFTERY ONE TIME OF CHICAGO RECORD ASSERTS FIRST CHAPTER [THEODORE] DREISER'S SISTER CARRIE IS WORD FOR WORD PLAGIARISM OF STORY YOU WROTE IN NINETEEN HUNDRED FOR RECORD. WE WOULD APPRECIATE YOUR RECOLLECTION OF THIS.

HERALD TRIBUNE

I could not get a wire to you last night as our local office closes in the early afternoon, when the operator goes home to milk the cow. Furthermore I was afraid to trust a long message to the operator so I simply wired you this morning:

MAILING STATEMENT REGARDING RAFTERY STORY ABOUT DREISER BORROWING MY STUFF.

I have just dictated the enclosed and you may do with it as you please. I am sincere in my statement that I do not wish to annoy Mr. Dreiser in regard to something which happened nearly thirty years ago. I haven't a copy of SISTER CARRIE at hand. If you care to dig up one and then get a copy of the fable which was printed in the first volume issued by Stone & Company in 1899 you can find out for yourself just how much resemblance there was between my paragraphs and his paragraphs. If you decide to print nothing whatever I shall be just as much pleased but if there is to be any publicity I think it only fair that you should use my statement or the essential parts of it.
I am, with best wishes

Sincerely,
. George Ade

You have asked me if Theodore Dreiser in his novel of Sister Carrie incorporated in one of his early chapters part of a story which I had written for The Chicago Record. Before I reply to your inquiry let it be understood that I am simply complying with your request to give facts. I am not stirring up any charge against Mr. Dreiser—not after all these years.

Along about 1898 I wrote for The Record a story in fable form called THE TWO MANDOLIN PLAYERS AND THE WILLING PERFORMER. In that story I had a character known as Cousin Gus from St. Paul. He was of the type then known as "a swift worker." Probably we would call him a "sheik" today, seeing that we have made such tremendous advances in recent years. In my little story I detailed the tactics which would be employed by Gus if he spotted a good looker on the train between St. Paul and Chicago.

When the very large and important novel called SISTER CARRIE came out I read it and I was much amused to discover that Theodore Dreiser had incorporated, in a description of one of his important characters, the word picture of Cousin Gus which I had outlined in my newspaper story and which later appeared in a volume called FABLES IN SLANG. It is true that for a few paragraphs Mr. Dreiser's copy for the book tallied very closely with my copy for the little story. When I discovered the resemblance I was not horrified or indignant, I was simply flattered. It warmed me to discover that Mr. Dreiser had found my description suitable for the clothing of one of his characters.

Many people came to me and called my attention to the fact that a portion of my little fable had been found imbedded in the very large novel by Mr. Dreiser. I figured that he had read my story in the newspaper and had found that my character in the fable was about like his character in the novel and that he absorbed the description and used it without any intent of taking something which belonged to some one else.

Most certainly I do not accuse Mr. Dreiser of plagiarism, even by implication or in the spirit of pleasantry. I have a genuine admiration for him. To me he is a very large and commanding figure in American letters. While some of us have been building chicken coops or, possibly, bungalows, Mr. Dreiser has been creating sky-scrapers. He makes the old three-decker novel look like a pamphlet. He is the only writer in our list who has the courage and the patience and the painstaking powers of observation to get all of one human career into one story.

Theodore Dreiser was born in Indiana and we other Hoosiers are very proud of him. I knew rather intimately his brother, Paul Dreiser, who wrote so many popular songs and the one song so highly esteemed here at home, THE BANKS OF THE WABASH. I was active in planning a memorial to Paul to be placed on the banks of the Wabash down near his old home. While we were planning the memorial I had some correspondence with Theodore Dreiser and also with Louise Dreiser who is supposed to have been Paul's sister but she wasn't. Paul made her take the name because it helped her to get theatrical engagements. She was from Paul's home town and her father and Paul were great friends.

I am rather sorry that some one has reminded The Herald Tribune, of which I am a constant reader and regular subscriber, that Mr. Dreiser got into his novel something which read like something written by me before his novel came out. It all happened so many years ago! It seems to raise the absolutely preposterous suggestion that Mr. Dreiser needs help. Anybody who writes novels containing approximately one million words each doesn't need any help from any one. As I said before, while most of our guild are at work on tiny structures which stay close to the ground, Mr. Dreiser is putting up sky-scrapers. If in building one of his massive structures he used a brick from my pile, goodness knows he was welcome to it and no questions were asked or will be asked. These are the facts in the case. Mr. Dreiser hasn't hurt my feelings at any time and I don't want to hurt his feelings now.
InLP

Ellen Moers, Two Dreisers *(New York: 1969), pp. 126–32, treats the plagiarism thoroughly.*

Ade wrote Mrs. John Kendrick Bangs, September 13, 1926 (InLP), giving a personal reaction to the plagiarism:

> I must confess I was flabbergasted to have some one rise up after all these years and accuse Mr. Dreiser of having purloined some of my vernacular. I hope to goodness that he was not annoyed or angried. You know, H. L. Menken [sic] says that Dreiser is the present day giant of American letters, but that he is, also, a "lonely and weather-beaten figure,"—a colossal genius camping alone on the heights. I am ready to admit anything that anybody says about him but, between you and me, he uses up so much language that, at times, he is mighty hard reading.

73 ☙ TO RUFUS LE MAIRE

Hazelden
Brook, Indiana
Sept. 14, 1926.

My dear Mr. LeMaire:

When I told you that I was out of the playwriting game I meant it and possibly you were joking when you tackled me to give you some tips, but I am going to send you a little story I heard the other day and maybe you can do something with it. It was told to me by Admiral [Hugh] Rodman who has retired from the Navy and has been helping to teach the boys at Culver Academy this summer. You may remember that he was with Admiral [Frank Edmund] Beatty in the North Sea all during the war and he is a great character. The story he told me was as follows: some years ago out in Honolulu a junior officer had been running wild every night in the tough part of town and finally the Admiral ordered a Court-Martial for him. Several friends of the young man went to the Admiral to plead with him but he was very strict and strait-laced and insisted that the boy be tried. The judges of the Court consisted of a Rear Admiral, two Captains and two Commanders, who seated themselves behind a long table and named another officer to question the witnesses. The accused was brought in and confronted with the charges and then they called the witnesses. The first witness was a large and highly decorated dame who told the Court that her name was Madame Clarice and that she kept a well-known resort on the Hula Hula Road. The officer who was asking the questions then told her to take a good look at the accused. She did so. Then he asked her, "Do you recognize him?" She shook her head and said, "No, I don't know him at all but I know all of these other gentlemen very well," indicating the five dignified judges behind the table. Whereupon they all fell out of their chairs and the trial came to an end. Of course, you could not use the skit which might reflect on the Navy but you could do this: have the curtain go up on four or five solemn and queer looking elderly birds back of a table set at stage right or left. Open the act by having the prosecutor address them, so as to put plenty of speed into the thing and get to the finish. The prosecutor might say: "Gentlemen, members of the discipline committee of the Men's Purity League, you know why this meeting has been called." They nod their heads in unison. The prosecutor goes on to say it has been reported that one of their members, young Mr. Abner Hemmingway, has been visiting a notorious cabaret, with one of these crazy names such as the Blue Goose or the One-eyed Pup or The Bucket of Blood. The prosecutor tells the members of the committee that this cabaret or night club is one of the toughest joints in the world. The doorman pats every customer as he goes in and if he hasn't a hip flask he can't go in. The dancers dance so close together that it would be impossible to put a razor blade between them. One of the judges wants to know if anybody ever tried to. The prosecutor says not that he knows of and the judge says it would be a mean trick. Bring in the accused and without mentioning the name of the particular dive have the prosecutor tell him that he, the defendant, is accused of frequenting low and disreputable dives and dumps where jazz music is played and the law is defied. Then the prosecutor says, "I will call the first witness," and he brings in a gal who is made up like a circus. Of course, the whole thing wants to be very brief. He would ask:

Q State your name.

A Do you want my real name?

Q No, just the one you are using now.

She gives a hifuluting name. When she comes in she may bow to everybody in the room in an impersonal way and the judges may all gaze at her, as if fascinated, but it must not be tipped off that she knows them or that they recognize her. The prosecutor says:

We want to know about an infamous resort known as (so and so). She replies: "It is not an infamous resort. It is a night club." He asked "What is the difference?" and she says they are running a nice place and after the patrons go blind they send them home. He asks: "Are you the keeper of that resort?" and she replies: "I am the hostess," and again he asks "What is the difference?" She replies that a keeper knows only a lot of rough characters but a hostess knows everybody. Then the prosecutor adopts a bluffing tone and says to her: "Now, I want you to come through and tell the truth. Take a good look at this man" and points to the accused and then the prosecutor asks: "Do you know him?" She studies him carefully and then pulls the tag line: "No, I don't recognize him at all." And then she arises and with a sweeping gesture to the men behind the table concludes: "BUT I KNOW ALL THESE GENTLEMEN VERY WELL." They should do a flop backward as the light goes out.

The trick of the thing would be to play it very straight and heavy up to the time that she pulls the surprize and, of course, the shorter and snappier it is made the better it will be. I have dictated this thing in a great hurry and, of course, I have not put in the proper dialogue or names or anything. I have no doubt that Lester Allen and Billie Halligan and some of your other boys could take and fix it up in a hurry. The story itself gets a laugh and I never heard it until the Admiral told me. Of course, my name is not to be used in connection with the skit if you should decide to try it out and my only compensation would be the privilege of buying some good seats when I am in town. I just happen to think that possibly the thing might be twisted into a snappy little feature. If you can do anything with it you are welcome to it.

I am, with best wishes

Sincerely,
George Ade

InLP

74 ☙ TO GRANTLAND RICE

Hazelden
Brook, Indiana
Oct. 26, 1926.

Dear Grant:

I am delighted to have a message from you and I am enclosing a little piece I wrote for the local paper. By the way, you might be interested in knowing something about the party on Sunday evening. It was too late in the season for dancing in the pavilion or sitting down to watch a picture and we could not seat one hundred and fifty people for card games. So we had a Monte Carlo party.

As each guest entered the house he was given an envelope containing $5,000 in stage money, marked in various denominations. We had desperate gambling games in operation in every room in the house so as to keep the crowd spread out. We had games as follows: one roulette, one hazard, three old army games, two free for all crap games, one wheel of fortune for cash, one paddle wheel for fancy baskets, dolls, boxes of candy etc., and one Keno or Beano game for an assortment of prizes including aluminum ware, glassware, dolls, strings of beads etc. etc. The persons having the most money laid up after four hours of gambling won the prizes.

This kind of party is the wildest and most hilarious thing you ever heard. Before we got through Sunday evening the crap shooters were rolling for a hundred thousand a roll. Even the local Methodists and leaders of the Klan cannot bring the law down on us because it is not real gambling. No one can lose anything. Of course, having it on Sunday evening was a scandal but everything we do on any evening is a scandal.

My plans for the winter are indefinite. I am not very keen to go back to Belleair. The place is too darn sporty. If you go to the parties you cannot do any work and if you don't go to the parties you might as well live on a desert island. I am thinking of doing some cruising this winter. I had a month in the West Indies last Spring on the California and enjoyed every minute of it. It was my seventh cruise to the West Indies. It is the best 30-day trip in the world.

I trust that Mrs. Rice is staggering with renewed health and that you are well and happy. By the way, Purdue is out of the joke division. We played a close game with the Navy with hardly any practice before the game, defeated Wabash, held Wisconsin to a tie, and licked Chicago. I am afraid Northwestern is a little too husky for us but we should clean up on Indiana. Anyway, we are out of the cellar and going strong. Jimmy Phelan is a good coach and we have a Freshman team almost as good as varsity. We are beginning to get some results from years of patient battling.

I am, with best wishes

Sincerely,

InLP George Ade

Grantland Rice, the author-journalist whose column, The Sportlight, *syndicated 1914–1930, was a friend of Ade's. On occasion Ade sent Rice items for his column.*

75 ☙ TO THOMAS MEIGHAN

Hazelden
Brook, Indiana
Nov. 29, 1926.

My Dear Tom:

First off, let me thank you for the golf clubs which were sent on by Gene [Sarazen] and which are beauties. I have not tried them out because we have had practically no golfing weather since you were here and I have been away much of the time.

I am sending a copy of this letter to Mr. [William] LeBaron and also returning to him the three magazines he sent me a long time ago through you. Pardon the delay in reporting but I have been terribly busy while at home. I will give you a condensed opinion which may not be worth a darn. I think the title is good and would excite interest and look well on the printing and signs—"Once a Gentleman." The story is well written in spots and at other times it is rather crude. The general idea of a menial or underling masquerading as an aristocrat or nobleman is very old, of course, but all of the sure-fire material is old. It was used very effectively in "The Tailor-Made Man." I understand that you might make radical changes in the story but you could not use the story at all without making Tom a valet or man-servant and I doubt if the people who go to see him on the screen would care to see him in that kind of a part. Unless you would explain in the early story or the text that he came of a family which had been in service and which brought him into America where he had ambitions to be a man instead of a man's man. It is pretty hard to make a hero out of a valet or barber unless you have him an aristocrat who is merely pretending to be a menial. William Gillette had a fine play written by [James] Barrie, I believe, called "The Admirable Crichton." A few people were stranded on a desert island and the moment they found themselves helpless and away from civilization, the butler took command of the outfit by sheer force of his superior intelligence and dominated all the scenes and the girl fell in love with him and then a rescuing party arrived and the moment the party found itself in contact with the outside world, the butler lost all his importance and became a servant again. This type of play has more meaning in Great Britain than it would have here.

In the magazine story Tom has a love affair with the good looking housekeeper. I would be doubtful about that. It might be hard to get people excited over an affair between a clothes brusher and a furniture duster. I have felt often that you should not play, too often, the rugged he-man with hair on his chest who commands the love of the beautiful heiress, but, at the same time, I doubt if you would feel at home playing the part of a man servant because of a prejudice in this country against any male who makes his living by doing house work. I am compelled to say that I don't see much in the picture except the title. In the great mess of material which I submitted for OLD HOME WEEK, and none of which was used, I had the story of a young fellow who was brought up by a grouchy uncle and a kind but pious aunt. The boy comes to visit the relatives and finds a stranger standing across the street looking at the old homestead. It is another uncle, the black sheep of the family, who ran away from home years before and whose picture is turned toward the wall. The bad uncle takes a liking to the young fellow. Later on the young fellow is down on his luck and busted and desperate when he gets word that the bad uncle has died and left him everything. In the story I submitted we made it a circus. Why not a string of race horses and let the nephew go against all of the difficulties and dangers which are waiting for any green horn who breaks into the horse racing game. Of course, he will have to win the Derby and the girl at the same time by getting her and her horrified relatives out to the track where they are carried away by the excitement, as any one will be who goes to a real big race. Why don't you get out at a race track for once and own a string of horses? That is one thing you haven't done in the pictures although we talked once about a picture called ON HIS UPPERS in which you lost everything and became a hobo and finally met out west the news-stand girl who had been your friend and who had become an attractive young widow and saved her from a gang of sharpers, of which you were supposed to be a member.

I am just hanging along here and expect to start south next week and be in Florida by the 15th. Along in February I may take a cruise to the Mediterranean if [John] Jenks does not make out on me.

Give my best wishes to Mrs. Meighan.

Sincerely,

InLP George Ade

Once a Gentleman *was never filmed.*

William LeBaron, editor, playwright, was associate producer of Famous Players Lasky, 1924–1927.

76 ☙ DUPLICATE NEWS LETTER FROM MR. AND MRS. GEORGE MORSE, JOHN JENKS, VINCE SHEKLETON AND GEORGE ADE, MAILED SOMEWHERE IN FRANCE

March 4, 1927.

As we wound up the preceding letter we were heading close up to the most notorious rock in the world—the huge boulder known as Gilbraltar. Beyond some low-hanging storm clouds it was standing up very majestically from the sea, a bright sunlight beating down on it. By the time we were in the sheltered harbor alongside of it and ready to land, the clouds had closed in and rain was falling. We went ashore on the first tender and found ourselves in Great Britain, beyond all doubt. The rugged architecture, the painful cleanliness, the dignified soldiery, the blue-and-white signs above the shops, the crowded show-windows, the soft aroma of Scotch Whisky in the air, and even the overcast skies and damp pavements were sure reminders of dear old England.

Gibraltar is a huge mass of green-covered rock towering above the narrow entrance to the Mediterranean. It is honeycombed with tunnels, which the visitor is not permitted to see, and from those tunnels there are peek-holes out of which guns can be pointed in any direction. Only a few years ago the fortress could have blown to pieces any ship trying to get in or out of the Mediterranean. Now we have the sub-marine, to say nothing of the air-plane, and there is a question as to the defensive value of the stronghold. At least, it is most interesting, because there are soldiers all over the place. Sprawled along the base of the rock is a town with a population of 25,000 and, it being a free port, prices are low and the shoppers off the ships lose all control of themselves.

We are not going to describe all the places we visit. Go to your encyclopedias and histories and you will find all of the interesting dope which one might send you if we could take the time to write it down.

We drove around Gibraltar and then across a neutral zone to the town of Luica, in Spain, and the moment we motored across the frontier we were in another world—of squat houses, gay colors, bad pavements, noisy talk, squalor, poverty, making up in smells what was lacking in sanitation. Senoritas, smeared with mouse-colored powder, leaned from the windows above and brave Spanish gentlemen, urgently in need of shaves and clothes pressing, lunged gracefully along the untidy side-walks. We visited the bull-ring and saw a good fight between two sturdy donkey-drivers and waved away whole regiments of begging children. It was the first time in Spain for all of us and we were glad that we organized our own excursion instead of taking the Cook trip, which was merely a ride around the town. We did not go ashore in the evening as Gibraltar is not a lively spot after dark, but early next morning Mr. Jenks, Mr. Shekleton and Mr. Ade stole a ride ashore with the second and third cabin passengers who went in by the 8 o'clock tender. Many of them were Jews, headed for the Holy Land. When they got together in a group, you couldn't see them for the whiskers. On the dock we picked up an enterprising guide who had helped us the day before, and he secured a car for us. We motored around the bay to Algeciras, a Spanish town west and opposite of Gibraltar. We saw a farming district which was very productive, growing mostly wheat and beans and potatoes and also we saw a pasture full of long-horned fighting bulls.

Algeciras is an old and interesting Spanish town. We visited the room in which Lloyd George and the delegates from several great powers met in 1905 to determine the future policy of the civilized world regarding Morocco. The conference gave Morocco to Spain, which was like presenting a friend with a rattle-snake. We went to a most attractive tourist hotel above the town—the Cristina—surrounded by palms and tropical plants. Then back to Gibraltar for a little frenzied shopping before going aboard to sail at 1 o'clock. All of which was on Monday, Feb. 28th. Tuesday, March 1st, at sea, was the loveliest day we have found since leaving New York. Early yesterday morning we looked out of our ports at Algiers, which was a huge panorama of white buildings rising in a crescent shape to the very tops of the mountains circling the bay.

We can't begin to tell you about Algiers. It has been the high spot—one half a beautiful and cleanly metropolis and the other half a rocking bedlam. When you are in the French quarter you can well imagine that you are in Paris. When you are in the native quarter you can well imagine you are in the Old Testament which has been scrambled, stood on edge and saturated with all the disagreeable odors in the world. We climbed up and down slippery and slimy and gloomy chasms and tunnels, surrounded by dusky and dirty men, women and children in rags and nighties, through an atmosphere which could have been cut up into cubes and taken away as souvenirs.

Mrs. Morse was so fascinated by the picturesque Arabs that she picked up one of the ragged babies, heavily encrusted with dirt and germs, and carried it for a while finally restoring it to the mother, an estimable one-eyed woman, who was so flattered by the attention paid to her offspring that she shook hands with Mrs. Morse and wished her well during the remainder of her visit to the Old World. All of which did not happen, the facts being, that Mrs. Morse, who discovered anti-septics, is said to have returned to the ship and taken a bath, after filling the tub with Listerine.

We drove all around the city, finally escaping from a Cook guide who was leading us to all the places we did not care to see. Luncheon at the St. George, a lovely hotel on a terraced hill and bordered with palms and lemon trees. At the hotel Messrs Jenks and Ade met Charley O'Brien, an old friend who lived at the C.[hicago] A.[thletic] A.[ssociation] for years. He had been at the hotel for two months and enjoyed it, even though surrounded by frozen-faced British wearing monocles and prominent front teeth.

We couldn't tell all about Algiers without copying pages from the guide-book. It was a most interesting spot—a strange mixture of the modern and ancient civilization in full bloom and the dregs of humanity steeped in ignorance and filth, too poor to have much of anything except religion.

It is now Thursday, March 3rd and we are headed over a smooth sea toward Villefranche, the port of Nice and Monte Carlo. Our fellow-passengers are late in coming out. They were ashore last night, dancing and hunting up a second-rate African imitation of night life in Paris.

Something about the weather. Algiers has been cool and wet for two months. We needed our overcoats at Gibraltar. The only real summer weather was at Madeira. We are not suffering from the cold but we wear light woolens and take our wraps along when we go ashore. We have not seen any Palm Beach suits or straw hats. In other words, you do not, at this season, get Florida weather in the Mediterranean.

Mr. Jenks and Mr. Ade will join up with an old friend, Fred Babcock, at Villefranche tomorrow morning. We will have a full day and evening around Nice and Monte Carlo and sail for Naples early Saturday morning, arriving there Sunday for a motor ride to Pompeii, Sorrento and Amalfi.

P.S. Mr. Ade won the ten dollar decimal pool today, the first lift in the clouds.

InLP

Ade may have intended the newsletters written while on this Mediterranean cruise for publication.

George Morse, the zoologist, was the director of the Shedd Aquarium, Chicago, Illinois.

John Jenks, a Chicago businessman, was a long-time friend of Ade's, who traveled with the author frequently in later years.

Vincent Shekleton was a partner in Shekleton Bros., Chicago real estate subdividers and developers.

77 ☙ TO JOHN N. WHEELER

Hazelden
Brook, Indiana
May 31, 1927.

My dear John:
I have your letter and also the script which I will go over, very carefully, at once. I did not know that you were going to have some one tackle this stuff and I will tell you very candidly that I do not wish to sign my name to work done by some one else. This is no reflection on Mr. [Ring] Lardner who, probably, is more up to date and snappy than I am, but I just have the very emphatic feeling that any writing man of any standing whatever would never wish to have his name used on material that he had not prepared himself. It is really against the rules. Furthermore suppose we go ahead and market, as well as we can, this little batch of material, what are we going to do after we use up this stuff? It will then be up to me to come across with something or other and I will be right back where I was before—up to my eyes in the weekly release grind. I am supposed to sit down now and get up material for a book and I cannot do it if I go right back on the old routine again.

I feel most uncomfortable about this arrangement which you have made with Mr. Lardner. Once or twice before to fill a gap he padded out some pieces for me and did the work well but the point is that every man has his own style and his own way of doing things and I just know that I could not go into this kind of an arrangement.

I am, with best wishes

Sincerely,
George Ade

InLP

John Wheeler was associated with the Bell Syndicate. Ade wrote John McCutcheon, Autumn 1924? (InLP): "Jack Wheeler has been very fair with me and has succeeded in selling a lot of old stuff that was warmed over so I have a feeling that I should stick with him and give him the first option on anything I do."

78 ❧ TO RUTH M. WOODWARD

Hazelden
Brook, Indiana
July 1, 1927.

Dear Ruth Woodward:
I am glad to have your letter and I congratulate you on having the courage to sit up and wise-crack while you are still in the shadow of the hospital. I have been to the hospital a few times but I never volunteered. I do not like the gentle odor of disinfectants or the cold professional air of the hired help. I am wondering if you were ever in a hospital where they had one of those sepulchral annunciators which keeps repeating in every corridor the name of some Doc who is needed at once in some other ward to help a patient die. I admire good nurses but I think there are too many rites and ceremonies connected with the noble profession of nursing. Just when the sufferer wishes to be let alone the angel in white insists on doing something which can be recorded on the chart and make it look like a real chart.

We have no further news regarding our robbers. They are all in jail but my personal property is still at large. Chirk up if you can and use a little Christian Science.

I am, with best wishes

Sincerely,
George Ade

InLP

79 ❧ TO WILLIAM SHAW

Hazelden
Brook, Indiana
Sept. 4, 1927.

Dear Mr. Shaw:
I will try to answer your questions the best I can. I have lived at

Hazelden and tried to keep a garden going since 1904. The name Hazelden is a variation of a family name, Hazelton, and also it was a good name when we moved out here as the house was surrounded by hazel brush. I don't think I have any unusual passion for flowers. Of course, my mother always had an old-fashioned garden. My father often told me of the gorgeous floral displays on the open and unbroken prairies away back in the fifties. Along in late summer the rank flowers, mostly blue or yellow in color, grew many feet tall. The traveler, winding across the prairie on one of the trails, would have to stand up on the seat of the vehicle in order to get his bearings and for miles he would see an expanse of these gay flowers.

I am trying to find a copy of an article in which I spoke of the plan for a park in every county and a scheme for preserving plant life.

In my garden here I have favored the old-fashioned and wild flowers because they seem to fit in with the old-fashioned architecture and the natural condition of the landscaping.

I will be more than glad to receive some prints.

I am, with best wishes

Sincerely,
George Ade

InLP

Ade wrote Mrs. J. Bennett Lowe, September 26, 1939 (InLP), that he named his estate in honor of his grandmother's sister Ann Hazelton.

80 ❧ TO THOMAS B. WALL

Hazelden
Brook, Indiana
Sept. 4, 1927.

Dear Mr. Wall:
I am much interested to have your letter. It is true that while I was in London I was writing an article for the Cosmopolitan Magazine and I said that the average American was poison to the British and could not help feeling a chill in the air. I said this because I knew it to be a fact. I have visited London many times. I like the atmosphere of the town and I revel in the play houses and always put in many happy days shopping but this year I discovered that I was an

object of frigid suspicion. I do not wave the flag or force myself upon strangers or talk in loud tones or patronize the most lowly. I am quite sure that the so-called "typical American," as imagined by the English, is a rare specimen and not typical at all. My father was born in England. I have every reason to entertain a friendly regard for the cousins, but I am not going to undertake any demonstrations of affection for cousins who insist upon regarding me as a crude barbarian and who kick me on the shins, even when I am keeping perfectly quiet and trying to behave myself.

Some of the data and statistics you send are most interesting and I have no doubt they are reliable.

I am, with best wishes

Sincerely,
George Ade

InLP

81 ☙ TO LOUISE DRESSER

Hazelden
Brook, Indiana
Sept. 9, 1927

My dear Louise Dresser:
I am interested to have a letter from you. Of course, nothing would make me happier than to deliver to you a story which could be worked up into a good picture but I am not sure that I have the knack of outlining the kind of stories that the directors like.

I saw THE GOOSE WOMAN several times and it was a beautiful character performance that you gave. It is the kind of story I could not do on a bet. The things I have done that are worth anything at all are shy on heavy melodrama and run more to comedy. I had a story outlined once but never did anything with it. It was called AUNT FANNY FROM CHAUTAUQUA. A very rich man with a modern family gets word that his sister, whom he has not seen for many years, is coming to visit him. He has a large country place and the young people are getting ready for an important house party. They know nothing about Aunt Fanny and the fact that she is about to land in on them is bad news. Father has only one picture of her and that was taken at the World's Fair in Chicago and shows her as a funny looking little country girl. It appears that she is forty or forty-five years old. To a flapper of 18 that is just the same as ninety. Besides she comes from Chautauqua, the home of piety, prayers and psalm singing.

The idea of the comedy would be to demonstrate that a good many women of 40 who do not live in the cities are still snappy and up-to-date. The aunt lands in and sizes up the situation. The guest of honor is a rich and distinguished bachelor, one of these handsome dogs of the Louis Stone variety, a little gray around the temples, but very good looking and what the young girls would call "dis-tang-gay." The bachelor is just what Aunt Fanny is looking for. He is a little older than she is and has a fine social position and money and looks so there begins a battle between the flappers and the old maid. They plot to expose her real age and her country breeding and she evens up by cooking all sorts of things for the bachelor and making him talk about himself. The young ones are trying to impress him with their importance, the old one is trying to impress him with his importance. Of course, for the purposes of the drama the older one must win out. I will confess that this outline, as far as we have got with it, doesn't contain very much drama but possibly a few exciting episodes could be worked in. As I said, I probably could not do a real serious play and I don't know that this story which I have vaguely in mind would work into anything, although the character of Aunt Fanny would be a good one.

I am, with best wishes

Sincerely,
George Ade

InLP

Aunt Fanny from Chautauqua *was published posthumously in* One Act Plays for Stage and Study *(New York: 1949).*

82 TO FLORENCE IRWIN

Hazelden
Brook, Indiana
Sept. 20, 1927.

My dear Miss Irwin:
I have your letter with the enclosures and I want to tell you that I am interested and sympathetic but the fact of the matter is that I definitely stopped writing for the stage a good while ago. I haven't on hand a script which would be any good for you and it would be

a miracle of miracles if, without any idea as a starter, I could sit down now and hastily prepare something that would be any good for you. It would have to be done hastily as I have taken on certain contracts for syndicate stuff, stories and magazine articles which will keep me busy for a long time to come. I am mighty sorry.

I never heard before that there was any question as to the ownership of the play. I sold the script outright to your sister May [Irwin] for $200 and supposed that she simply had it put away somewhere until she took it out and tried it at Boston. I never wept over the fact that I might have collected thousands of dollars in royalty. When May bought the play I was an unknown, at least as a playwright. She took a gamble on a little story I had and won out and I was very pleased when the play made good. I am sorry now that she is not disposed to let you use the piece but I haven't any pull with her or the husband and, as I have already said, I am not in a position to fix up something and send it on.

I am, with best wishes

Sincerely,
George Ade

InLP

Florence Irwin had been stopped from using Mrs. Peckham's Carouse *by her sister Mae, who demanded a $50 a week royalty, and stipulated that her sister use the play only when playing Chicago and cities west of Illinois.*

Kurt Eisselt was Mae Irwin's husband, press agent, and manager.

83 ☙ TO F. A. HOOPER

Hazelden
Brook, Indiana
Oct. 14, 1927.

My dear Mr. Hooper:
I am interested and flattered to have your suggestion that I do a little piece about EUGENE FIELD. Possibly I could look at the data and give you the condensed information you desire but I have a feeling that the contribution should be written by Charles H. Dennis, Managing Editor of the Chicago Daily News, who wrote the book EUGENE FIELD'S CREATIVE YEARS, published by Doubleday Page & Company. Francis Wilson wrote a good little

book about Field. Mr. Dennis and Mr. Wilson knew Eugene Field much better than I knew him. He was associated with an older set of men about the time that Brand Whitlock, Peter Dunne, John McCutcheon, Ray Baker, and a lot more of us were breaking into the game in Chicago. When I began to do a department on the old MORNING RECORD, I was assigned to the desk which Field had used. By that time he was in ill health and what ever writing he did was done at home. You had better find some one who was intimate with him and I think Mr. Dennis is the man.

I am, with best wishes

Sincerely,
InLP George Ade

F. A. Hooper had asked Ade to write a biography of Eugene Field for the Encylopædia Britannica.

Francis Wilson wrote The Eugene Field I Knew *(New York: 1898).*

Charles H. Dennis, Eugene Field's Creative Years *(New York: 1924), pp. 313–14, gives an account of the beginnings of Ade's years as a columnist.*

84 ❧ TO MILDRED V. HAXTON

Hazelden
Brook, Indiana
Nov. 2, 1927.

Dear Miss Haxton:

Replying to your inquiry as to whether or not the author usually selects a title before he writes his story, I should say that usually he has a title in mind but often enough he changes it after the script is completed and then after that very often the title is again changed at the suggestion of some magazine editor or publisher who wishes to put a popular label on the work. Very often a title is selected and a story is built around it. I have written some plays which really started with titles which were felt to be unusually good. I mean THE COLLEGE WIDOW, FATHER AND THE BOYS, JUST OUT OF COLLEGE, BACK HOME AND BROKE, and THE SLIM PRINCESS. These are titles which helped the stories. Anita Loos had a very tame and meaningless title for a story but Ray Long, Editor of the Cosmopolitan, had her to change it to GENTLE-

MEN PREFER BLONDS and the title helped to make the play a great success.

I am, with best wishes

Sincerely,
George Ade

InLP

85 ❧ TO JOHN N. WHEELER

Hazelden
Brook, Indiana
Nov. 13, 1927.

My dear John:
I went to French Lick a week ago and was called home by the sudden death of my brother Joe [Ade] and I have neglected my correspondence.

I have a letter from [Art] Helfant which I will answer in detail soon, although I wrote him briefly this morning. Regarding the three strips, which were rejected by the Philadelphia Ledger, I don't know what in the world to say about them except that I think they are very proper and Presbyterian as compared with most of the stuff that is being printed these days. We cannot now recall them. You might say to the Ledger that in the future we will try to avoid putting into the strips anything which could bring the blush of shame to the face of a very old person. I am sure the young ones will think they are very mild.

I await, with some interest, a report on the syndicate as I really hope that we will succeed in getting some money out of them sooner or later.

I am with best wishes

Sincerely,
George Ade

InLP

Art Helfant drew Fables in Slang, by George Ade *for the Bell Syndicate. The comic strip ran in 1927.*

Ade wrote John Wheeler, Sept. 10, 1927 (InLP):

> I think we should remind Mr. [Art] Helfant that we are not going after the kid trade and that he should avoid making his people too low comedy. Make them good comedy characters but don't make

them look too much like monkeys or we will fail to please the people who have been interested in the fables.

Ade wrote Wheeler, Oct. 5, 1927 (InLP):

I am sending you two more strips. I shall be keenly interested to know how Mr. [Art] Helfant feels about this stuff I am sending on. I don't wish to insult his imaginative intelligence by giving him too many directions and in the future I will not indicate anything about the pictures unless he wants some tips. As it is, I have made the suggestions very brief.

It might be a good idea to let the prospective customers know that a good deal of the material contained in the new series will be entirely new. You might get up a sample sheet including new stuff sent in and ask the editors to look at it and note that we are giving a new kind of treatment to the fable material.

86 TO WILLIAM HERSCHELL

Hazelden
Brook, Indiana
Nov. 23, 1927.

Dear Bill:
I am enclosing a brief tribute to our old friend Tom Taggart and I hope it will be what you want. I am glad to join with you in this

little movement because Tom who really had done something for his fellowmen has been the target for a lot of cheap abuse.

I did not see you at Bloomington last Saturday but I hope you were there. We were scared pink for a while but everything turned out all right.

I am, with best wishes

Sincerely,
George Ade

Enclosure:

In 1892 I met Tom Taggart. He was Chairman of the Democratic State Central Committee and I was a newspaper correspondent, come down from Chicago to learn the truth regarding political conditions in Indiana. He aroused my wondering admiration at our very first meeting because he looked me in the eye and gave me some facts, instead of dealing in evasive generalities.

That was thirty-five years ago and I have kept track of him, with a friendly prejudice in his favor ever since. We have met countless times. I never came up on him, from behind, that I did not find him performing some act of gracious courtesy, binding up a wound, dealing out the soft answer that turns away wrath, or giving some other evidence of the fact that he is a kindly man of large sympathies and abounding charity. All he ever needs, at any

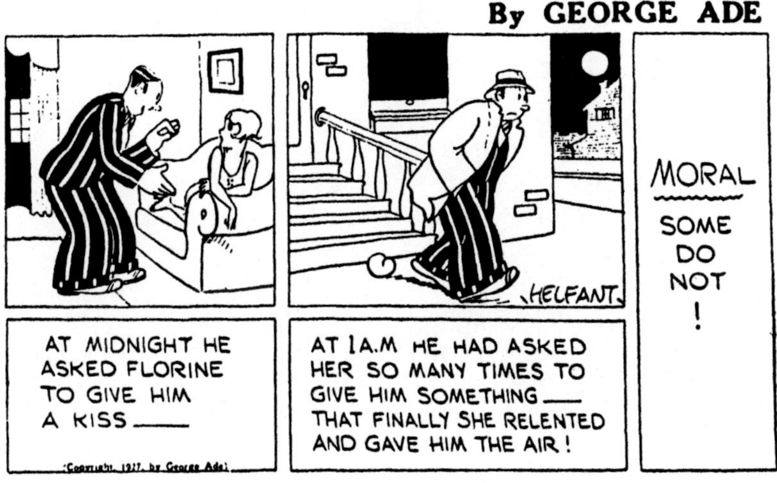

time, is a strand of sleigh-bells and a few reindeer to be a real Santa Claus.

He has done more for Indiana than any one hundred of his critics, all of whom are narrow between the eyes and have dark minds. Our state educational institutions were starving until he arranged to have them fed. In the United States Senate he always voted right. He is a beautifier of landscapes, a builder of highways, a promoter of good feeling and prosperity and decent toleration. We honor ourselves in honoring him.
InLP

87 ❧ TO VICTOR RICHARD RUBENS

Hazelden
Brook, Indiana
May 27, 1928.

Dear Mr. Rubens:
Here is a hard luck story regarding the use of tobacco, which I regard as the most amiable, genial and tolerable of the smaller vices. I learned to smoke, by painful efforts, when I was a small boy, starting in on corn-silk and graduating up to the stub-tailed cheroots, which came in small paper boxes and sold three for a nickel. During my collegiate days I smoked cigarettes and a pipe. The Lone Jack and Marburg mixtures were very popular in the eighties. I hope that they are still used by discriminating pipe smokers. The favorite cigarettes were Sweet Caps and Richmond Straight Cuts. We all knew the ancient wheeze to the effect that it was a Richmond Straight Cut that finished Richard III.

For many years after I took up the writing game I smoked whatever was readily obtainable, with a preference for a mild Havana Cigar of the Panatella shape. In November, 1918, just as I got through with some war work and the Big Trouble was ended, I was put flat on my back for a month by an attack of illness. Of course, while I was propped up in bed I did not smoke. When I convalesced and tottered back to my usual haunts I learned that I had retained a modicum of my normal thirst but I had lost all desire to smoke. I would light a cigar or cigarette and take a few puffs at it and experience a sense of disappointment and discontinue the effort. For ten years I have not smoked. I love to see other people smoke and I select cigars and cigarettes with great care for my friends who have not enjoyed the misfortune of being cured. I wish I could smoke now but I can't.

I am, with best wishes,

Sincerely,
George Ade

InLP

88 ❧ TO FRANKLIN P. ADAMS

Hazelden
Brook, Indiana
June 9, 1928.

Dear Frank:
I am glad you are tackling that piece about the old Olymp and I will give you all the help I can. I was a regular there for several years and when I start digging I will turn up some antiquities, I can promise you. I know of a man who can give you a world of stuff. Chris Lane, who was one of the favorites at the old house, singing extemporized songs the same as Rolling Mill Kelly did years ago and Harry Breen later on, is now connected with the Benson amusement agency in Chicago. The thing to do is to get hold of Chris and Abe Jacobs and then consult the files of the old Clipper and I think you will strike a rich lead. [Joseph] Webber and [Lew] Fields were often on the bill. You must get a picture of young Mule Hoey, brother of old Hoss, the only comic who ever combined a ballet skirt with a full set of whiskers. I remember the Lorenzo Brothers who tore paper and also the Leonzo Brothers who did wild west melodramas at the Clark street dime museum. They featured the trained dogs and when a female of the troupe gave birth to a litter [William F.] "Biff" Hall announced that the boys were going to send out a number two show the next season. We will fix it up later on to get together but we will need Abe Jacobs and also some list of the troupers. The house did not advertise in Chicago except by hand bills.

I am interested to learn that Chase Osborn is living near you. He is an interesting character and, if encouraged, will talk to you.

I am, with best wishes

Sincerely,
George Ade

InLP

Franklin P. Adams, whose column "The Conning Tower" and other writings gained him a place at the Round Table, had been friends with Ade since the two had worked on Chicago papers. Ade wrote Richard Welling, a New York attorney who collected Ade's books, May 14, 1938 (InLP): "I knew Frank P. Adams about that time [1899]. He was a student at the Armour Institute. Even at that time, he was doing a little writing and he would bring an occasional contribution to my column."

See Franklin P. Adams, "Olympic Days," Saturday Evening Post, *201 (June 22, 1929), 18+. The Olympic Theater was a third-rate vaudeville house in Chicago which Ade frequented in the 1890s.*

Chase Osborn was governor of Michigan, 1910–1911.

89 TO SAMUEL FRENCH, INC.

Hazelden
Brook, Indiana
June 27, 1928.

Gentlemen:

I suppose there is no sadder moment in the life of an author than when he is compelled to return a check sent to him by a publisher. The enclosed letter and remittance from you to me will explain itself after you have carefully gone over it again. I was delighted and surprised to receive a check of this size but when my assistant and I began to check over the items we found on page 6 some addition which filled us with grief, because there was an error of $1,000 and it was not in our favor! I hope I have not brought trouble upon one of your valued employees by calling attention to this error. Perhaps the sportsmanlike thing for me to do, in order to protect your bookkeeper, would have been to pocket the check and say no more about it, but, it seems, there is one New England conscience out here in Indiana and so I am sadly returning the whole thing and will ask you to go over it again and send me the amount really due, which I fear is exactly $1000 less than the amount you sent.

I am, with best wishes

Sincerely,
George Ade

InLP

90 ☙ TO CHARLES L. JEWETT

Hazelden
Brook, Indiana
June 28, 1928.

My dear Colonel:
I have your letter and I have been brooding over the thing. You are dead right that some one should put a lot of stress on the fact that the battle against prohibition should be based upon the consideration of taxes. I have a feeling, however, that I make a fool mistake every time I dabble in politics or issues of a political nature. I have friends in both parties and what little reputation I have acquired or what success I have made has been due to the fact that I have been friendly with a large number of people and have avoided making enemies. Just at present I have no connection with any newspaper or magazine which would permit me to do any preaching and I doubt if I would be acting wisely in getting too much mixed up in this prohibition fight which will be, for the next few months, a party issue. I am disgusted with the general hypocrisy and evasion shown by party leaders in regard to the enforcement of the Amendment and the Volstead Act. They sit in their rooms and drink and then go outside and talk dry. It is the hardest thing to find, even in this part of the dry belt, a man who will not take a drink when he gets a chance. Also, he will sit in a private room and curse the dry enactments, but when he gets out before the Methodists, Baptists and bigots and W.C.T.U's he either dodges the whole issue or says, vaguely, that he is in favor of law enforcement. I don't think the issue can be sidetracked for ever and I know that a lot of men must show their courage by coming out and battling for a commonsense solution of the problem, but, just now, I haven't the ambition or disposition to be the head crusader.

I am, with best wishes

Sincerely,
George Ade

InLP

Charles L. Jewett was a New Albany, Indiana, lawyer.

The W.C.T.U. (Women's Christian Temperance Union) was founded in 1874, "banded together for the protection of the home, the abolition of the liquor traffic and the triumph of Christ's Golden Rule in custom and in law." This largest and most active temperance organization exerted considerable influence during Prohibition.

91 ❧ TO ARTHUR WELLS

Hazelden
Brook, Indiana
July 7, 1928.

Dear Mr. Wells:
I am interested to have your letter and the sheaf of material which I shall carefully preserve. As I told you, this is a new game for me and I am not sure that I can be of any help to you. Whatever I do I will do because of my interest in all "troupers" and not for revenue. I have at this moment a freak idea which might be worth considering if it has not been done by others in your line of work. Open the act with a fake microphone all set and adjusted for broadcasting. You come out and talk into the "mike" announcing the name of a fake station in the town where you happen to be playing and say you have a very interesting program ahead and then you can read it into the mike, using a number of "locals," naming people in the town in a way that will give offense to no one. If there is a confirmed old bachelor in the town have him sing a sentimental love song. Name the local celebrities and say they will do their stunts, etc. Then announce that you yourself will be the star of the program, whereupon Mrs. Wells, as the prima donna could come in and insist that she is the star of the program and you could open with a brisk quarrel in front of the "mike" with thousands of people listening in. After you start on your act as agreed upon you would not have to pay much attention to the microphone but you could give novelty to your act by having a super in a messenger's uniform bring in many telegrams from people listening in, some praising you some praising the lady and possibly some finding fault with both of you. These could come from out of the way places and you might have some of them come from notables. Also you might ring in telephone calls from local people. The main idea would be to have fun with the radio. Possibly including imitations of some of the well-known entertainers. You would have time to study them up. This idea may be worth nothing and possibly it has been worked before in your line of entertainment but I have not seen the kind of act I am suggesting. I shall be pretty busy for a week or two and away from home most of the time but later on we can talk over this idea or some new ones which may occur to me.

I am, with best wishes

Sincerely,
George Ade

InLP

92 ☙ TO DONALD FREEMAN

Hazelden
Brook, Indiana
July 10, 1928.

Dear Mr. Freeman:
I have your inquiry and I am not going to cast a ballot for anyone but I will tell you what I think of the candidates and the parties at this time. The Republicans start with a big edge because they have reduced taxes for those influential citizens everywhere who provide campaign funds and know how to mold public sentiment by indirect methods. Their candidate has been a most useful citizen but I do not think he will ever be a popular figure. I think he is too clammy and autocratic. The party has treated the farmers of the middle west with extreme contempt. It is bad enough to starve to death without being scolded about it. The Republicans deserve defeat for their absolute cowardice and hypocrisy regarding Prohibition and the Volstead Act. The national and state legislators and the delegates to all of the conventions sit in their rooms and drink anything that comes out of a bottle and has an alcoholic content and then march over to the convention hall, stepping high, and vote for "rigid enforcement." They do not believe in it and if enforcement ever became rigid they would suffer greatly but they continue to enact the sickening farce because they are afraid of the Anti-Saloon League, the Baptists, the Methodists and the W. C. T. U.

The Democratic party is certainly a medley, an olio, a crazy quilt and an assortment of odds and ends. This year it has a good candidate. Sooner or later we should elect a Catholic to the Presidency just to prove that we are living in the 20th century instead of the 18th and that witch-burning and religious persecutions are no longer the pastimes of a free and intelligent people. Al Smith is entitled to all the praise in the world for his courage and sincerity in saying the truth about the 18th Amendment and the Volstead Act. He said what 10 thousand politicians in the Republican party knew to be true but were afraid to say out loud. He will develop great strength in the east and in the cities and will be ambushed by all of the Protestants and fanatics and bigots who have dark minds and are narrow between the eyes. When I check up on the principal opposition to Governor Smith I am tempted to vote for him because I do not wish, at any time, to be found in the same camp with the mental dwarfs and perverts who are raging against him. I think he would be a much pleasanter room-mate than Herbert Hoover. I suspect that Mr. Hoover would expect his room-mate to press the Hoover trousers and take orders every morning from an efficiency expert by the name of Herbert Hoover. Al knows how to sing a song and to him the world is an alluring spectacle. No one can deny that Mr. Hoover has been a real humanitarian but he does not sing. He has filled many a stomach but probably never made a heart beat any faster. If he is elected, our beloved country will continue to be run on a factory system of scientific management, and prosperity will continue. If it continues much longer in the present direction, we who have invested our money in farm lands will be playing checkers in the large red-brick poor-houses which dot the middle west.

I am, with best wishes

Sincerely,
G. A.

InLP

93 ❧ TO MARGARET M. SCOTT

Hazelden
Brook, Indiana
Oct. 9, 1928.

Dear Miss Scott:
I am rather out of contact with the old-fashioned Christmas. Perhaps the old-fashioned Christmas has passed on, with many other Victorian institutions. I can remember distinctly when Christmas meant bob-sleds, sleigh bells, skating on the open ponds of the wind-swept prairies, possibly a tree at the M. E. Church, and, without fail, hanging up all the stockings on the evening of December 24th. We really believed that Kris Kringle could beat all of the [Charles E.] Lindbergh records established later, and proceed from house to house, all the way from Maine to California, and go down chimneys which were not large enough to take care of a nest of barn swallows in the summer time. I am a bachelor but if what they tell me about the young people is true, they can no longer be fooled by any myth regarding a very old gentleman driving reindeers. They probably know what they are going to get, a week before Christmas, and what the darn things cost. However, I am just talking from hearsay. I have been south every Christmas for a number of years, and down there the only special observances seem to be the playing of golf by the adults and the exploding of firecrackers by the young ones. There is no suggestion of Christmas when the

beach is crowded with bathers. I have always been in favor of Christmas and I hope that somewhere it is still being observed.

Yours truly,
George Ade

InLP

Margaret M. Scott was an officer in the Woman's Press Club of Indiana. She had written Ade, November 17, 1924 (InLP), requesting a Christmas message to be used at the meeting. Ade sent the following answer: "We have come to 'peace on earth' because we are worn out from fighting. Now let us have 'good-will toward men' because we are decent and want to behave ourselves."

The above letter was probably prepared for the Christmas meeting of the Press Club.

94 ❧ TO FRANKLIN P. ADAMS

Hazelden
Brook, Indiana
Oct. 21, 1928

Dear Frank:

Yes, I have read the Edna Ferber book and I thought she did very well in describing the Carry Watson establishment in view of the fact that she had never, I hope, visited same.

As for the Olympic [Theater], I am pleased to inform you that I wrote it. For several years I was a Monday afternoon writer and I knew every act on the bill, also, the after pieces put on by Frank Hartwell after one rehearsal, with all the actors doing ad lib stuff.

You speak of your picture on a Worlds Fair pass. I have my pass put away somewhere and the photograph is terrible. You may recall that I secured, from the official photographer, at the Fair, the unimproved prints of William Dean Howells and Archibald Forbs, the British war correspondent. I showed these photos to a number of police officials in Chicago and asked them, secretively, if they could identify the boys. Most of them said that William Dean was a confidence man and that Archibald was a yegg. It made a dandy story which I must dig up and reproduce some time.

I am, with best wishes

Sincerely,
George Ade

InLP

Carry Watson ran a Chicago purlieu which Edna Ferber used as a model for "Hetty Chilson's place" in Show Boat. *It is interesting to note that in evoking Chicago in the nineties Miss Ferber mentions Ade as one of the devotees of Billy Boyle's Chop House.*

In a manuscript notation on a letter from Douglas Silver to Ade, December 20, 1926 (InLP), Ade recorded that the passport picture story was published in The Chicago Record.

95 NEWS LETTER NO. 7 FROM GEORGE ADE AND OTHERS

Peking, China
8 February, 1929.

In the previous letter, mailed from that fascinating but frozen little "Sacred Island" in the Inland Sea of Japan last Saturday, the 2nd, we apologized because we had so little to tell. Be assured, good friends, who are far away, that since Saturday we have had so many strange and bewildering experiences that this letter could take up ten pages without telling half of the story.

After we got clear of Japan we headed to the Northwest. It was cold in Japan, but before we got through with our Polar expedition we had discovered a new brand of cold weather. . . . Last Tuesday morning, the 5th, we arose at an early hour and looked out of our port-holes and learned that the big BELGENLAND was crashing her way through floating ice floes. We were many miles out from the port of Chinwangtao. The temperature was just about zero. We peeked out and saw, several miles away, a good-sized steamer trying to break through the ice and get to us. Here was an experience not on the program. When we looked over the prospectus of our cruise around the world we did not see any pictures of large steamers fighting their way through ice eight or ten inches thick. We anchored well out in the harbor and our tender, which was really a tramp steamer of good size, bucked the ice and finally came alongside, but we were hours late in getting ashore and, oh, what a frigid ride it was from the steamer to the landing.

We were all day Tuesday getting from Chinwangtao to this most marvelous and interesting and frost-bitten town. It is the most spread out place in creation. When you go anywhere you ride for miles and miles. The Imperial City and the Forbidden City and the Legation Quarter have the widest streets in the world and the buildings seem to be set miles apart. In the native quarter the streets are not so wide and they have a seething, swarming population suggesting bee-hives, if you can imagine bees with high cheekbones, breathing steam. The wind blows most of the time and dust is everywhere. We have ridden for miles and miles, visiting temples and palaces of incredible size and beauty, some of them slightly gone to seed and others filled with the most wonderful museum displays of Chinese art dating away back to B.C., when our ancestors were living in trees. . . . All of our party, including Mr. and Mrs. [Bob] MacKay, Mrs. [MacKay] LeRoy, Mr. and Mrs. [Dave] Noyes and Mr. [Ray] Rice, have been comfortably housed at the Grand Hotel de Pekin, a large and modern establishment in the heart of the Legation neighborhood, a little run down because conditions have been so unsettled in recent years that the tourists have been timid about coming up to Peking. . . . We cannot undertake to tell you of the marvels of the Imperial City and the Forbidden City and the Summer Palace and the lofty gates and the rambling walls. You will simply have to go and read up for yourselves. We have been very cold while sightseeing, but we have been dazed and fascinated by what we have seen. Also, we have gone a little loco on shopping, because the rugs and the porcelains and silks and linens and what not are different from anything we have struck before and prices seem low, although we shall have to pay an 11% tax on anything we take out.

We had an interesting experience Wednesday evening, when we attended a reception given by Lady Bredon, said to have the most beautiful home in Peking, with over three hundred rooms, stored with art treasures of every kind. When we arrived at the reception a fire was raging next door, and our hostess was in a state of collapse, while her twenty-five or thirty boy servants were out fighting the flames. Later we went to the large and beautiful home of Mrs. William J. Calhoun, who used to be Lucy Monroe of Chicago. Her husband was formerly Minister to China and she is about the most popular and best known woman in Peking. She has converted an old temple into a beautiful residence and lives in much splendor, although we have quietly agreed among ourselves that we would not care to live in Peking forever. . . . We have shopped to the limit and viewed such a panorama of Chinese life that our heads ache. . . . Tomorrow morning very early we take a train back to the frozen port and head south for Shanghai. Very soon we shall be in warm weather. The warm weather will be welcome. Most of us have sniffly colds. Otherwise we are all right.
InLP

Ade wrote John Wheeler, October 4, 1928 (InLP), proposing to do a series of autobiographical recollections for newspaper syndication while on this round-the-world cruise:

> I will have with me a former Secretary [Ray Rice] who is lightning fast and accustomed to my dictation and we could send stuff back from various points and keep the thing going. I don't know just how it will work out but I will sit down this morning and make a lot of notes and then I will dictate or write out for you what I think would be one of the releases and you can size it up in a hurry and decide whether or not it is any good. It seems just now that the boys who break up their stuff and discuss a large number of topics —serious, semi-serious and comical are more entertaining to the average reader than the fellow who delivers a broadside.

The Log Book series Ade describes was never published.

Robert MacKay had played in the Broadway production of Ade's Father and the Boys.

96 ☙ TO REX S. GAY

Hazelden
Brook, Indiana
May 22, 1929.

Dear Rex:
I am interested to have your letter and I think I can give you the dope you want. The two big gamblers from Chicago about the time of the World's Fair were Mike McDonald and George Hankins. Mike had a high rolling place at 76 S. Clark. It seems to me that the numbers then started at Madison Street. Anyway Mike's place was south of Madison on Clark and on the west side of the street. The Hankins place was north of Madison on the west side of the street and south of the alley between Madison and Washington. It was a big place and was known as the dinner pail game because it invited the patronage of the small-fries. It had a pool room on the lower floor and every kind of gambling game above. Jeff Hankins was a brother of George. He was a partner also for a while and then had a place of his own. Joe Ullman ran a place at 2 Theater Court, just back of the old McVicker theater. Others who ran houses were John Condon, Sid McHie (now retired and respected citizen at Hammond), Harry Romaine (for many years after at French Lick), Cy Jaynes. I forget which one of these owned a place at 14 Quincy Street. There were two or three well-known places on Quincy Street

and a half dozen or so along Clark Street, but Mike McDonald and George Hankins were the best known of the lot. I might add that George had a wife named Effie Hankins who ran a well known bagnio. George and Effie made enough money to build a beautiful stone mansion in Michigan Avenue near 18th which may be standing now. After they went broke Ald. John Powers bought the house for May McKenna with whom he was hooked up.

I am certainly glad to be back home after a tedious tour and I am getting all rested up. Come down and see our golf course. It is better than ever before. Jim Rathbun and Joe Reeve are here and wish to be remembered.

I am, with best wishes

Sincerely,
George Ade

InLP

Rex Gay was a novelist and screen writer.

97 ❧ TO LOUIS F. SNEDIGAR

Hazelden
Brook, Indiana
Aug. 14, 1929.

My dear Red:
I have your letter and here is what you may want:

Last winter I made a cruise around the world. It was supposed to be a pleasure cruise. We were on the same ship for nearly five months, much of the time looking out at a wide expanse of empty water and living on cold-storage food. When you eat certain kinds of food which has been in the ice-box for three or four months it is just the same as trying to eat an inner tube. It tastes like nothing whatever. It is just as tender as a piece of buckskin and it provides no nourishment. We went up to the north of China where it was 10 below zero. Soon after we were down on the Equator and 120 in the shade. Now, I had been around the world once before and I am still wondering why I went again when I might have gone to Florida and had good food all of the time and pleasant surroundings and a civilized climate, never very hot and never very cold. I have said it many times and I will say it again, because it is the simple truth, that the climate of the east coast of Florida is the best winter climate in the world, and I have tried them all. Nothing can stop people from going to Florida every winter. The man who can afford to go to Miami Beach and can get away and remains up in the Polar regions to shovel snow and have the flu and nurse his chilblains, is simply wrong in the head.

I am, with best wishes

Sincerely,
George Ade

InLP

Mayor Louis F. Snedigar had asked Ade for a favorable comment on Miami Beach to read on radio.

98 ❧ TO FRANKLIN P. ADAMS

Miami Beach, Florida
Dec. 8, 1929.

Dear Frank:
I am interested to hear from you and I am compelled to reply that various press agents at different times had me engaged to all of the young ladies mentioned in your letter and several others including some I never met. Because I didn't run around much with the gals back of the foot lights the publicity boys seemed to think it was a great joke to float these wild-eyed stories about my pursuing Dorothy Tennant or Helen Hale or Irene Frizelle or Elsie Janis. The story about Tennant was the one most widely circulated although I knew her very slightly and had spoken to her timidly a couple of times at rehearsals.

I trust you are well and happy.

Sincerely,
George Ade

InLP

Dorothy Tennant starred in The College Widow.

Helen Hale starred in Peggy from Paris.

Elsie Janis, So Far So Good *(New York: 1932), p. 94, recalls her rumored betrothal to Ade:* "In the play [*The Fair Co-Ed*] I was engaged to marry half of the college, which necessitated my wearing a string of fraternity pins. George Ade started my collection by giving me his Sigma Chi pin. The humorous gesture was taken seriously by the press and my engagement to George was announced."

1929

Amy Leslie (Mrs. Lillie West Brown Buck), the daughter of the editor of the Lafayette paper for which Ade worked, shared her reviewers' tickets with Ade when he was a cub reporter in Chicago. It was rumored that the veteran drama critic was in love with Ade.

This previously-unpublished sketch of Ade and his dog Spry was found in one of Mildred Gilman's scrapbooks.

1930-1944

"More margin. More margin!" The cry penetrated every ear. The deafening sound of the Wall Street crash depressed America. Because he had invested in land, Ade was not devastated by hard times. He did experience difficulty in selling his writing. He kept a hand in his craft by voluminous correspondence. Ade reminisced in print and with cronies about happier days. There were annual sojourns to Miami Beach, fellowship dinners, and occasional attacks on the New Deal. The liberal newspaper man became increasingly conservative as he watched the changes of the century. The Second World War disrupted the habits of the nation. Ade followed his established routine. Stoically the country gentleman, who had been intermittently ill for some years, continued to send his best wishes until his death in 1944.

Ade, who believed in Emersonian individualism, was himself capsuled by the philosopher:

> If the single man plant himself indomitably on his instincts, and there abide, the huge world will come round to him.
>
> —Ralph Waldo Emerson, *Literary Ethics*

99 ❧ TO MRS. CARL F. WERTZ

Miami Beach, Florida
January 12, 1930.

Dear Mrs. Wertz:
I find it a little difficult to comply with your request, but I am quite sure that when your boy is a little older he will find that the most useful thing he can read will be [Ralph Waldo] Emerson's essay on "Compensation." I believe absolutely in the philosophy advanced by Emerson that we must pay for whatever we get in this world and that the books must always balance.

The most useful lesson for a young man is that he will not get something for nothing—that he must go out and earn the things that are really worth while.

Sincerely,
George Ade

InLP

100 ❧ TO THOMAS B. COSTAIN

Hazelden
Brook, Indiana
Aug. 20, 1930

Dear Mr. Coston [*sic*]:
I am glad to have your letter of the 15th and to learn that the [James Whitcomb] Riley material which we succeeded in getting to you a little ahead of time is satisfactory. I felt sure that you would be compelled to make some cuts in the stuff but the important thing was to get to you some copy which was acceptable. Riley had his own way of saying everything and it struck me that these brief extracts would prove to be delightful reading. Your publication date, September 17th, is entirely satisfactory to the book publishers as, I believe, that the book is to appear on October 7th, Riley's birthday. Your P.S. indicates that you might be willing to look at some other manuscript. I have in mind an article dealing with the influential pioneers of this part of the world. They were of a type that has disappeared. They wore broadcloth on Sundays and Henry Clay collars and were rather stiff-necked and autocratic but they were the real barons of their day and most of the towns in this region were named for them and they had little in common with the happy-go-lucky

pioneer who lived in a log cabin and devoted much of his time to hunting and fishing. There are many rare stories to tell about these old birds who came out here early and grabbed practically all of the land in sight. One of them was Peter VanRensselaer of the aristocratic New York family. At one time he owned thousands of acres in this region and the city of Rensselaer is named for him. The piece would be out of the ordinary and it is one I want to write some time because I am old enough to remember some of these distinguished early settlers and they were really great men.

I am, with best wishes

Sincerely,
George Ade

InLP

Thomas Costain, associate editor of Saturday Evening Post, *1920–1934, later wrote popular novels, e.g.,* The Silver Chalice, *1952.*

In "Riley and His Friends," Saturday Evening Post, *September 27, 1930, Ade made use of material from* Letters of James Whitcomb Riley, *ed. William Lyon Phelps (Indianapolis: [1930]).*

Ade's "Prairie Kings of Yesterday" appeared in the Saturday Evening Post, *July 4, 1931.*

Ade wrote John Wheeler, June 29, 1926 (InLP), criticizing the Post: "I have no desire whatever to write for The Saturday Evening Post. My stuff does not conform to their style. I try to keep my copy boiled down to the limit. I go over it and try to take out superfluous. They print page after page of padded stuff. Much of it is good and much of it is not."

101 ❧ TO JAMES KIRBY RISK

Hazelden
Brook, Indiana
Sept. 17, 1930.

Dear Kirby:
I have your letter of the 15th and I can hardly find time to tell you all of the things I have done around Purdue. When the Memorial Gym was planned and Purdue had to raise a certain sum to meet an appropriation by the state, the University fund was still short $2500 on the last day and I chipped in with the amount required. I helped out on the Harlequin shows for a number of years and bought the boys about $2000 worth of scenery, including the plush drop curtain still in use. I directed the building of the Sigma Chi

house and spent about $25,000. Also I handled the alumni magazine for a number of years. Dave Ross discovered the site for the Stadium and showed me the layout. We bought sixty-five acres of land for $40,000 and later matched up contributions made by alumni so that our total contribution to the project was somewhere between $60,000 and $70,000. I have no accurate record of the amount we spent. It is not my desire to blow about the things I have done for Purdue because I derived a real pleasure from getting in on such large and worthy enterprises. You must remember that Dave Ross and I are old bachelors. Every person who begins to grow old must adopt something. Old maids adopt cats and canaries. Dave Ross and I adopted Purdue. It is only fair to add that Dave has done much more for the University than I have done. The amount of work he has given to the school and the amount of money he has given, without many people knowing about it, entitle him to first place among the alumni and I want it distinctly understood that I am not presuming to put myself in his class as a Purdue benefactor.

As I wrote before, I have no suggestions to offer as to placing the story. The young lady could find no better medium than The Saturday Evening Post.

I am, with best wishes

Sincerely,
George Ade

InK

Kirby Risk, a friend of the university, was always interested in spreading information about Purdue's benefactors, and in helping young people further their talents.

102 TO CLAUDE G. BOWERS

December 19, 1930

Dear Mr. Bowers:
I am more than interested to have your letter and in due time I shall sit down and try to get together some notes of that "swing around" in Indiana when Jim, [Sam] Blythe and John McCutcheon and I and some more of you were guests. What you heard about the trip is more or less true. I shall try to tell you what impressed us at the time and I think the most remarkable thing about Bev was that he could arise in his place at any time day or night and make a whale of a speech.

Last week I re-read "The Tragic Era." You certainly shattered some of my early idols, although I think I had figured out the low-down on most of them before I read your book.

I am glad that you are going to do the life of [Albert] Beveridge. I knew him for many years. He was a senior at DePauw when I was a freshman at Purdue and I had him under observation for a long time and admired him very much and wish at times that he had played a little politics and moved up to the high places where he belonged.

I am with best wishes,

Sincerely,
InK George Ade

Claude G. Bowers had written The Tragic Era; the Revolution after Lincoln *(Cambridge: 1929). He had queried Ade about the 1908 campaign train for his forthcoming study,* Beveridge and the Progressive Era *(Boston: 1932). In pages 295 and 296, Bowers describes a campaign tour through the state by train in 1908. According to Bowers, Samuel G. Blythe, George Ade, John McCutcheon, and Kin Hubbard were along and the "company of wits" was "a bit boisterous in its mirth." Although Ade seems to disagree with Bowers, the biographer cites letters from Ade, McCutcheon, and Blythe as sources.*

Ade wrote John McCutcheon, September 10, 1932 (InLP): "Have you read the book by Claude Bowers about BEVERIDGE? It mentions you several times and there is one rather cryptic mention of the both of us as if the biographer had learned that you and I and Beveridge had been sporting around together and there was some talk about our doings but the biographer does not go into detail. He is not talking about the tour through the state in 1910, which was a wild sort of a picnic, but about something earlier."

103 ❧ TO JOSEPH REEVE

[Miami Beach, Florida]
[December–January, 1930–1931]

Under-Cover News

Here are some news items which have not been printed but which come from pretty reliable sources.

Mr. [George W.] Wickersham called on Pres. [Herbert] Hoover

early in December and privately reported to him that his Commission had decided that the solution of the Prohibition problem lay in permitting 4% beer, repealing the Volstead & Jones acts and letting each state take care of enforcement. The President hit the ceiling and said he never would agree to such a program. Evidently he is still very much under the domination of extreme Drys. He told Mr. Wickersham that the Commission report would not get his support if it compromised with the Wets. So the Commission is now at work on a report which will embody what Hoover wants instead of what the Commission really believes. It is said that the President is being influenced by Mrs. Hoover, who is rabidly dry. The President used to drink a cocktail once in a while and take a little wine.

Congressman Fred Britten says that the Wets in Congress are not thinking of any repeal of the 18th Amendment or the Volstead or Jones acts but they are organizing to ham-string all appropriations for enforcement. Many Congressmen and Senators listed as drys would be glad to nullify Prohibition enforcement if they could do so without getting in wrong with dry constituents. By voting for economy they can make the 18th amendment as null and void as the 14th and 15th amendments, which ceased to operate the moment Congress failed to vote any money to enforce them. Britten thinks that after another Congressional dictum no money will be voted to enforce Prohibition and that even in the serving Congress the Wets have a chance to keep down the appropriation and make enforcement even more of a joke than it is at present.

The anti-Thompson forces in Chicago are really afraid that Big Bill [Thompson] may be elected again, although they believe that his mental and physical condition will prevent him from doing any effective campaigning. Judge [Jonathan H.] Lyle cannot beat him at the primaries. Lyle is now in the spot-light as a brave and holy crusader and is entitled to credit for recent successful articles on the gangsters, but his previous private record will not bear inspection. The wiser politicians of both parties agree that "Tony" Cermak is the one man who can certainly defeat Thompson. He is not a righteous reformer but would be an improvement. If Thompson is nominated, the Tribune and the News will probably support an independent republican candidate, already selected, the real idea being to prevent Cermak to eliminate Thompson. Many of the most useful and influential citizens of Chicago admire Cermak and have confidence in him.

About two months ago Al Capone sent a bunch of killers to Chicago to "get" the Federal officials who have started to put the Capone organization out of business. The plot was discovered and the killers were trailed. They got cold feet and disappeared. Jack Guizik gets five years in Leavenworth for failing to make proper income tax returns. Al Capone has never filed a report. The Federal officials are planning to get him but they hope to get him dead and not alive. It is hoped he will make some move, when and if taken into custody, to justify a killing. He is in more danger than ever before. At present he is in hiding but two weeks ago he was at his home on Star Island, Miami Beach, and talked for two hours with Walter Winchell, of the N. Y. Mirror. "Al" was playing cards with three friends but he had a huge "gat" on the table in front of him. He explained, "I've got to the point where I dont trust any one." He said he had nothing to drink on his premises because, "If they found anything here, they'd frame me."

He was sore because Chicago papers did not give him credit for running free soup kitchens in Chicago. During the interview Al's little boy sat a few feet away reading "Tarzan of the Apes."
InK

Joseph Reeve was Ade's secretary, 1923–1944.

George W. Wickersham was the head of the Law Observance and Enforcement Commission. The Wickersham Report, January 19, 1931, made it clear that the Eighteenth Amendment was not enforceable.

William Hale Thomson was mayor of Chicago for three terms, 1915–1923 and 1927–1931. Anton Cermak was elected mayor in 1931.

Ade wrote risque material on separate slips of paper which he included in letters to select friends such as Ort Wells, John Jenks, Charles Fernald, and O. O. McIntyre, who were appreciative of ribaldry. Because of his reluctance to dictate this material to the female stenographers he used in Florida the following stories and jokes were sent to Joseph Reeve to be inserted with mimeographed newsletters. None of these insertions is dated or signed. The manuscript copy is comparable to the author's handwriting 1930–1941. The following selected items appear in the order in which they were clipped together in the Joseph Reeve papers.

> Why is our beloved President [Franklin D. Roosevelt] like a constipated osteopath or a pregnant whore? Ans—He doesn't know his business.
>
> An old maid by the unusual name of Miss Smith had saved up $600. She went to her Jew lawyer and said she wanted to put $300 into a trust to provide her with a proper funeral and a well-chosen burial lot. The other $300 she had decided to spend on one wild bust-over

of the hilarious indiscretion she had always craved. The lawyer said he would attend to all the details. He consulted his wife "Times are hard," he explained. "Why shouldnt we have that three hundred?" "Sure," said the wife. "Its all business." And the lawyer said hed be home at nine o'clock the next morning. Next morning he didnt appear. The day wore on. The anxious wife called his office. No one had seen him. At last she succeeded in getting through a call to the old maids apartment. Friend husband answered the phone.

"What's the matter?" she asked.

"It's all right" came back over the phone. "Miss Smith has decided to be buried in the Potter's Field."

N. Y. magistrate goes to big dinner drinks cocktails & everything. Sick on way home & throws up all over himself. Suspicious wife waiting up. He tells her he could not get taxi on account of drunken bum next to him leaned on him and vomited. He says "I turned him over to a cop and when his case comes before me tomorrow morning I'll give him six months.—Next morning, while on bench he gets phone call from wife.

"Has that case come up yet?"

"No, but when it does I'll give him six months."

"Better make it a year. He s--t in your pants too."

104 ❧ TO A. A. MERCEY

Hazelden
Brook, Indiana
July 17, 1931.

My dear Mr. Mercey:

Having worked around newspaper shops for a good many years I continue to be interested in daily papers. They have been dying off lately as if stricken by some fatal epidemic. The information that some one is going to start a new paper causes almost a thrill. I don't know what your newspaper is going to be. If it is to be independent you have my sympathy because you will have to be a tight rope walker to go along and maintain a neutral attitude. If you are to be Republican you have my sympathy because you will have to do some tall writing to explain why the [Herbert] Hoover program for continued prosperity and general employment failed to show up when it was needed. If you are to be Democratic you have my sympathy because you will be trying to win a general election with a minority of voters, one half of whom are deacons in the church and the other half of whom have signed up with the Demon Rum.

Editing a newspaper is the most interesting work in the world. It is a great life if you don't weaken but I began to weaken a little after conducting a two-column department for many years and writing more words than you will now find in the Encyclopedia Britannica. At any rate, I can play safe and congratulate you on your heroism.

I am, with best wishes

Sincerely,
George Ade

InLP

A. A. Mercey founded the Vincennes *[Indiana]* Times.

105 ❧ TO ALEXANDER GUERRY

Hazelden
Brook, Indiana
Nov. 7, 1931

Dear Mr. Guerry:
I am interested to have your letter and I am very glad to send to you, for your Freshmen, the kind of message which I have tried to deliver to many Freshmen in whom I have been interested. So-called words of wisdom from the old fogies do not always impress the young people but I know that my advice has been good.

The important thing for any Freshman to have in mind at the beginning of his college career is to do his college work more than well and postpone the more pleasurable college activities until later on. What I mean is that if a Freshman will get high grades in mathematics and the sciences and his lab work during his first year, all the work after that will be easier. If, however, he gets away to a bad start and does not get the fundamentals into his head and does not form habits of industry and does not impress upon his instructors the fact that he is dependable, he may have a very hard road to travel before he takes his degree.

I know that in my own case, the fact that I got very high grades in the first year, gave me a friendly standing with the Faculty and helped to carry me through the later years.

I am, with best wishes

Sincerely,
George Ade

InLP

Alexander Guerry, president of the University of Chattanooga, had asked Ade and other notables for messages to be read at freshman orientation.

106 ❧ TO GRANTLAND RICE

Miami Beach, Florida
Dec. 4, 1931.

My dear Grant:

I am submitting to you a couple of things which you may use for your book if you desire. One is the newspaper account of the Purdue game with Iowa in 1929. You can easily cut it down. The second would be out of the ordinary. It is the third act of THE COLLEGE WIDOW. This stuff becomes interesting largely from the fact that this play was the first successful play dealing with college life and absolutely the first play on the American stage with football as a central theme. The wise men of the theater said that the public would not be interested in college life or college sport. I think an introduction should reveal the fact that the half-back's father went to Europe thinking that the boy would play on the Baptist team and that the college widow of the Presbyterian school vamped him and induced him to come to the little college of which her father was President. The old man returns from Europe and picks up a paper and finds that his boy is playing against the college he has endowed and that explains his arrival during the game and his determination to take Bolton out of the game. Remember this, football plays on the talking stage on the silent screen and on the talking screen which have been written in the last twenty-five years, every one of them has been a carbon copy of THE COLLEGE WIDOW. It had to be because we used the only workable plot—the player who was fighting against odds and who wins for his team when everything looks dark. No reader should criticize this work until he takes into consideration the fact that this was the first of the football plays and that it deals with the game of 1905. The scene always went big because we played it with two companies—one on stage and one off stage. The large company off stage supplied the songs and yells and worked very carefully on the cues so that the moment the dialogue on the stage ceased the yelling and singing began off stage and the moment the turmoil in the arena quieted down the talk in front was taken up again. By using this method we got a real effect and maybe it would be interesting to reproduce the whole act.

I am, with best wishes

Sincerely,
George Ade

InLP

Grantland Rice and H. Powel edited The Omnibus of Sport *(New York: 1932), which contains "The Fable in Slang of the Caddy Who Hurt His Head While Thinking," the third act of* The College Widow, *and an extract of this letter.*

107 ☙ TO W. B. SKERRYE

[Miami Beach, Florida]
Dec. 19, 1931

Dear Mr. Skerrye:
I have you letter of inquiry. I had some Latin in High School, but I did not get any in my College course, because I attended Purdue which does not offer the Classics or the so called dead languages.

Although I did not become well acquainted with Latin, I honestly believe that a good working knowledge of it is of the utmost value to any man who expects to be in the writing game, because the most useful and expressive words in our vocabulary are of Latin origin and the delicate shades of meaning can be revealed only to students who know something about the Latin origin.

I have a suspicion that a great deal of "practical" knowledge which is forced upon students in our modern schools is forgotten soon after they leave school, but anyone who has acquired his Latin will never forget the essentials of it.

I am, with best wishes.

Sincerely,
George Ade

InLP

108 ~ TO JULIAN STREET

Hazelden
Brook, Indiana
May 29, 1932.

Dear Julian:

I have postponed replying to your last letter of inquiry because I wanted time to look up some dope, including some from John McCutcheon, but he is quite ill and on his way west, so I will take a little time off this Sunday morning and attempt to help you out.

You are right about our accepting conditions as we found them without endeavoring to investigate causes or psychoanalyze ourselves. For instance, I lived in Chicago all during the nineties when it was the wildest and most wide open town in the world and to me all the conditions seemed perfectly proper and natural and the picturesque trimmings of city life.

I think you can get more material about Rome and Capri than I can give you as I remained only a day or two. Of course, you know that the present Lord LaScalles [Henry Ulick Viscount Lascelles, Earl of Harewood] who married Princess Mary, was attached to the British Legation in Rome and wore the enormous monocle and he is the bird who arranged to meet Jim Stutesman at Peru and hunt the Incas.

The Ross-Ade Stadium was promoted by Dave Ross and myself. He is now President of the Board of Trustees. It is exactly the size of the original stadium near Athens and will seat about 23,000. It has a beautiful sight on a hill top overlooking the Wabash Valley and the playing field, because of soil and drainage conditions, is said to be one of the best in the country.

Now regarding George Barr McCutcheon. He continued as City Editor of the LaFayette Evening Courier long after John [McCutcheon] and I went to Chicago. He wrote many plays and novels and submitted them to managers and publishers but they were turned down year after year. One day he came into our office in Chicago and said that Herbert Stone had offered him five hundred dollars cash for the script of a novel. I advised him to accept it but not to promise any future deliveries at any rate. My argument was that if Stone got the book cheap he would boom it and spend on advertising the money which might otherwise be paid in royalties. I told George that if he made good on this first book he could name his own terms on later books but he simply had to get a start somehow and so he signed the contract and took the five hundred dollars. The book was GRAUSTARK which brought him fame and fortune. When it became generally known that he had received only a small sum for the book, I was blamed for giving him bad advice but I still think the advice was good because if he hadn't accepted that offer maybe he never would have found a publisher.

When George was about 18 he became stage struck and joined a traveling company. He changed his name to George Emerson and had this name painted on his trunk and below his name the words COMMEDIAN, the spelling is his. The show busted over in Illinois and he walked all the way home. The family living out at Elston, a suburb of LaFayette, were at Thanksgiving dinner when they saw George looking in the window. They brought him in and thawed him out and asked him to sit down and have some dinner but he said he had just eaten a hearty meal over at the junction. As a matter of fact, he had not eaten for two days. Finally he was persuaded to sit down and have a bite and they did not get him away from the table until late in the evening.

I don't know the story about George and the girl and the buffalo coat but John [McCutcheon] took Fannie McGrath to an entertainment at Purdue one night and drove her over in a buggy behind a famous white horse which was later sold to Charles J. McCarthy, the actor, and appeared on the stage all over the country as one of the horses in THE STILL ALARM. When John came out to drive home the boys had taken the wheels off his buggy and hidden them. He looked for the wheels and could not find them. By that time it was too late to 'phone. He could not leave that valuable white horse over at Purdue, so he marched down Chauncy Hill, across the levy, up Main Street and all the way home, leading the horse and Fannie McGrath on his arm.

While he was at Purdue his father was sheriff. John was only sixteen. His family lived in the residence of the jail and he helped supervise the prisoners. One day a tough criminal knocked him aside and jumped through the doorway and ran into the open street. John got a revolver and chased him five blocks and into a lumber yard and popped at him five times before the prisoner threw up his hands and surrendered. He got a great write up in the local papers.

I am not sure about Jake Sharp but I think he is dead.

I am going to call it a day but I will help you later on if you have any special queries.

I am, with best wishes

InLP

George Ade

Julian Street was collecting anecdotes for a series of articles, "When We Were Young," Saturday Evening Post, *205 (Sept.–Dec., 1932).*

According to John McCutcheon, Drawn From Memory, *p. 179, George McCutcheon billed himself as "George M. Clifford, Commedienne."*

109 ❧ TO WILL R. WOOD

Hazelden
Brook, Indiana
June 12, 1932.

My dear Will:

I am interested to have your letter. Some of the recent political developments have been so sudden and to some people so surprising that it is pretty difficult to size up the situation. Your recent action in Congress and the definite stand taken by the state convention on the Prohibition issue undoubtedly have helped to improve the general situation so far as the Republicans are concerned. I need not tell you that the G.O.P. ticket in general will be up against two discouraging factors, namely, the rather appalling and prolonged business depression and the fact that Mr. [Herbert] Hoover has few of the qualities of a popular idol and is strangely lacking in the arts of diplomacy. These general conditions may give you a handicap in this district but I think that will be the only handicap you will be against. Because of your outspoken and sensible declaration regarding Prohibition I think you will gain a hundred votes in the district for any ten you might possibly lose. Only the extreme drys persist in believing that every man who thinks that Prohibition has been a legislative failure therefore believe that the old-time saloon was a blessing and that booze should be freely retained and that it is absolutely all right for a man to get pickled and go home and beat his wife.

The general reversal of sentiment, even in the outlying and rural districts, has been almost astounding. Newton County has always been listed as bone dry but every delegate to the state convention voted for the Henry Marshall platform.

I think that a little later we can get a pretty good outline on this district. So far as I am concerned I am for you and will help you in any way I can. It would be a calamity for this district to lose the services of the most useful member of the House of Representatives. It would be stupidity to put into Congress a man who would not be in a position to help the people of his district by acting as an intermediary between his district and the many departments of the Government. You know what I mean by that. Probably your most important work has not been on the floor of the House. Regarding any possible opposition within the party, it is true that some of the more temperamental of the Republicans have been all lathered up over the demand for repeal but I am quite sure that you have done all that a sane and well-balanced man could do in carrying out the wishes of your constituents. It is a good time to remember that a man may have convictions without going absolutely off his nut and turning cart wheels.

As you know, I have kept pretty well out of politics for a good many years but I do not hesitate to express myself very candidly regarding your case and if I can be of service to you later on I will be glad to hear from you or the members of your committee, but I will not make any speeches.

I hope to be at the convention for a day or two but it may be a rather tame affair.

I am, with best wishes

Sincerely,
George Ade

InLP

Will R. Wood was a congressman from Indiana, 1915–1933.

110 ❧ TO ORSON C. WELLS

Hazelden
Brook, Indiana
July 15, 1932.

My dear Ort:

I am interested to have your letter and I am sending a book to Sam Blythe in this mail and I am going to write to him and have him give me some more information about Langdon Smith as many people who get the book want to know more about him and I can tell them very little except that I met him several times when we were covering big assignments. Any dope you can give me will be welcome.

I am interested to read what Sam Blythe says about [Herbert] Hoover. He may be right. Up to the present time it is pretty hard to find, out here in the country, any one who says he is going to vote for Hoover but I believe there will be a growing distrust of [Franklin D.] Roosevelt. The voters have always been a little scared of an emotional leader of the [William Jennings] Bryan type. For about a year Mr. Roosevelt has worked a little too hard at being a candidate and has been over eager to enlist the sympathy of the hard-luck boys and put a lot of blame on the rich, forgetting that there are no rich any more. I have no use for Hoover whatever but I am leary of any statesman who writes a piece every week for the Liberty Magazine, which is about the lousiest low-class publication in America, especially since Bernarr McFadden took charge of it.

I have been pretty well most of the summer but feel a little low when I get tired or over work and the doctor says that I have a low blood pressure when I get in a condition of fatigue. It is said that a low blood pressure will not kill you but it will make you feel like Hell. However, I am doing quite a lot of work. If I cannot get any revenues from the farms or from the so-called securities I just can't figure any way of getting it except by grinding out copy and even the editors are not willing customers these days.

I am, with best wishes

Sincerely,
George Ade

InLP

Orson C. Wells had been a newspaper boy in Lafayette. He became a successful businessman in Chicago, and made a million dollars in Wall Street. He and Ade traveled around the world together in 1910, and took several trips to the West Indies.

Ade had an edition of Langdon Smith's poem Evolution *privately printed in 1932. Ade wrote a brief introduction. See Russo, p. 149.*

Sam Blythe was a news correspondent, publicist, and magazine writer.

111 ❧ TO WILLIAM A. ALEXANDER

Hazelden
Brook, Indiana
Aug. 13, 1932.

Dear Mr. Alexander:

I am more than grateful to you for sending me exactly the information I wanted regarding Mary Hartwell Catherwood. I have under way an article dealing with celebrities who have lived in this region up here. I was quite sure that Mrs. Catherwood lived at Hoopeston, Illinois, for a while but I also remembered that, late in the nineties, she helped give a two-night show at Indianapolis for the benefit of the Benjamin Harrison Memorial Monument Fund. We had on the bill: Gen. Lew Wallace, James Whitcomb Riley, Charles Major, Mrs. Catherwood, Booth Tarkington, Meredith Nicholson, George Barr McCutcheon, Evaleen Stein and one or two more. Riley had not appeared in Indianapolis for years and he was reluctant to go on the program because he said people had lost interest in him! When he walked out on the stage the whole assemblage stood up and cheered. I remember that Gen. Lew Wallace gave some quiet confidential advice to Tark, Nicholson, George McCutcheon and me while we were waiting in the wings. He said: "You are younger than I am and have not made any public appearances and I want to give you some good advice." We assured him that we would be grateful and he said: "Just before you walk out on the stage, take your forefinger and run it along the fly of your trousers to make sure that everything is buttoned up." Come to think of it, it wasn't such bad advice.

Thank you again. I am, with best wishes

Sincerely,
George Ade

InU

W. A. Alexander was librarian at Indiana University.

Authors' Readings for the Harrison Memorial Fund occurred May 30 and 31, 1902. The letter to James Whitcomb Riley, appealing to him to participate in the program May 31, was signed by the chairman, Charles W. Fairbanks, and the Hoosier authors who read selections of their works. Marcus Dickey, The Maturity of James Whitcomb Riley *(Indianapolis: 1922), pp. 383–384.*

Shumaker, A History of Indiana Literature, *treats all of the Hoosier authors Ade mentions.*

112 ❧ TO C. M. LINCOLN

Hazelden
Brook, Indiana
Aug. 18, 1932.

Dear Mr. Lincoln:

Thank you very much for your letter about Langdon Smith. What you say about him seems to bear out my own observation and what others have told me. He was a very quiet fellow of a rather grim disposition and very much self-contained but you are right when you say that he was a corking descriptive writer. What you say about the typewriting machine happens to interest me greatly. I have always believed that one who used a machine could turn out copy more rapidly but also I have been convinced that he is all of the time tempted to become verbose and repetitional and violate the old rules for good writing which advised simplicity and directness. I never have written a line on a typewriting machine. All of my copy, from the time I began to report for a LaFayette paper forty-five years ago has been done with a very black pencil on soft paper. I have written a lot of bad copy but the good copy I have turned out and peddled to advantage would not have been as good if I had rattled it off on a typewriter. When a man writes by hand the tendency is to adopt a compact style and cut out the superfluous adjectives and go by the nearest possible route to the point which he is attempting to make.

Thank you for your letter and I am glad you liked the little book. I am sure that Langdon Smith would have been properly flattered to know that a few of his admirers were keeping his memory green and I am equally sure that he would not have given way to any emotional outbursts.

I am, with best wishes

Sincerely,
George Ade

InLP

C. M. Lincoln, former Sunday editor of the New York Times, *had known Langdon Smith when he was a reporter on the* New York Herald. *Smith left the* Herald *and joined the staff of the* New York World, *and then wrote for the Hearst Service.*

113 ❧ TO I. L. PADDOCK

Hazelden
Brook, Indiana
Oct. 29, 1932.

Dear Mr. Paddock:

I was very much interested and some what flattered to have your character estimate based on the sample of my handwriting. I think you have made a very good character reading in most of the particulars.

I am, with best wishes

Sincerely,
George Ade

InLP

Dear Mother:
I suppose you received the cable announcing our safe arrival in London. We had pleasant weather nearly all the way — only one bad day and on deck it was so warm that one seldom wore our overcoats. As this is my fourth visit to London. I feel at home here.

Portion of letter to Adaline Ade (see page 38).

I. L. Paddock, a graphologist, had written Ade the following analysis (InLP):

> One of the first things that I notice from your handwriting is the entire absence of conceit or pride in your nature. You do not have any false ideas about values and this ability that you have to put yourself on a plane with the other person is a very valuable one indeed.
>
> You possess a congenial, easy flowing, diplomatic nature and you get along with others quite successfully and you are quite clannish in the selection of your intimate friends. You possess a good deal of ease of expression, as well as an emphasis of opinion that causes what you say to carry authority.
>
> You are direct both in thought and action. When you have something to be accomplished you may be rather careless of details, you

possibly will take short-cuts, yet you keep your central purpose firmly in your mind and accomplish this goal that you set for yourself with a minimum of effort and delay. You are the type of person to do away with all that is unnecessary and superfluous.

You have an excellent sense of values rather than being particularly extravagant or wasteful. You realize the value of time as well as money, and anything of an extravagant nature is distasteful to you, although at times in order to satisfy some whim or desire that you have, you may somewhat depart from this angle of your nature.

You possess a good deal of adaptability and originality, you do things in your own way, could have made a success of several different professions, show ability to concentrate for hours at a time on anything that interests you in the least.

Your head maintains the balance of control over what you do rather than your heart. Your judgment is good, you are deliberate and analytical in what you do rather than being hurried and somewhat lacking in confidence.

114 ❧ TO JOSEPH H. MC CONNAHEY

Hazelden
Brook, Indiana
Nov. 1, 1932.

Dear Sir:

I am interested to have your inquiry in regard to "American Humor." The word HUMOR has been so passed around and variously used that it means almost anything from a vaudeville stunt up to a President's Message. I never have pretended to be a humorist. In all the stuff I have written for syndicates and magazines I have simply tried to tell the facts about certain people and their peculiarities, using as few words as possible, and taking the liberty of expressing myself in idiomatic language or the vernacular or slang or whatever you choose to call it. In the case of Mark Twain, he loved to write in a playful mood and everything he wrote was underlaid with truth. He did not hesitate to use words that helped him to express himself. Will Rogers plays havoc with the English language but his work is effective because he is telling the plain truth about something and doing it in the unconventional way.

I am, with best wishes

Sincerely,
George Ade

InLP

115 ☙ TO CYRIL CLEMENS

Hazelden
Brook, Indiana
Nov. 2, 1932

Dear Mr. Clemens:

You have asked for an expression which it is very difficult to formulate. The average reader can get very little out of Josh Billings by sitting down and reading him today. The same is true of Artemus Ward and many more of the old timers. On the other hand, Mark Twain improved with age because he always dealt with truth and human nature and treated them in a playful mood. I have no doubt that Josh Billings deserved all the popularity that he acquired but I cannot candidly say that he was a great humorist because I have read only a few of his writings, not because I have any prejudice against him but I don't like to do any reading which involves hard labor.

I am with best wishes

Sincerely,
George Ade

InU

Cyril Clemens, Josh Billings, Yankee Humorist *(Webster Groves, Mo.: 1932), pp. 170–71, quotes this letter. The "hard labor" to which Ade refers is the penetration of dialect employed by humorists Josh Billings (Henry Wheeler Shaw) and his rival Artemus Ward (Charles Ferrar Browne).*

116 ☙ TO CHARLES B. DILLINGHAM

Hazelden
Brook, Indiana
April 6th, 1933

Dear Charley:

I am returning to you the script and I will make a few comments on it. It is all good stuff, but for a periodical such as the Post you want to be more explicit and permit yourself to ramble in all directions. You cannot give the Post the kind of stuff it wants if you sit down and go through the drudgery of writing everything out in longhand. You want to give your views on a lot of things connected with the theatre and give your impressions about the speaking stage and the pictures and the old-time actors. The stories are all right and should not be omitted but I think you should open up with a little talk on the fact that no matter where a man or woman is born if he or she has the theatre in the system it will break out, and then you can say, for instance, Fred Stone was the son of a humble barber in a little town in Kansas and go through the list and show that the stars you have managed and the prominent people with whom you have associated came from all sorts of places and I dare say that most of them had humble beginnings. I would soft-peddle the fact on page 1 about Mr. [William Randolph] Hearst and his newspapers because the Post and Hearst are not too friendly. I would devote hundreds and hundreds of words to Charles Frohman as one of the most unusual characters of his day. Tell how he started. Bring out the fact that he doubled the royalties of every playwright. Tell what happened to the stars he managed and how they became rich while he remained poor. Tell all about his habits and his avoidance of publicity and his pleasant eccentricities, and don't be afraid of writing too much about him.

At different times you mention Mr. Frohman but all of your stuff about him and all of the other topics is written in the concise boiled-down, tabloid style which you probably acquired on the New York Sun, the best newspaper ever published. What you want for the Post is to be verbose and voluminous. Get a good, fast stenographer at your elbow and just prattle and prattle and prattle on every kind of topic connected with the theatre and have the stuff double spaced and then when you go over it you can cut out and interline and edit and rearrange and you will get ten thousand words while you were feeling around trying to get one thousand words by old-fashioned writing. For instance, on page 2, you tell something about Flo Ziegfield, but you want to tell twenty times as much as you have told here. Also, tell a lot about Elsie Janis. Women everywhere are interested in her and all of the old play-goers have a lingering affection for [Dave] Montgomery and [Fred] Stone.

Go into more detail about Julia Marlow and Charles Major and Clyde Fish [Fitch]. Tell all you know about them that is fit to print. Remember that readers are more interested in people and the qualities which made these people great or notorious or spectacular. You have had a wonderful career and you have rubbed up against a marvelous bunch of people, but in your writing so far you were merely giving a glimpse of each one instead of giving an analysis and a long, pleasant, rambling talk about each one. To cite another instance, on page 8 you mention William Gillette and Annie Russell and Ida Conquest and tell a nifty little story at the finish, but the chapter which you now have headed "William Gillette" should be expanded into about 1500 words.

I have looked over your stuff and page after page simply reeks with names of people you knew well and regarding whom you had inside information and you simply must open up and talk about them and talk very candidly and say what you think of them, even if you happen to offend somebody. As I run over the pages I think the rule for you to follow would be to get the old stenographer and start in on page 1 and take every name of every celebrity as you come to it and tell how you met the person under discussion and whether he or she made slow headway or fast headway and what enabled him or her to get along, etc., etc. On page 29 is the chapter about Fred Stone and it is very, very short. It should be twenty times that long. I knew him very slightly but I could write forty times as much about Fred than you have written, for instance, how George Castle, of the Orpheum Circuit, barred them from the vaudeville theatres because a girl greatly admired by Castle was in love with Stone. After Fred and Dave made their enormous hit in "The Wizard of Oz" they used to walk down the street from the Grand Opera House, where they were playing, to the Olympic [Theater, Chicago], where George Castle had a big office with a plate glass window opening out on Clark Street. Fred and Dave used to put their faces up against the window and make faces at him for an hour at a time. They had him nuts and he appealed to the police but the police came over and nearly died laughing. His health failed very rapidly and he had to be taken to a rest cure and I think the boys were to blame.

No need of my going through the pages and enumerating the names. The pages you have already prepared are simply crowded with the names of people you know about and you should tell about them in a very intimate way. You need not specialize too much on stories but don't omit any story that is good, but tell all of the unusual things that happened to these people and if they had the artistic temperament tell about them, and so on and so on. I am sure you get my idea. If you want to sell this stuff to the Post you should turn in to them a total of at least sixty to seventy-five thousand words—enough material for a good book. Whatever you do, don't be afraid to dwell lovingly on trivial things, because the people love to read trivial things. They should rather read, even now, what Lillian Russell ate for lunch every day than to read all the stuff ever written by the twelve Apostles. I am sure you get my idea.

Best wishes.

Sincerely,
George Ade

InLP

Charles B. Dillingham, the vaudeville impresario, was working on a book of his theatrical memories. He had sent Ade a draft which consisted largely of anecdotes. The Saturday Evening Post *had agreed to publish the copy and Horace Liveright wished to print the memoirs in book form. Later the* Post *turned down the manuscript. Dillingham also submitted his recollections to* Cosmopolitan, *but they were never published.*

117 ❧ TO ANN LIN CARR

Hazelden
Brook, Indiana
July 16, 1933.

Dear Miss Carr:

I wish I could tell you a great deal about General Lew Wallace who was a kindly soul. I never visited his home but met him at Indianapolis when all of the identified authors of Indiana lined up to give a two-nights show for the benefit of the Benjamin Harrison Memorial Monument Fund. General Lew Wallace and James Whitcomb Riley were our headliners but I remember also Booth Tarkington, George Barr McCutcheon, Meredith Nicholson, Charles Major, Mary Hartwell Catherwood, Evaleen Stein, Kin Hubbard and several more. I remember the General lining up some of the younger men, back of the scenes at the English Opera House, and giving us some good natured advice about getting ready to walk out in front of the footlights and deliver something to a large and critical audience. I remember that his advice dealt largely with a general preparedness of the wardrobe rather than any special training of the vocal cords. Strangely enough, the most interest[ing] sessions I had with General Wallace were at the Republican National Convention in 1892 at Minneapolis. He was a delegate and we lived at the same hotel. I was then a traveling correspondent for The Chicago Record. We walked from the hotel to the convention hall several times and he told me a lot of interesting stuff which I do not distinctly recall because it dealt with his experiences in various parts of the world and was of a rambling and good natured character. A very likable man and a writer of such distinction that he has helped establish a general suspicion that Indiana is the natural breeding place for bona fide authors.

I am, with best wishes

Sincerely,
George Ade

InLP

Ade wrote Charles A. Kiler, December 24, 1942 (InLP): "I met him [General Lew Wallace] a few times and he was a great old fellow. While he was Governor of New Mexico and writing "Ben Hur," it seems that "Billy the Kid" stood outside his house for awhile trying to make up his mind whether to kill him or not. He decided to let him live, which was very considerate of him."

118 ❧ TO RUSSELL DOUBLEDAY

Hazelden
Brook, Indiana
July 26, 1933.

Dear Mr. Doubleday:

I am interested to have your letter. The story about Lilly Mars was one of the most captivating things that [Booth] Tark[ington] has ever done. Perhaps I can tell of one yarn which you may edit up to suit yourselves.

Some of us were walking with him along Meridian Street in Indianapolis. He was on his way to make a call on some lady who had been hospitable and he carried a large bouquet to be presented to his recent hostess. Across the street he saw a portly negro wench, waddling along with a bundle of "wash." Tark saw her and suddenly left us and walked across the street, confronted the portly negress, removed his hat and made a sweeping gesture with his hat and a low bow. Then he poured upon the dark lady the most lavish compliments ever bestowed any member of her sex, removed the covering of the bouquet and presented it to her. We had to walk all the way back with him while he bought another bouquet but Tark was smiling and happy. He had defeated the conventions, brought a burst of sunshine into the life of a lowly worker and given a certain dark female something to talk about for days to come.

I am, with best wishes

Sincerely,
George Ade

InLP

Doubleday Doran and Company had just published Booth Tarkington's Presenting Lilly Mars.

119 ❧ TO CARL F. ACKERMAN

Hazelden
Brook, Indiana
Aug. 25, 1933

Dear Mr. Ackerman:

I am properly flattered to have your letter of the 22nd. At the convention of the country editors I rather opened up and told what was on my mind because it seems to me that a vast majority of the little weeklies are muddling along and using antiquated methods in getting out a paper. They do not seem to realize that conditions have changed entirely in recent years, that the weekly paper and the daily papers and the radio and even the telephone have established themselves as such huge agencies for the spreading of news and entertainment and comment that the country editor must not try to compete with them and must focus all of his attention upon the little empire in which he dwells. The happenings which were events in 1900 are now trivial incidents and yet the average weekly gives most of its space to tedious routine news, the only value of which is that it brings into the paper a great many names of people who like to find themselves mentioned in public print. In every community there are burning local issues and these are mostly ignored. The really important news concerns the yield of various fruits and orchards and gardens but the editor seldom prints any news about the crops. He does not do enough commenting in a friendly way or in a critical way on subjects that keenly affect the local welfare. The country editor who writes ponderous editorials on big national topics is just a nuisance to his subscribers. He need not ignore the N.R.A. or the Farm Relief Board or any of the agencies intended to bring us back to happier times. What he should do is find out what all of his townspeople think of these issues and all the other issues that are engaging public attention. In short, he should print a newspaper for his own community and let the rest of the world go by. If so he will get out a paper that even his most cordial enemies will be compelled to read every week. I thank you again for your friendly letter. I really believe that you are the first human being who ever suggested to me that I might make a success from the teaching profession.

I am with best wishes

Sincerely,
George Ade

InLP

Carl F. Ackerman was dean of the Columbia University School of Journalism.

Ade's speech appeared as "Practical Pointers for the Editors; George Ade on Newspapers," National Printer Journalist *(August, 1933).*

The NRA—National Recovery Administration—was supposed to provide for government direction of an upswing in the economy. The accomplishments of the NRA were social rather than economic.

The Federal Farm Board paid farmers to regulate production in accordance with the government plan. Those who coooperated were to get a larger income from reducing production than noncooperators received from increasing it.

120 ❧ TO DAN RESNECK

Hazelden
Brook, Indiana
Aug. 27, 1933.

Dear Mr. Resneck:

I have your inquiry from Kentland and will answer briefly and according to my best ability. In nearly all of my writing I have tried to be a realist and to tell about people and things as I saw them, endeavoring to find the element of "human interest" and possibly some phases which might be amusing or entertaining. I have not had in my mind's eye a very definite or very critical audience but I have attempted to interest all people of fair intelligence who might have an abiding interest in plain people and every day happenings. I cannot give the names of the "literary masters" who might have influenced my preferences or affected my style but I suppose I was very much under the influence of [Charles] Dickens when I was young and later I no doubt got some inspiration from Mark Twain and Robert Louis Stevenson. In regard to my short stories written in the vernacular, I have merely entertained the hope that because they told the truth about people and events of contemporary interest they might be of interest to coming generations as a partial record of our times.

I am, with best wishes

Sincerely,
George Ade

InLP

121 ☙ TO FRANCIS SONDAY

Hazelden
Brook, Indiana
Sept. 3, 1933.

Dear Mr. Sonday:

Only a straggling few theaters in the larger cities are holding out and battling for the spoken drama. The so-called "week stands" are no longer dependable and few of them offer any proper housing for a traveling theatrical company. The one-night stands, commonly known as the "road" are just about extinct. Plays which are to be performed on a real stage by real people must take in money at the box office or they will no longer be presented. The stage entertainments of former days which tried to open in New York and then tour the country had to be commercial propositions and they had to show a profit, whether they were approved by the critics of the drama or not. All of us know that the spoken play, for which there is an actual hunger among people who love the theater and honor the traditions of the theater, will disappear from the earth unless it is kept alive by separate community efforts, each community making its independent production, regardless of New York productions, or money making managers or syndicate bookings or any of the old-time machineries. In the future a city such as Indianapolis must depend for good plays on the Civic Theater or on productions which are made by amateurs in organized groups. The large and flamboyant screen play-house has very little history, no tradition, and no rules of construction which are not subject to revision every twenty minutes. They are improving their output but most of the picture dramas are addressed to the intelligence and the cheaper emotions of the immature gigglers and gum-chewers. It seems that if we want plays, and not spectacles, we must depend upon our civic theaters.

I am, with best wishes

Sincerely,
George Ade

InLP

Francis Sonday, publicity manager of the Civic Theater, Indianapolis, had asked Ade for his opinion of community theater.

Ade was president of the Civic Theater, 1916–1917.

122 ❧ TO J. M. ERWIN

Hazelden
Brook, Indiana
Sept. 12, 1933.

Dear Mitt:

I am delighted to have your letter with the clipping by Willis Abbot, but I must set you right on a few things. I was not President of the organization which planned the reunion. It was Barney Mullaney who did most of the work and presided at the dinner. Regarding Willis Abbot, you should remember him, he was on The Times at Chicago in the early nineties and later came back on the American, an ardent [William Jennings] Bryan man and a two-handed drinker who could not carry his rum because he was too frail and intellectual. Finally the Christian Scientists got hold of him and straightened him out and he was managing editor for several years and is still one of the editorial directors of The Monitor. He is well into the seventies. I think the most interesting fact about him is that he was the original or proto type of the Little Rollo stories, written by his great uncle, Rev. Jacob Abbot, the historian. All of the honest-to-God boys detested Little Rollo and I think Willis tried to live down his early shame by getting stewed on all occasions. Anyway, they have him all laundered and dried out now and his grandfather would be proud of him.

I am enclosing to you a copy of my address and also a copy of newspaper given out at the dinner and I have marked with pencil those who were present at the dinner. Possibly I have missed some of them. Among those who did not contribute to the paper and who were on hand might be mentioned: George Bolling, F. M. Brazelton, C[harles] H. Dennis, Allen Eddy, W. J. Etten, Gilson Gardner, Ed Harden, Clarence Hough, Helen Follett, Louis Lamb, Elton Lower, Harry New, of Indianapolis, Oppie Read, Dr. Louie Schmidt, Slason Thompson, and I think that is all. We were together at luncheon and the dinner at the Federal Building was really quite an affair because we had present only men who had actually attended the Fair and written about it. I must have met 40 men whom I had not seen in years and, I must confess, that I had come to believe that most of them were safely put away in the cemeteries. Thank you for writing your pleasant letter and if I ever do go traveling again I may walk in on you. I am, with best wishes

Sincerely,
George Ade

InLP

1933

The newspaper veterans of the Columbian Exposition of 1893 had a reunion at the Century of Progress, August 12, 1933.

123 ☙ TO HARVEY WOODRUFF

Hazelden
Brook, Indiana
Oct. 5, 1933.

Dear Harvey:

In 1905 I was the owner of a one-cylinder Juggernaut with a curved dash and a steering helm and a crank on the side, the same as a hand organ. At the request of the makers I wrote a little book about the car, the title being THE ROLLING PEANUT. I am trying very hard to find some copies of this little book, and I thought maybe you would print this letter and let your millions of readers know that I will be glad to negotiate for any copies, which may be sent to Brook, Indiana. If you sneak this letter in I will pay you by sending you the following items for your column:

"I can remember way back, when morning papers came out in the morning."

"Pearl Putt, who lives near here has been made the Queen of our golf club."

"Bob Fitzsimmons thought he could sing. If you wanted a good interview with him, all you had to do was praise his rendition of 'Sweet and Low,' which was his favorite."

"Two hours before Fitz met [Peter] Maher he hopped off the train at a lonesome railway station in Texas and indulged in a 'wrasling' match with a full-grown bear, chained to a pole in front of a saloon. His manager, Martin Julian, tried to stop the battle but he was afraid to go near the bear."

I am, with best wishes

Sincerely,
George Ade

InLP

Harvey Woodruff, the former sports editor, wrote "In the Wake of the News," a sports column. He published an extract of this letter, Chicago Tribune, *October 15, 1933.*

Ade did The Rolling Peanut *in 1904 for the Olds Motor Works. This rare pamphlet is in the Ford joke book tradition.*

124 ☙ TO FRANK J. WILSTACH

Hazelden
Brook, Indiana
Nov. 7, 1933.

Dear Frank:

Although I knew you had been grubbing for similes since 1849 I had no idea that you had built up a volume of such size and comprehension and value. The book is a wonder and as a volume to have on the table when you are stuck it is worth its weight in gold. No union author would ever steal a simile but he might get a lot of ideas from a book like yours.

Charley Price was right when he said the first fable ever written was the one about sister Mae. I did it just for a fill in one day and then found that the public liked it and I started doing one a week. The version which you print was not exactly the first version but I condensed the stuff before I put it into a book.

I must tell you about Ambrose Bierce. When I wrote my first little fable I tried to make it different by modernizing the scenes, using the capital letters at random and taking the utmost freedom with the current vernacular. I knew that Aesop had written fables also [John] Gay and various Frenchmen. I did not know then or until years later that Bierce had written some fables on the coast. Years after I had trailed along with a succession of authors who had written fables in every generation for centuries I learned, to my amazement, that Ambrose Bierce said I had stolen his idea and degraded it. I understand he felt that way about a lot of people and I am sure I never could have convinced him that I was simply giving a weak imitation of a great but misunderstood genius. It is pretty hard now to find anything that he wrote but anyone out west can tell you what he said about somebody else. Thank you again for the picture and the enclosures.

I trust you are well and happy.

Sincerely,
George Ade

InLP

Frank Wilstach, whom Ade had met when he arrived in Lafayette in 1883, had sent Ade the revised and enlarged edition of Dictionary of Similes *(Boston: 1930). In this edition Wilstach listed 27 Ade similes.*

Charles Wilson Price was the editor of The Electrical Review.

John Gay published his first series of Fables, *1727; second series, 1738.*

Ambrose Bierce brought out Fantastic Fables, *1899. The cynical facade Bierce employs makes his productions differ entirely from Ade's* Fables in Slang, *1899.*

125 ☙ TO FRANK C. EVANS

Hazelden
Brook, Indiana
Nov. 13, 1933.

Dear Mr. Evans:

I have taken occasion, several times when being interviewed, to say that one of the most dismal aspects of the depression out in the country is the general dinginess that is overtaking everything. A neat looking farm building which has been recently painted is a positive novelty. Even if the farm revenues have not yet shown up we went ahead and painted three sets of improvements this year and will do the other three next year. Those that have been repaired and tidied up and painted look like a million dollars compared with most of the nearby so-called improvements. I surely do hope that good Indiana farm land will get out of the hole sufficiently to pay the taxes and the upkeep. One of the first things I did after I made the loan from you last year was to pay $1800 on the semi-annual taxes, the total being around $2300. The farm manager put in $500 as his share. He had a little more than that but he couldn't put in every blamed cent because he had expenses coming up all of the time. For years when I was travelling around over the world I made inquiries about good productive land and I learned that any land which would grow a variety of crops for the feeding of human beings or animals without being irrigated or heavily fertilized would sooner or later become worth four or five hundred dollars an acre if near a big city. My brother Will [Ade] and all the wise birds at home told me to steal my money in the city and buy farm lands and then I could sit back in my years of retirement and enjoy a lovely income. Now there ain't no income from the darn stuff. I think it is entirely because of the fact that the world has become motorized but I am not proposing any remedies. When I am in Florida I live at a little house at 1331 Fourteenth St., Miami Beach and it is really a matter of economy to live there instead of at one of the big hotels as a bachelor simply cannot camp off by himself in an apartment building.

I am, with best wishes

Sincerely,
George Ade

InLP

Frank Evans was a partner in Evans DeVore Company, Crawfordsville, Indiana.

Ade rented the Spanish style house at 1331 Fourteenth Street in Miami Beach in 1932 and every subsequent winter that he spent in Florida.

126 ❧ TO CHARLES EVANS, JR.

Miami Beach, Florida
Jan. 18, 1934.

Dear Chick:

I am delighted to receive from the Farm the little book written by your mother and inscribed by you. It is a most interesting and well told story. I am reminded that my father, after he was eighty years of age and we had induced him to retire from the bank, wanted to write a book about our county. We had a lot of material and I helped to arrange it and had five hundred copies printed by the Bobbs-Merrill Company. I think my dad gave most of them away before people had time to buy them. I felt, as I know you felt, that the greatest obligation is to the parents. All the other relatives do not amount to a darn. I mean that very rarely does a man have a real sense of obligation in regard to any of his kin except those who really did something for him.

I am spending my second winter in a comfortable house down here and I enclose a picture of it. My health is good and my conduct has to be nearly all right or my health wouldn't be good.

Best wishes,

Sincerely,
George Ade

InLP

Lena Young Evans had published a children's book, Little Pioneer, *Junior Classic Series (New York: 1932).*

John Ade published Newton County: A Collection of Historical Facts and Personal Recollections concerning Newton County, Indiana, from 1853–1911 *(Indianapolis: [1911]).*

127 ☙ TO JAMES D. RATHBUN

Miami Beach, Florida
Jan. 24, 1934.

Dear Jim:

I am enclosing copy of my letter to Joe [Reeve] which may give you the news and I will answer the inquiry from Nellie [Rathbun]. **** Paul Dresser, who wrote THE BANKS OF THE WABASH, THE BLUE AND THE GREY and many other popular songs, was an older brother of Theo. Dreiser. The latter gives his birthplace as Terre Haute but I always understood from Paul that they grew up in a little town on the banks of the river, north of Terre Haute. [Born] Dreiser but Paul changed his name because it looked better on show bills. He started out in a minstrel show and was on the stage several years, playing the plumber in [Charles] Hoyt's very successful farce, "A Tin Soldier." Then he became a song writer, living in New York most of the time, making a lot of money and spending it as fast as he got it. It is only in recent years that I have heard it suggested that Theodore wrote part or all of the verses of THE BANKS OF THE WABASH. It will be agreed that these verses are much superior to those usually found in a popular song. James Whitcomb Riley admired the lines especially the one about "through the sycamore the candle lights are gleaming." I have been slow to believe that Theodore wrote any part of the song because he has never been addicted to poetry or sentiment. Louise Dresser's father was a locomotive engineer and he was a great friend of the two Dreiser boys. Her name is not Dresser at all. She has a jaw-breaking German name. When she came up to Chicago to get a job on the vaudeville circuit, Paul took her in hand and told her she would have to change her name. He had an inspiration. "Call yourself Dresser," he said, "and I'll tell all the agents you are my little sister." He was popular and influential and she went on the stage made a hit as a vocalist she married Jack Norworth and later divorced him and Jack married Nora Bayes, the two of them singing "Harvest Moon" better than anybody has sung it since then. Louise married Jack Gardner, formerly on the stage but now one of the executives of the Fox Film Corp. Louise will be remembered especially for her work in "The Goose Woman" and "State Fair." Theodore Dreiser is still alive and living in New York, a very grim and disagreeable and cantankerous individual who is "agin" almost every thing. He lacks the sense of humor but his huge realistic novels dealing with the more sordid aspects of American life deserve the credit they have received. They include AN AMERICAN TRAGEDY, THE TITAN, JENNY GERHARDT and several others not so well known. It is said that he is more popular in England than he is here at home. I will relate some thing about him which will give you a line on his gloomy attitude towards things in general.*** Recently we held at the Exposition in Chicago a reunion of newspaper and magazine writer[s] who had reported the Fair forty years ago. Barney Mullaney, our president, heard that Theo. Dreiser had written about the old Fair and invited him to join our group and attend the reunion. Dreiser wrote back that he could not lend his name to the enterprise until convinced that it was actuated by some serious purpose. As there couldn't possibly be any serious purpose in a lot of newspaper boys getting together for one day to whoop things up, Barney wrote a polite letter to go to the devil.****I am greatly interested in the news regarding W. T. [McCray] and like you I am wondering what it means.

Regards to all,

Sincerely.

InK George Ade

Louise Dresser's real name was Louise Kerlin.

Theodore Dreiser, one of the editors of The American Spectator, *had asked Ade for a contribution. Ade wrote Dreiser, January 27, 1933 (InLP), and sent* The White Ewe *which Dreiser rejected. This play appeared in* Esquire *(January, 1934).*

128 ঌ TO MAY ROBSON

Miami Beach, Florida
March 5th, 1934.

My Dear May Robson:

I meant to write you a letter when I heard about your birthday and congratulate you upon the fact that you are younger than I am—and I am a bounding athlete.

My birthday came on February 9th. I hid under the bed all day and there was no publicity or broadcasting. Attend to the following: George Washington saved the Colonies, retired, was called upon by a grateful country to serve *two terms* as President, after which he spent many years at Mt. Vernon, passing away at a "ripe old age," if you will permit me to exhibit my originality by coining a phrase. Yes indeed! And when the venerable Father of Our Country (if it still is one) went to all of his rewards, he was just as old as I am *now*, at present. No further comment required.

For many years I have been your slavish admirer, so please accept this letter as a bouquet from a juvenile to an ingenué.

Sincerely,
George Ade

DLC

May Robson (Mrs. Augustus H. Brown) was a popular actress and comedienne at the turn of the century.

129 ❧ TO DAMON RUNYON

Miami Beach, Florida
March 8, 1934.

My dear Damon Runyon:

Up to date you have batted one thousand with those stories in Collier's. I cannot begin to tell you how much I liked them because you not only get a story but you spice it with the correct vernacular of the non-virtuous night-hawk and what's more, you bring out his singular point of view, which combines the innocence of childhood with all of the less gentle traits of the Bengal tiger. I'm not a raver by habit. Some of my other preferences are P. G. Wodehouse, Harry Leon Wilson, Westbrook Pegler and, with reservation, Irvin Cobb, when they are hitting on all cylinders.

Sorry I was not in the other evening when you called. I think it was the day of the party for Eddie Cantor. As a matter of fact, I received no invitation or notification and neither did John Golden and so we must not be accused of running out on our little pop-eyed friend. Please drop in again and maybe I will be at home.

Convey my best wishes to Mrs. Runyon,

Sincerely,
G. A.

InLP

Damon Runyon had been publishing a number of stories in Collier's *since 1931. "The Lemon Drop Kid" and "Princess O'Hara" which appeared in the February and March issues may have inspired Ade's praise.*

P. G. Wodehouse, the English humorist, is particularly remembered for his creation of Jeeves, whose name became a synonym for butler.

Harry Leon Wilson was a novelist, humorist, and playwright. He collaborated with Booth Tarkington on The Man from Home.

Westbrook Pegler was an author and columnist whose irrascibility made him a most controversial pundit for decades.

Irvin Cobb, prolific humorist and novelist, also took character parts in films.

Eddie Cantor was a comedian who rolled his eyes and perfected a gentle, nervous style that won him long popularity.

John Golden was a dramatist and screen writer. Ade wrote a tribute to him in Three John Golden Plays *(New York, 1925).*

130 ❧ TO AUSTIN P. SIMS

Hazelden
Brook, Indiana
March 15, 1934.

My dear Mr. Sims:

I was, to use an old slang phrase, "knocked a twister" when I received your letter and the two copies of the Post and the pictures taken at the dinner given by George Harvey for Mark Twain.

You speak of Biff Hall, he was one of my best friends and I succeeded as President of the Forty Club. *** I knew John Murdock when he married the girl with the auburn hair. He took Amy Leslie and me to dinner with the said wife one night and forgot all about the cocktails until the ice cream was being served and then he had them brought on. He is still on deck.**** I knew Lillian Russell and Ed. Rice of EVANGELINE fame. I did not know Harry Hunter, the lone fisherman, but I knew big George Fortescue who played the large dame. *** For many years Eddie Foy was one of my best friends. A great fellow. At first I didn't like him.*** I have seen all the plays you name and I met all the troupers you mention including William Russell. The summer before Bill Hodge opened in the MAN FROM HOME, he visited me for two months in order to get a correct line on the yap Hoosiers. I wonder why he came to my house.*** What am I to do with the treasures you sent on? Most certainly I had a great kick out of them.

Sincerely,
George Ade

InLP

George Harvey, author and editor, was president of Harper and Brothers, Mark Twain's publisher.

William T. (Biff) Hall died May 16, 1903. Ade, who had been vice president, served as president of the Forty Club, 1903–04.

John J. Murdoch was one of E. F. Albee's partners; Murdoch produced theatricals west of New York.

Edward E. Rice composed the score of Evangeline, *1874. Rice was the first to label an extravaganza a "musical." Lillian Russell played in this burlesque by J. Cheever Goodwin. Harry Hunter played the Lone Fisherman, a character who did pantomimic commentaries of other characters on stage to underscore their ridiculous condition. George S. Fortesque played Catharine. This role was always transvestite. Allen S. Jackson, "Evangeline Forgotten American Musical,"* Players Magazine, *44 (Oct.–Nov., 1968), 20–25.*

William Hodge had appeared in the New York production of Ade's Sultan of Sulu. *He stayed at Hazelden in 1912 to prepare his role in* The Man From Home *by Booth Tarkington and Harry Leon Wilson. Kelly,* George Ade, *p. 216, suggests that Hodge used Joe Ade as the model for his characterization.*

131 ☙ TO JOHN G. JENKS

Hazelden
Brook, Indiana
April 22, 1934.

Dear John:

Well, we are all back again, including Spry and his lady friend and I still insist that motoring is the hardest work in the world. I am not going to tell you the story of my life this morning. Poor Tom [Meighan] wired me that he hadn't been able to read my opus because he fell off the wagon on his birthday but as soon as he was able to read he would let me know. In the meantime no word of any kind from Hollywood. The stuff should have arrived there about a week ago and the Lord only knows when Winnie Sheehan ($250,000 a year) will find time to read it or whether Bill Rogers will be pleased to discover that Louise Dresser's part has been fattened up. He is the most cunning fox in the game. No one except Bill Rogers ever had a chance to score a hit in a Bill Rogers picture and if they did you name one of them. Charles Dillingham told me all about him. When he went in to pinch-hit for Fred Stone he kept changing things until he had all the fat in the lines and collected practically all the gate receipts. At the same time, the newspapers were praising him for his unselfish loyalty to Fred. All of which is under your hat. I want to do business with him but I know what I am up against.

I can get wholesale, in the name of the Club, from Grocery jobbers the ordinary cooking bourbon and gin at very low prices but I will be glad to take a case or two of Berry Brothers. I enclose a letter and a copy of my reply which explain themselves.

You mention going to the "circus." What circus? I will write you more at length later on. This is clean-up day.

I am, with best wishes

Sincerely,
George Ade

InLP

Spry was Ade's dog.

Ade sent Tom Meighan a copy of his scenario of The County Chairman, *which the Fox Film Corporation released in 1935.*

Fred Stone, who had starred in Ade's musical, The Old Town, *1910, broke both legs in a plane accident and was unable to star in* Three Cheers, *which opened October 15, 1928. Will Rogers substituted for Stone, and, according to the critics, saved the show.*

Ade wrote Joseph Reeve, March 24, 1934 (InK), that he was upset because Louise Dresser was not pleased with the character part he had written for her in the film version of The County Chairman.

132 ⁂ TO WILLIAM ALLEN WHITE

Hazelden
Brook, Indiana
June 22, 1934.

Dear William Allen White:

I wish I could be present for that dinner for Ed Howe. He deserves more than a dinner. Some one should give him a week's board. To me he continues to be a revelation and a marvel although he would scorch anyone who tried to put either of those labels on him. No other writer of our day has such a mountainous fund of candor and courage and common sense. I would say that he never seems to be right at the time he is speaking but everything that he says is correct and true when you check up on it, ten years after he has delivered it. He speaks out in meeting when all others present are looking out of the window and trying to conceal the surging convictions. His nearest prototype was Benjamin Franklin. Both were print-shop men who pitted the human race and cussed it and doctored it, all at the same time.

I sincerely hope he gets the large party he deserves.

I am, with best wishes

Sincerely,
George Ade

InLP

William Allen White, the publisher of the Emporia Gazette, *had asked Ade to send a message to be read at the Topeka, Kansas, Chamber of Commerce banquet in honor of Edgar Watson Howe, a journalist and novelist. Like Ade, Howe was an apostle of common sense who preached the gospel of the middle-western small town.*

133 ❧ TO WILL H. HAYS

Hazelden
Brook, Indiana
June 24, 1934.

Dear Will Hays:

I am interested to have your letter. A few days ago I sent Steve [Hannagan] a large nucleus for his shelf. In checking over your list I cannot discover that you have a copy of the best looking book that ever had my name on the cover. It is called FORTY MODERN FABLES and the typography is beautiful, regardless of any other possible merits. I have salvaged three copies of this book and I am glad to send you one of them. I believe that you now have what might be called a complete collection. It does not include some little volumes which I prepared as souvenirs for the Indiana Society of Chicago but so few of these were printed and they are so hard to find that probably it would be useless to search for them. I am sending a little book about John Hertz, given out at a dinner I pulled for him.

We are between the devil and the deep blue sea out here in Indiana. The Republicans have nominated for Senator, to succeed himself, that oleaginous and unspeakable tadpole, Arthur Robinson. It will be a crime against the state if we return to the Senate a chattering demigogue who has earned the contempt of all the other senators. The Democrats have put every independent voter on the spot by nominating [Sherman] Minton at the dictation of Paul McNutt. Unless you have been in the state during the past year you cannot understand how general and deep seated is the resentment against McNutt. He has turned the appointive power over to a lot of second-story men and door mat thieves and the result has been a slaughter, reminding one of the Custer massacre or the Spanish Inquisition. We find an army of Republicans in angry revolt against Robinson. We find an army of Democrats, especially those who have been friendly with Earl Peters, in open mutiny against McNutt. Party lines will be shot all to pieces.

In this district, Fred "Buckskin" Landis probably will be sent back to Congress to enliven the capitol even if he isn't strong enough to throw any switches, single handed.

Convey my best wishes to Mrs. Hays.

Sincerely,
George Ade

InLP

Steve Hannagan was a publicist and journalist in New York.

Arthur Robinson was senator from Indiana, 1925–1935.

Sherman Minton was senator from Indiana, 1935–1941.

Paul V. McNutt was governor of Indiana, 1933–1937. Ade wrote Joseph Reeve, February 19, 1933 (InK): "I rate he [McNutt] is now dictator of Indiana. A dictatorship is the ideal form of government if the dictator is honest and intelligent and has guts." *During McNutt's first year in office the Indiana General Assembly passed 292 acts and resolutions, many involving governmental centralization and economies.*

Ade and John Hertz, the founder of the Yellow Cab Company and chief of the Hertz Drive-Ur-Self Corporation, had become friends when both worked on the Chicago Record. *Ade's booklet,* John Hertz, *which he had printed in lieu of giving a speech, was reprinted in the* Miami Daily News *and the* Miami Herald, *February 6, 1930. Ade arranged the dinner. He wrote introductions for the various speakers, and had John Golden, the dramatist, serve as toastmaster. Golden read Ade's remarks.*

Frederick Landis was a congressman, 1903–1907. The politician and author died November 15, 1934.

134 ❧ TO CHARLES J. WINNINGER

Hazelden
Brook, Indiana
June 27, 1934.

Dear Charley:

I am delighted to have your letter because you have been my favorite actor ever since Edwin Booth died and I caught you in the parade at Eau Claire.

The sad facts in regard to THE COUNTY CHAIRMAN are that M.G.M. bought the talking rights and recently sold them to Fox [Film Corporation]. I understand that Fox had [Will] Rogers in mind for the title role but I do not believe they have any definite plans regarding the piece. This is all too bad as the part would fit you and you could play it as well as you do your trombone.

Your letter has been most welcome. I am away out in the country and away from things in general but getting along all right and behaving myself and working hard. John Jenks was down here last week and I shall visit Judge [Kenesaw Mountain] Landis [this?] week. As for the Landis party on July 10th I have had no invitation but maybe I could suck around and get one. However, I doubt if I could be in the far east on that date. I have so many dates with women, being booked weeks ahead, that I find it almost impossible to escape them. Which reminds me that not long ago a tormenting old lady asked me, "Why did you never get married?" I don't know whether it is mine or whether I remembered it, but I said, "Because her father didn't own a shot gun." Go ahead and put that into the Maxwell House Coffee release for the family trade. We get you on the air every week and we long for television so that we can get a peek at your smiling mug.

I am, with best wishes

Sincerely,
George Ade

InLP

Charles Winninger wanted to play the lead in the film version of The County Chairman. *Ade wrote Jack Gardner, December 26, 1934 (InLP), that he had Will Rogers in mind for this part.*

Ade tailored the lead in The Hero of Eagle Creek *for Rogers, but this scenario was shelved when the actor-humorist was killed in a plane crash, August 15, 1935.*

135 ☙ TO JOHN L. V. WILLIAMS

Hazelden
Brook, Indiana
June 22, 1935.

Dear Mr. Williams:

I have your letter and I wish that I could put my hand on some letters from Brand Whitlock. I knew him for many years and heard from him once in a while but I have no dates and the letters are put away in the archives somewhere. To me the most interesting biographical fact regarding Whitlock is that he started out, in his newspaper days, to write sarcastic and humorous stuff. He had the "joshing" style so popular with the New York Sun. If the editor wanted to poke fun at some ceremony or some celebrity he gave the assignment to Whitlock and some of his reports were classics. After he became a lawyer and was Mayor in Toledo he became a serious uplifter but in Chicago he was known as a witty commentator. I recall that in telling of a performance given by the tragedian, James Owen O'Connor, he said that the actor's voice sounded as if he might be "standing too close to the 'phone." He was a member of the famous White Chapel Club but he was one of the sedate and temperate members who sat back and enjoyed the ribald talk but did not have much to say. He was a very fine character and deserved all of the attention he is now receiving.

I am, with best wishes

Sincerely.

InLP George Ade

John L. V. Williams of Appleton-Century Company had requested correspondence for inclusion in The Letters and Journal of Brand Whitlock, *chosen and edited with a biographical introduction by Allen Nevins (New York, 1936).*

136 ❧ TO LOIS COY

Hazelden
Brook, Indiana
Oct. 25, 1935.

Dear Miss Coy:

I have your letter of inquiry and I fear that you have sought information from one not very well qualified to answer your question as I am not affiliated with any church. However, I do think that the church is necessary in modern life because people cannot get the comforts and consolation and the promises for the future which they find in church relationships by scientific research or a study of philosophies. Our churches inspire faith and arouse emotions which are useful to the well being of the world and so, I think, they are necessary.

I am, with best wishes

Sincerely,

InLP George Ade

137 ❧ TO HARRY B. MARTIN

Hazelden
Brook, Indiana
Nov. 8, 1935.

Dear Dickey:

I am exceedingly interested to have a message from you and to learn that you are working on a book dealing with the history of golf in this country. I began trying to play golf in the nineties, at Exmoor, near Highland Park, which then had only a nine-hole course. I have no recollection of playing with George Barr McCutcheon but I did play some with John McCutcheon. The Maskell ball was just coming in and the boys were beginning to get more distance. I remember when I began to play the scores were computed on a Bogie basis and 165 yards was considered a full swipe. For instance, if a hole was over 330 yards long, Bogie would be 5 as the player would not be expected to be on the green in two strokes and, usually, he was not. The bunkers were built straight across the fairway at right angles to the line of play and about a hundred yards apart and the player was supposed to hop over them. The greens had not been built up or landscaped or heavily trapped and most of them were flat. I remember that as late as 1913 when I laid out my first long course, I had Tom Bendelow help me. He was well known as a pro and a designer of courses and was plenty capable but a lot of country courses were being opened about that time and the clubs out in the country could not afford to pay for blueprints and expensive construction and Tom would lay out a course in one day. He would pick out a likely spot for No. 1 tee and put a stake in the ground and mark it and then he would walk out until he thought he had come to a good place for a cross bunker and he would put down another stake and then go ahead and mark another bunker and then decide where to put his green and where to put the traps around it. As his services came to $25 a day the country club seldom kept him longer than one day because, after he had given them a rough sketch and a few directions they were ready to begin work on their course. Tom was a little ahead of the period when one modern green, highly elevated and undulated and deeply trapped, would cost as much as one of the old-fashioned courses.

Charles MacDonald, who had played golf in Scotland, was the daddy of the game in the region of Chicago and his son-in-law, H. G. Whiggam, a talented young Englishman on the staff of The

Tribune, was an early national champion because he had learned to play in England. Even at that time the Egan boys, and Chandler in particular, were the prize exhibits at Exmoor and they played great golf even with the ancient tools. I remember that every fellow was trying to use a "cleek" and some of us had "baffies" and the mashie was usually described as a "lofter." Possibly if you write to John McCutcheon, care the Chicago Tribune, he can induce his uncle, Charley Atkinson, to give you some interesting dope regarding the early days in Chicago. I am enclosing a couple of postcard pictures of our little course here. It has been going since 1913 and during that time we have had a lot of good players here and some interesting events. On September 18th, 1918, we had a tournament and raised over $5000 for the Red Cross, a record for Indiana.

I wish I could give you something really worth while but my recollections are a little hazy and indefinite. I only know that I was crazy about the game for years and it makes me sad to realize that I am no longer permitted to play. I am getting ready to motor away on Monday for Miami Beach and my address will be 1331 Fourteenth Street until next April. If you are in Florida this winter I certainly hope to see you.

I am, with best wishes

Sincerely,
George Ade

InLP

H. B. Martin was collecting material for Fifty Years of American Golf *(New York: 1935).*

A cleek *is an iron-headed golf club with a straight narrow face and a long shaft.*

A baffy *is a short wooden club having a face with a deep pitch or loft.*

In a Hazelden Country Club bulletin, March 5, 1934 (InK), Ade was trying to raise funds. He included a history of the club in this communication:

> It started 24 years ago with about 40 members, all from Kentland and Brook. The "course" was nine approach-and-putt holes in the Hazelden grounds. No great expense involved. Dues nominal. Annual dinner in my house. In 1913 we moved out into the pasture and opened a nine-hole course, total length only 1500 yards. I put in water system supplied from pump on home grounds. The club began to assume part of expenses but all landscaping to date has been a private enterprise. We improved the course and made it longer. In 1916–17 I built the log cabin. Later the club enlarged and improved the building. We put up a locker building. It cost

$5000 and the club paid for it in no time. The dues became $50 a year. We offered playing memberships at $20 a year but not one member accepted the cut rate. Everybody had money. The club had a balance in the treasury—and wasted it. We tried operating a restaurant in the cabin and lost heavily every year. We kept on improving and modernizing the course, the club beginning to pay for renewals and repair of machinery and tools. It did not pay taxes on land or improvements and has not paid any of these taxes for the past two years. The club has used a truck every day during the season year after year, but never has owned a truck. In recent years it has paid the gasoline bills. It paid part of the $1750 expended on the tennis court. The club, co-operating with Mrs. James, has made the restaurant much less expensive. Club members, by private subscription last year, paid for the beer license and put in the playground for children. It would take a Philadelphia lawyer to figure the equity of the club in the real estate and buildings. This is nothing to worry about as the entire proposition will pass to the club in due time.

138 ❧ TO WILLIAM HERSCHELL

Miami Beach, Florida
January 30, 1936.

Dear Bill:

Replying to your letter of January 20th:

My first visit to your city was along about 1880, when I went with my Father to attend a convention of Bankers. I remember that we stayed at the old Grand Hotel, which seemed to me very large and gorgeous. Also we went to the Grand Opera House and I saw young Minnie Maddern (later to become famous as Mrs. Fiske) appearing as a tom-boy in "Fogg's Ferry." She was certainly a very nimble and talented young girl and she must have been very young, because when she died a few years ago I discovered she was just about my age. As I was only fourteen when I saw her on the stage she must have been a very juvenile star.

My second important visit to your town was on the occasion of the funeral of Thos. A. Henricks. Once more I stopped at the Grand Hotel, and while I was getting my dinner someone stole my first tailor-made overcoat from the check room. I had played hookey to come down to Indianapolis on the excursion and I got a grand scolding from home when they found I had made the trip without any permission from home, and had lost my overcoat. I went back to

Purdue and put on my old coat, and in a few days I received the new coat that had been stolen. Your vigilant police had found it at a pawn shop and ever since that time I have had a very exalted opinion of your police force.

Indianapolis was still a country town when I saw it in the '80's, but to me it was New York, London and Paris all rolled into one.

I hope the above will be what you want. Always glad to hear from you.

Sincerely,
George Ade

InLP

William Herschell was a feature writer for the Indianapolis News. *He published collections of verse which had originally appeared in his columns. Sentimental excursions, such as "Ain't God Good to Indiana," are typical of Herschell's contributions.*

Thomas A. Hendricks was governor of Indiana, 1872–1876. He became vice president in 1884 and died in Indianapolis, November 25, 1885.

Ade tells of the coat theft while in the state capital to see a theatrical performance, "Recalling the Early Tremors of a Timorous Playwright," *The Players 14th Annual Revival of* The County Chairman, *etc. [1936].*

139 ☙ TO STUART GATES

Miami Beach, Florida
March 18, 1936

My dear Stuart Gates:

Your father has been good enough to send me some samples of your work for the newspaper and I have been interested to read them and to discover that you have a sprightly style and the faculty of observation and a good sense of humor. Writing from long experience I would like to suggest that you do a lot of writing on all sorts of topics and make it a rule to read books and articles written by authors who have a command of correct and graceful English and, also, make it a rule to read the good newspapers, such as the New York Times, so that you may absorb the essentials of good reporting. The way to learn to write is to keep on writing, and when you are reading keep a dictionary at your elbow and check up on the words which are new to you or whose real meaning might be in doubt. Build up your vocabulary but do not strive to put into your stock too many long, unusual or freakish words. A simple and direct style is always the best. If you want to find out what excellent use may be made of old and simple words read Robert Louis Stevenson. Among the authors of today who have a style that is worth study I would suggest [Booth] Tarkington, [Rafael] Sabatini, [Joseph] Hergesheimer, [W. Somerset] Maughn, [*sic*] and even [H. L.] Mencken. I am not suggesting that you imitate any one of these first-class masters of English but if you read them you will naturally fall into the way of expressing yourself in the proper words and phrases. The field of advertising offers a fine chance for any young writer and if you are properly interested in your work and keep pegging away I am sure that you will make good. Certainly you have my best wishes.

Sincerely,
George Ade

InLP

Booth Tarkington, novelist, is best remembered for Seventeen, *1916,* The Magnificent Ambersons, *1918, and* Alice Adams, *1921.*

Rafael Sabatini, the historical novelist, created swashbuckling adventures, such as Scaramouche, *1921, and* Captain Blood, *1922.*

Joseph Hergesheimer wrote The Lay Anthony, *1914,* Java Head, *1919, and other forgotten works. Clifton Fadiman aptly labeled Hergesheimer, "The Sargent of the modern American novel."*

W. Somerset Maugham was a novelist and playwright; his best work is generally considered to be Of Human Bondage, *1915.*

H. L. Mencken, critic, gadfly, and sage, contributed The American Language, *1919, and numerous other works which prove Mencken to be "a highly sanative enzyme in the body politic."*

140 ☙ TO THOMAS MEIGHAN

Hazelden
Brook, Indiana
April 29, 1936.

My dear Tom:

I am addressing this letter to your hotel on a guess that you have not yet moved to the country. If conditions are the same with you as with us there has not been much evidence of spring out in the country. We arrived home on the 17th without mishap and almost immediately ran into mean weather including one snow fall which completely covered the ground. Now we are having warmer weather and plenty of rain and the trees are beginning to green up. I have been hoping that you landed back in New York feeling improved and that you are keeping up the gain which you made in Florida. When you feel so disposed I shall be glad to hear from you. By the way, I mailed to Frances [Meighan] a photograph which was almost the same as the one she wanted. I could not find a duplicate of the one printed in the magazine. Of course, I was shocked and grieved to learn of the death of Pete Dunne. He had a very keen mind and wrote very beautiful and vigorous English. He was made famous by his Dooley stories but his editorials were the best things he ever wrote because he had a caustic wit and a very distinctive style and a fine command of words. It happens that I never was very friendly with Percy Hammond although I had a proper respect for his ability. Many years ago, while I was spending much of my time in Chicago, I met him and Eddie Cooke and George Kingsbury in front of the Sherman House one day and, in the course of idle conversation, I mentioned the fact that I had been invited to join the Friars Club in New York and made some inquiries about it. I did not know that Hammond had been put up for membership at the Friars and turned down because some of the boys connected with the stage had it in for him. It seems that Hammond thought I was riding him and that I knew about his experience at the Friars and after I left him and the two others he opened up on me and balled me out. After that he never missed a chance to give me a dirty crack and, naturally, I resented all of the cruel and superfluous things that he said about me and I never spoke to him again afterwards. One interview with him would have cleared up the whole misunderstanding. He was a very interesting and capable writer and I have read his stuff with a good deal of interest.

John Jenks is loitering around Chicago but threatens to go on to New York during May and you may see him. He has suggested that I go with him and I have some cordial invitations from the Players Club to be at the first performance of the revival of THE COUNTY CHAIRMAN on May 25th but I think I might as well give up the idea because I have not made any long trips lately and I don't think I had better take a chance. I get no further word regarding Ort [Wells] and I take it that he has escaped from the hospital. Things down here in the country have been very quiet but the country club will open the season with a dinner on Friday evening and already we have had a good many players on the course which came through the winter in grand condition. I continue to feel pretty well and I suppose I am planted here for another long run.

Convey our best wishes to Frances [Meighan]. Joe [Reeve] is writing this letter and he is now as fit as a fiddle.

Sincerely,
George Ade

InLP

141 ❧ TO CARL N. WEINSTEIN

Hazelden
Brook, Indiana
Aug. 5, 1936.

My dear Mr. Weinstein:

Replying to your letter of inquiry, I am compelled to say that the literary work I am doing at present is not sufficient in bulk or importance to bear any important relation to present trends in the work by American authors. I think we may discover, however, by looking over recent outputs, that there is a marked tendency among American writers to favor biographies dealing with our more eminent people, novels which try to illuminate some of our more important periods and also many efforts to analyze the threatened revolution in our economic affairs and general form of government. It seems to me that all of these "trends" are encouraging and educational and will help to give us a better understanding of our own country. The fact that many fiction writers favor mystery stories is not to be deplored because most of these stories provide good entertainment.

I am, with best wishes

Sincerely,
George Ade

InLP

142 ❧ TO GEORGE VAUGHN

Hazelden
Brook, Indiana
Oct. 29, 1936.

Dear Professor Vaughn:

I have postponed replying to your letter of inquiry because I doubt very much if I am qualified to speak with any authority regarding the need of a "spiritual awakening." I think our greatest national handicap at present is the willingness and the desire of so many people to live at government expense and get money from the government on any sort of pretext. If you would define a spiritual awakening as a renewed enthusiasm for the activities of the orthodox churches, and especially those of Protestant persuasion, I must say frankly that I do not discover any tendencies in that direction. I think we need a revival of the spirit of independence and unselfish patriotism and a return to the old-fashioned virtues of economy and saving. I fear that we are suffering from a lack of moral fibre and have taken the wrong slant on what our government really should undertake to do for us. Frankly I have no recipe for insuring a return to the cardinal virtues.

I am, with best wishes

Sincerely,
George Ade

InLP

George Vaughn was a professor of law at the University of Arkansas.

143 ❧ TO MIRIAM NESBITT

Hazelden
Brook, Indiana
March 6, 1937

My dear Miriam Nesbitt:

Thank you very much for your long and entertaining letter. Because you have told of so many interesting experiences on the west coast I realize that I should repay you by sending you a real news letter from here but the sad truth is that I have not been anywhere or done anything much since you left.

You asked about "Gone With The Wind," I read it with the greatest interest and I think it is a wonderful book to have been turned out by a young woman with so little training in the game of fiction writing. It has drama and sustained interest and good dialogue and distinct characters and everything needed to make it a book of absorbed interest. You asked if I am writing anything. I regret to say that since my illness I have not had enough ambition to sit up to my desk and do a blessed lick of work. I live in hope that later on I may have more pep.

Regarding the use of a typewriter, I own one but I never have used one—all of my work has been done in long hand and most of it with a pencil on soft yellow paper. I believe that writing in long hand helps one to be more concise. Those who type their stuff are tempted to become verbose because it is so easy to write.

Thank you again for your friendly letter. Best wishes.

GA:B Sincerely,
InLP George Ade

Miriam Nesbitt had played the female lead in the Chicago and New York productions of Ade's The County Chairman.

144 ❧ TO QUINCY HOWE

Hazelden
Brook, Indiana
May 6, 1937.

Dear Mr. Howe:

I am interested to have your friendly letter of inquiry in regard to that "autobiography." My good friend [O. O.] McIntyre always means well but I regret to say that he was not very accurate when he said that I was hard at work on my memoirs. I should be but I am not for the simple reason that I am not feeling sufficiently rugged and ambitious to do very much work and I cannot make any definite promises for the future. Thank you for your interest in the uncertain project and possibly it may develop into something later on.

I am, with best wishes

Sincerely,
InLP George Ade

Quincy Howe of Simon and Schuster wished to consider Ade's autobiography for publication. Although Ade had written a number of reminiscences for Hearst's International, *1925–1927 (see Russo, p. 239), he never showed any interest in collecting these pieces in a book.*

Ade wrote Cyril Clemens, January 13, 1936 (InLP), and Franklin P. Adams and David Hazen, April 3, 1937 (InLP), of his unwillingness to write his memoirs or to have another author do a biography. Carl Van Doren had suggested Hazen collaborate on Ade's memoirs. Fred C. Kelly, who wrote Ade's biography, urged the author to write his autobiography for years.

145 TO FRANKLIN P. ADAMS

Hazelden
Brook, Indiana
May 22, 1937.

My dear F.P.A:

I have your letter of inquiry and this time the old memory expert cannot give you any help. Perhaps one reason is that I did not usually ride on the street cars when going to and from my daily task because [John] McCutcheon and I lived on the near North Side and walked to work. It may interest you to know that each of us carried a walking stick. I have been addicted to the walking stick habit all of my life, not because I needed support but because when I carried a "cane" I always knew what to do with at least one of my hands. Also, I am glad to recall the fact that each of us usually spent ten cents every morning for a white carnation and tried to put a little brightness and sentimental decoration into the murky atmosphere surrounding us. Probably if the verse regarding Faultless Chips had been set to music I might remember it. I seem to remember only the verses which were set to music and sung at the Olympic Theatre. If you can remember all of those old street car slogans you are several up on me. I am interested to hear from you again and sorry that I cannot supply the words which will explain why Daisy flew into a passion. Glad to hear from you again and hope you will soon find yourself doing the kind of work which gives you the most satisfaction.

I am, with best wishes

Sincerely,
George Ade

InLP

Franklin P. Adams had queried Ade about old advertising posters on Chicago street cars, such as the slogan for Faultless Chips candy.

146 TO WILLIAM FRED KURFESS

Hazelden
Brook, Indiana
June 9, 1937.

Dear Fred:

I am interested to have your letter with the news from the front.

I sincerely trust that you will not become privately engaged in any argument with Mr. [John L.] Lewis or his gang because, just at present, they have too much ammunition and too much help from the powers that be. I am convinced that the present drive against invested capital is not so much an attempt to better the condition of the working man as to raise the power and prestige and money resources of the C.I.O. I am inclined to think that Mr. Lewis and his associates will over-reach themselves and that their desperate plans to capture all the machinery of our government will not go through.

Probably you know that Margaret [Rathbun Harding] is down here. She was over here on Saturday with her new husband, whom I met for the first time. He seems to be a very amiable young man and I am sure he is devoted to Margaret. Jim [Rathbun] reports that she is feeling well and gaining weight every day and that is good news.

I didn't know until now that you had become a collector of letters and autographs. Most certainly you have made a good start but you should be warned that when a man gets a mania for collecting he will starve his family and go without clothes in order to enjoy his fad. You ask if I ever come to Chicago. I simply don't go anywhere except to picture shows in nearby towns. I do not feel that I could qualify as a house guest at present and so I linger by my own fireside. By the way, the Sigs are going to have their round-up here two weeks from today, the 23rd, and I hope you may find it possible to be among those present. Convey my best wishes to Ardis [Ade Kurfess] and the boys and remember that you will always be welcome down here.

Sincerely,

K George Ade

James and Nellie Rathbun's daughter Margaret married George Harding.

Ade wrote William Fred Kurfess, June 28, 1937 (K):

> I rejoice with you in the apparent collapse of the attempt by the C.I.O. to coerce the workingmen and compel them to pay tribute to Mr. [John L.] Lewis. It seems to me that he has all the ear-marks of a dangerous character and I cannot believe that he is working for the welfare of the mill hands as earnestly as he is seeking power for himself. It would be a calamity if a man of his methods became a real factor in politics. It will be a blessing to the general public if he is squelched. Things have come to a pretty pass when work-

ingmen who are satisfied with their pay and with working conditions are not permitted to deal with their employers direct instead of taking orders from some trouble-making outsider. I sincerely hope that your company will come through all right and today all the indications are that the independent companies have won their battle.

147 ❧ TO CYRIL CLEMENS

Hazelden
Brook, Indiana
June 10, 1937.

Dear Mr. Clemens:

I have your postcard inquiry. I think the quotation you have in mind goes as follows: "A man can afford anything he can get and a woman can afford anything that she can get a man to get for her." It may be that I used "fellow" and "girl" but I believe the above is the way I wrote it a long time ago and I seem to remember that it was used as a moral for one of the fables but, for the life of me, I cannot lay my hands on the book which might contain it.

You ask if I ever met President [Warren] Harding or President [Calvin] Coolidge. I met both of them. Long before Harding was President I met him here at my home place when he came through here on a speaking tour and had a pleasant visit with him. While he was President I met him several times in Florida and became rather friendly with him. He was a very likable man. I met Coolidge while he was President and tried to interest him in a matter which did not seem to arouse his enthusiasm and I think he looked out of the window most of the time while I was trying to talk to him. I did not hit it off with him very well. If you want some further report of my impressions I will be glad to send it.

I trust you are well and happy.

Sincerely,
George Ade

In

Ade had gone to see Calvin Coolidge to seek clemency for Warren McCray.

148 ☙ TO MASON PETERS

Hazelden
Brook, Indiana
July 16, 1937.

Dear Pete:

I am more than interested to have your friendly and entertaining letter. Also, I am properly flattered to learn that you have been telling the students of the summer school something about the Sultan of Sulu. When we slipped into New York without any advance ballyhoo and made a hit I experienced one of the real satisfactions of my career as a playwright. The New York critics were kind enough to discover that the play was really a satire and not just another one of those things. Certainly I am flattered to learn that you still agree with the critics.

Well, I am leading a very quiet and lazy life here at the old homestead. Recently the hot weather has wilted me and I am a little below par just now but able to be up and about. You may be interested to know that Ort Wells is in the care of a nurse up at the Chicago Athletic Club. His old gall bladder is pestering him and he has what Tad used to call a "bum ticker." All of his friends hope that he will kick out of the present attack even as he has recovered from several previous attacks. He was down here last month with Kenesaw Landis, John Jenks and Charley Hermann and seemed to be rather sprightly at that time. Certainly he and the others cleaned up on a lot of fried chicken and we put in a grand day digging up the past.

What you say about the communistic influences working around under the surface out your way is most interesting and in line with what seems to be happening in a good many places. The powers that be are trying to make us all over again with a new recipe and the procedure strikes me as being rather cock-eyed. You will be interested to know that Charley Carson is here frequently and often speaks of you and your brother Bill [Peters]. When you are heading for New York I hope you may find it possible to visit the farm. I don't get to Chicago very often but I might connect with you up there if you will let me know your plans later on. Best wishes

Sincerely,
George Ade

InLP

Ade wrote Robert E. Sherwood, October 24, 1941 (InLP) in behalf

of Mason Peters. Sherwood, the playwright, had recently been appointed director of the overseas branch of the Office of War Information:

> I have known him for many years and I am glad to give you certain facts regarding him which may arouse your interest. During the first World War he was connected with the Intelligence Department in Washington and rendered valuable service which was approved by his superior officers. He will be glad to give you the details. He was publicity man for the Henry W. Savage Theatrical Enterprises for many years and had experience as a working newspaper man. He is alert, intelligent, sophisticated, shrewd, and extremely capable. He has an ambition to connect himself with your branch of the Government Service.

149 ❧ TO PHILIP HORTON SMITH

Hazelden
Brook, Indiana
October 22, 1937

My dear Mr. Smith:
I am interested to have your friendly letter and I wish that I could take time to write a small book about Gustav Luders. He was a very interesting person. He was of German birth and spoke with an accent. He had been an orchestra leader before he began to compose musical plays. He was rather good-looking, with a blonde mustache and the manners of a prince, a great favorite with the ladies and an expert at hand-kissing. He was very sensitive and very temperamental, given to bubbling enthusiasm over some new composition, followed by deep despair if he failed to win approval. His manners were above reproach and he was an interesting and delightful companion. In some ways, he was quite irresponsible because he was always falling in love with some woman other than his wife. During these affairs he was effusive but they did not last long or lead up to anything serious. I agree with you that he wrote a great deal of delightful and entertaining music, and I can assure you that he had a most genial and appealing personality.

I am most grateful to you for your reference to my work of long ago, and I thank you, especially for remembering "The Sho-Gun" which, I think deserved more attention than it received. Perhaps you know that my nephew, John Plugge, is a demon collector. He has dug up a lot of my stuff that I had forgotten all about. He has shelves filled with it and the Lord only knows what he will do with all of this material, but he continues to be very keen about assembling it.

Thank you again for your letter.

GA:JS Sincerely,
InLP George Ade

Gustav Luders wrote the scores for Ade's The Sho-Gun *and* The Fair Co-Ed.

Philip Horton Smith was a friend of John Ade Plugge, who had suggested that Smith write his uncle for information about Gustav Luders, whose scores Smith collected.

150 NEWS LETTER FROM MIAMI BEACH

December 11, 1937

Perhaps you will be interested to learn some of the facts in connection with the sudden passing away of our old friend "Skillet" Leslie, ex-governor of Indiana and late president of the Standard Insurance Company. I had no intimation that he was here until I received a phone message from Mrs. Leslie Thursday afternoon (December 9th) saying that he and she had arrived that morning and that he was in the St. Francis Hospital here in Miami Beach. She said that he was very tired from the railway ride and weak, because of a recent heart attack and that I had better postpone my visit to the hospital until Friday morning. I did so and when I went into his room at the hospital about ten o'clock Friday morning (yesterday) I found him propped up in bed and smoking a cigarette. He greeted me with his usual cheerful grin and reported that he had passed a fairly good night. The ride on the train from Indianapolis had been bumpy and tedious and he said that he sat up most of Thursday night. A recurrent attack of angina pectoris (old-fashioned "heart disease") induced Mrs. Leslie to move him to the hospital soon after they arrived at the Colonial Hotel in Miami. Dr. [Arthur L.] Walters, who was with Harry in Purdue and who is now practicing in Miami Beach, was with him when I called yesterday morning. He seemed plenty worried. I suggested to Mrs. Leslie that while Harry was spending the proposed week in the hospital it would be much more convenient and inexpensive for her if she would stop with us, inasmuch as the large and comfortable room reserved every winter for John Jenks was not being occupied. She accepted and moved in yesterday, spending the afternoon with Harry at the hospital. He was feeling so much better late in the afternoon that, at his suggestion, she came back to our house. She had dinner with me last evening and just as we were leaving the table, soon after seven o'clock, a phone message from the hospital said that Harry was suffering from another sudden and serious attack. Dave [Curran] took her to the hospital as speedily as possible but Harry died just before she arrived. He was unconscious after the final attack. Dr. Walters phoned me the news and I gave it to the morning paper. Mrs. Leslie came back to the house about nine. She was bearing up bravely and has shown remarkable courage. Last evening I sent wires for her to many of her relatives and near friends. This morning she is out with Mrs. Walters to make some final arrangements with the undertaker and get ready to take the evening train for home. I understand the funeral is to be at Indianapolis at 1:30 Tuesday afternoon. Several of Harry's friends from Indiana have phoned to express their sympathy and offer their help but there has been nothing much for any of us to do except stand aside and experience a lot of real sorrow over the departure of a genial companion, an able executive, a square-shooter and a good scout in general.

InLP George Ade

Harry Guyer Leslie was governor of Indiana 1929–1933. After his term of office he helped organize the Standard Life Insurance Company of Indiana.

Dave Curran was Ade's chauffeur.

151 TO HORACE H. WALL

Miami Beach, Florida
March 31, 1938

Dear Brother Wall:

I am interested to have your friendly letter and the inquiry as to my early experience in the printing office. I never was a regular type, although I did a little type setting just for practice. My job in the printing office was to run the job press, operate the roller on the old Washington hand press, address and fold the single wrappers and deliver papers to the post office. I was a kind of a devil around the shop but I never became a regular type setter. I did write a few items for publication and some of my school essays were printed.

I am, with best wishes

GA:R
InLP

Sincerely,
George Ade

Ade is probably recalling his brief tenure on the Lafayette Morning News *in 1888. In the autumn of 1881 he had a school essay "A Basket of Potatoes" published in the* Kentland Gazette, *and he did perform menial tasks for his hometown newspaper in the 1870s.*

152 ❧ TO C. S. HAMMOND

Hazelden
Brook, Indiana
May 3, 1938

Dear Mr. Hammond:

I have your long and very entertaining letter and I have read it with great interest. I was especially entertained by what you had to say regarding Theodore Roosevelt. I was with him in 1912 and I still think that he was compelled to walk out of the convention because his delegates, who had been properly elected, were unseated by very unfair methods. He had a majority of the delegates and when he walked out he really took the convention with him. I don't believe that Mr. [William Howard] Taft could have been elected even if Teddy had supported him. The Democratic victories of 1910 indicated very clearly what was going to happen to the regular Republican organization in 1912. There is an old saying that it is difference of opinions that makes horse races. Evidently you and I do not see eye to eye regarding important issues just now, but I have no disposition to argue with you. As I said in my previous letter, I am quite sure that you are sincere in your beliefs and I know that I am. Both of us are so old that we will never listen to the verdict of posterity.

I have read your letter with great interest, and I am impressed by your friendly and tolerant attitude.

I am, with best wishes,

GA:JS
InLP

Sincerely,
George Ade

153 ☙ TO JAMES D. RATHBUN

Hazelden
Brook, Indiana
June 27, 1938.

My dear Jim:—

I heartily endorse the stand taken by Henry Marshall in his editorial urging Republicans to somehow or other arrange to throw their final voting support to Senator [Frederick] Van Nuys. In order to effect a coalition of Anti-New Dealers in both of the major parties so as to defeat any [Franklin D.] Roosevelt candidate nominated by the state machine.

It seems to me that the new alignment must be between those who oppose the New-Deal and those who favor it. The opposition to the Roosevelt program should not be divided. The old party lines are no longer clearly drawn and it behooves all voters who approve of the heroic battle waged by Senator Van Nuys against the more vicious Roosevelt measures to somehow manage to unite their efforts with those made by Democrats who will support the Senator.

If these two voting elements can be united in opposition to the state machines slavish adherence to any and all New-Deal measures we may count upon a victory over the Administration forces. It seems to me important that we should put expediency and our desire to overthrow the state machine above any mere partisan considerations which might be favored by some Republicans.

Our main purpose is to register opposition to the New-Deal and the only way we can do this is by contriving in some way to give our voting support to Senator Van Nuys.

I am with best wishes,

Sincerely,
George Ade

InLP

Senator Frederick Van Nuys was re-elected November 8, 1938. See John D. Barnhart and Donald F. Carmony, Indiana From Frontier to Industrial Commonwealth, *2 (New York: 1954), 483–86, for a consideration of Van Nuys' position and problems of the New Deal in Indiana during the late 1930s.*

Ade wrote to Cyril Clemens, October 24, 1939 (InU): "I supported [Franklin D.] Roosevelt in 1932 but not in 1936 and I will never support him again."

A number of recent historians agree that in 1935 a second New Deal began. During this complex period Roosevelt critics and supporters alike expressed grave doubt. See William E. Leuchtenburg, Franklin D. Roosevelt and the New Deal 1932–1940 *(New York: 1963), pp. 143–66.*

154 TO ARTINE ARTINIAN

Hazelden
Brook, Indiana
August 20, 1938

Dear Mr. Artinian:
I am more than interested to have your letter asking me to put an estimate upon the works of Guy de Maupassant. It happens that I was tremendously interested in his translated short stories and some of his longer works from the time I was in college during the eighties up to and including the time when I handled a short story department on the Chicago Record from 1893 to 1900. I was most enthusiastic about the work of this author because his style was so simple and direct and he did not cumber his manuscript with tedious description or needless adjectives. I loved his brevity and his clarity and the direct manner in which he scored every point. I am sure that he greatly influenced my style because my friends often told me that I was trying to be another de Maupassant. I never denied that I was somewhat under his influence. I still admire his stories and read them and in my humble opinion he deserves very high ranking in the history of world literature. In other words, he is my kind of an author.

I am, with best wishes.
GA:JSR
InLP

Sincerely,
George Ade

Artine Artinian included this letter in Maupassant Criticism in France, 1880–1940 *(New York: 1941), p. 129.*

155 TO GEORGE HIRAM BROWNELL

[Miami Beach, Florida]
[February, 1939]

Dear Mr. Brownell:
For a time the docs were stumped, but now they know what it is—the deadly W. P. Aitis. You can see the victims everywhere, poor

souls, leaning on golf clubs, against palm trees, lamp posts, buildings—even against each other. Some are so weak they can't lean. They lie in beach-chairs or flat on the sand sunning themselves. . . . That's my fix. When I once get into an easy chair with a good book the disease is at its worst. I am unable to rise—until next mealtime. But the Doc says I'm improving and may be able to sit up long enough in a week or two to write that [Mark] Twain yarn for you.
The Twainian George Ade

This letter was published in The Twainian, I *(March, 1939), 2.*

George Hiram Brownell, editor of The Twainian, *persisted and Ade produced* One Afternoon with Mark Twain *later on in the year.*

Ade wrote Cyril Clemens, September 26, 1939 (InU): "Mr. Brownell padded my manuscript a little and all of the stuff was not written by me, but I have been willing to accept the authorship."

WPA—The Works Progress Administration—provided public works projects often for unskilled labor to employ those out of work. Ade refers to the WPA, as did many, to indicate goldbricking.

156 ❧ TO BURT CORY

Miami Beach, Florida
March 12, 1939

My dear Mr. Cory:

I am more than interested to have your letter and clipping. Also, I am amused to know that you remember about my connection with the ill-fated Morning News of LaFayette. It was started by Captain Jim Jefferson in 1887 so that we could have a republican morning paper in LaFayette during the campaign of 1888, but it died before the campaign opened. I remember Jim Davidson, the foreman, and also the printers you mentioned, Eddie Bass, Red Kern, Buckey Bolan and Clarence Jones. I was just a terrified cub reporter and all of them were my friends. I think Sam Leffew was in the bunch also. After the News flickered I went over to the Call and worked for Sep[timus] Vater for practically nothing a week until Harry Kramer gave me a job with his medicine company and I stayed with it until I left for Chicago. I am delighted to have a friendly message from a member of our old gang and to get your report on what happened to some of the boys in the composing room. Jim Davidson was quite an elderly man and probably has been dead for many years. If Tom Burt is still living he must be quite old by this time. You ask me if I remember the Wise [Saloon] across from the Lahr House. I certainly remember it even if I did not get over there very often. It was a tough dump. Thank you for remembering me with such a cheerful message and you have my best wishes.

GA:B
InLP

Sincerely,
George Ade

Burt Cory was a substitute typesetter on the Lafayette Morning News.

157 ❧ TO ELMER ELLIS

Hazelden
Brook, Indiana
May 4, 1939

My dear Mr. Ellis:

I am interested to have your letter in regard to Finley Peter Dunne. We always called him "Pete." I knew him for many years in Chicago and saw him once in a while or heard from him after he moved to New York. He was a very good editorial writer and used beautiful English. He greatly admired Robert Louis Stevenson and Cardinal [John Henry] Newman. By mere accident, he began writing the Dooley sketches which made him famous. I think he would have preferred being an essayist or commentator. He was lively in conversation and had a scorching wit. He was inclined to be a little combative and held very positive views. He was a very interesting person. If you want to learn more about him, I suggest that you try to get in touch with some members of the Whitney family in New York. The elder [William Collins] Whitney, who was in [Grover] Cleveland's cabinet, admired Dunne and so did Payne Whitney and Harry Payne Whitney. You may know that Payne Whitney left him five hundred thousand dollars. H. J. Whigham still living in New York knew Pete very well. I somewhat lost track of him in the later years of his life, but I always had a great respect for him and a real admiration.

I am, with best wishes,
GA:JSR
InLP

Sincerely,
George Ade

Elmer Ellis was collecting material for Mr. Dooley's America A Life of Finley Peter Dunne *(New York: 1941).*

William Collins Whitney was secretary of the Navy under Grover Cleveland. When Whitney acquired the New York Morning Telegraph *he made Dunne editor and gave him one-third interest in the paper. When Harry Payne Whitney acquired his father's estate in 1904 he disagreed with Dunne and bought the editor's interest in the* Telegraph. *Ellis, pp. 187–89.*

Payne Whitney, another son of W. C. Whitney, with Francis Garnan and Dunne tried to save Colliers, *1918–19. When Robert Collier died he bequeathed his equity in the magazine to his friends, who gave the bequest to Collier's widow. Ellis, pp. 251–55.*

H. J. Whigham managed The Metropolitan Magazine *for owner Harry Payne Whitney. In 1911 Dunne did "From the Bleachers" for Whigham. This series of articles provides a key to the author's personal opinions. Ellis, pp. 240–41.*

158 ❧ TO WILLIAM FRED KURFESS

Hazelden
Brook, Indiana
May 16, 1939

Dear Fred,
I am interested to have your letter and delighted to learn that the broadcast over WLW came through alright. I think I have learned a little about broadcasting. I no longer stand close to the "mike" and shout. I move back a little and try to specialize on enunciation rather than noise.

This morning, Bill Rathbun drove up here with the rather alarming news that Nellie [Rathbun] had undergone two operations since arriving at the hospital. Naturally, I am disturbed and a little alarmed. Bill did not seem to know the exact nature of the operation and he was awaiting a later report from his father. I believe Jim [Rathbun] is due at Kentland today to sign up the diplomas for the high school graduates. Perhaps I shall hear from him later on.

You ask if I knew Orson Welles. I suppose you know that he is my namesake. He was named after me and Ort Wells and his full name is George Orson Welles. Ort and I were on a West Indies trip with Mr. and Mrs. Dick Welles of Kenosha. We became very friendly. Mrs. Welles said she was expecting a little stranger and if it turned out to be a boy, she would name him after or for us, take your choice. In due time, we received word that the baby was a boy and had been christened George Orson Welles. We did not suspect that our namesake would turn out to be a celebrity. I have not seen him since he was a small boy, but he has called on Ort several times in Chicago and, I believe, touched him once or twice.

I am interested to learn of your plans regarding Jimmy [Kurfess]. I have heard of the Todd School and I have reason to believe that it is alright. I suppose Jim [Rathbun] will keep me informed regarding Nellie, but if he is too fussed or busy, I will be glad to get word from you.

Best wishes to Ardis [Ade Kurfess] and the boys.

GA:JSR
K

Sincerely,
George Ade

Orson Welles, a young producer, narrated "Invasion from Mars," October 30, 1938. The realism of the show, intended as a Halloween joke, terrorized the nation.

159 ❧ PLANS FOR HAZELDEN "CELEBRITY" NIGHTS

Hazelden Country Club
Brook, Indiana
June 7th, 1939

Well, our first party in honor of a visiting notable, the one for Bob Zuppke on May 24th, was a terrific success. We had an attendance of 100 with plenty of singing and good fellowship and Bob stood the boys on their heads. We want to pull one of these parties each month. The next one will have to be on June 14th because of bookings at the club house later in the month.

I have tried to get either "Chick" Evans or "Red" Grange for the June party but without success. We don't want to miss a month and so, rather reluctantly, after talking with several members, I am offering myself as a pinch-hitter. Of course, I am not a visiting celebrity. I am just one of the neighbors and another club member. But, I am wondering if you and the other members would not be interested in a parade of the celebrities who have visited Hazelden since 1905. Our list of visitors is rather amazing. It includes William Howard Taft, Warren G. Harding, Charles Warren Fairbanks, Tom Marshall, Uncle Joe Cannon, Booth Tarkington, Harry Leon Wilson, George Barr McCutcheon, Kin Hubbard, Will Hays, Harry S. New, Albert J. Beveridge, Tom Meighan, Elsie Janis, and dozens of others. I have thought that you might be interested and amused to hear stories about them. If so, come to the party on Wednesday evening of next week.

We will assemble at my home and dinner will be served about 6:30 at the usual price, seventy-five cents. I hope that many of you will show up. I know what they say about a prophet in his own country. What's more, I am no spell-binder as compared with Zuppke. But I do believe I can tell you some interesting things about the head-liners I have entertained.

I am keeping my fingers crossed hoping that the party will not be too much of a flop. Make your reservation at once with Jim Montgomery, Brook; Al Cast, Kentland; Louis Engle, Fowler; Bruce Hornbeck, Goodland; John Colbourne, Morocco; Claude Hedworth, Remington; Peach Leopold, Rensselaer; John Bond, Earl Park.

Now, and this is *Important*. We have booked John T. McCutcheon and Gen. Charles G. Dawes for July 19th, Kenesaw M. Landis for August 16th, Nobel Kizer and the entire football coaching staff at Purdue for September 13th and "Chick" Evans for October 11th. We are holding in reserve some other celebrities and hope to greet them next year. Let's make each one of these parties a whooping success. I am hoping to see you about 6 P. M. on Wednesday evening of next week, the 14th.

George Ade
President

InLP

160 ❧ TO E. R. MASTERSON

Hazelden
Brook, Indiana
July 6, 1939.

Dear Mr. Masterson:

Your letter arrived after some delay. I knew Bat Masterson for many years and while talking to him one night in El Paso in 1896 I was surprised to learn that he had been born in the "old town" section of Watseka, Illinois, only fifteen miles from where I was born at Kentland, Indiana. I have talked with him by the hour about his experiences at Dodge City and I have listened in while he and Eddy Foy told of those good old days, Eddy being a song and dance man at one of the theaters. I had a very high regard for Bat who was very kind, gentle and absolutely honest and never bothered any one who didn't bother him. Of course, you knew that he and Col. [Theodore] Roosevelt were great friends and several times I talked with the Colonel about Bat. At this time I cannot go into the details but I shall be glad at some later time to give you in detail some of my talks with your uncle.

I am, with best wishes

Sincerely,
George Ade

InLP

E. R. Masterson was a grand nephew of Bat Masterson, the famous gun man.

Ade wrote to the Houghton Mifflin Co., September 10, 1932 (InLP), requesting a picture of Bat Masterson: "I was in El Paso just after Pat Garrett killed Billy the Kid and I saw plenty of bad men. . . . Eddie Foy, the famous comic, played in Dodge City for a long time, at one of the Honka-tonks [*sic*] when "Bat" was there. One night I sat between them for hours and I heard wonderful stuff regarding Dodge City."

Houghton Mifflin published Stuart Lake's Wyatt Earp, Frontier Marshall, *1931. Eddie Foy and Alvin F. Harlow,* Clowning Through Life *(New York: 1928), pp. 98–147, describe the actor's Dodge City days.*

161 ⁂ TO CYRIL CLEMENS

Hazelden
Brook, Indiana
July 7, 1939

Dear Mr. Clemens,
I have your postcard in which you ask me to recall what happened at the Republican Convention of 1912 in connection with Warren G. Harding. I attended the convention as a spectator and also as a rooter for Theodore Roosevelt. I was infuriated by the speech which Harding made. He compared Roosevelt with Benedict Arnold. I knew then and I know now that a majority of the delegates properly elected were in favor of Roosevelt. He was deliberately robbed of the nomination. When he walked out of the convention, he took with him a majority of the bona fide delegates. The Progressive party or the Bull Moosers turned out to be a rather strange conglomeration of odds and ends, but I still believe that Roosevelt was

justified in refusing to accept the nomination of [William Howard] Taft. It is all ancient history. Some of my standpat friends still hold it against me because I supported Roosevelt, but I still think that I was right. I still think that Harding's speech was a contemptible specimen of hide-bound party politics.

I am, with best wishes.

Sincerely,
George Ade

InU

162 TO EVERETT WATKINS

Hazelden
Brook, Indiana
July 7, 1939

Dear Everett:
I am interested to have your letter. Whatever you heard about the cyclone didn't begin to tell the story. The darn thing nearly ruined us. I am enclosing a bulletin which tells something about the storm and another regarding our Country Club.

You ask regarding "The College Widow." Well, as I look back to 1905, I realize that I was either very courageous and far-sighted or else very foolhardy. I wanted to write a play dealing with college life and football. No play dealing with those two subjects had ever been produced on the American stage. Henry W. Savage, who had been producing my plays, and many other wise people connected with the theater were of the opinion that the general playgoing public was not keenly interested in under-graduates or college athletics. I thought they might be if we treated the college students as human beings instead of little tin gods and produced a comedy instead of a melodrama. I did not make the mistake of picking out a big school, such as Harvard or Yale or Princeton. When I wrote the play, I had Wabash in mind. It is a sectarian school for men in a fairly small city and small enough to have its local characters and a provincial coloring. I tried to put into the play a lot of interesting "types" and evidently I succeeded. I wrote the play in three weeks about mid-summer in 1905 and it went into rehearsal in New York about August first. Strangely enough, my newspaper and theatrical friends who attended rehearsals did not show any enthusiasm for the play. I felt in my bones that they thought it was all about something in which most people were not greatly interested. We went down to Washington for a try-out week very early in September.

The opening was at the Columbia theater. Everybody connected with the enterprise was very dubious and apprehensive. We had attended so many rehearsals during which the lines were spoken to empty benches that the dialogue seemed to have lost all sense and flavor. I remember that on the afternoon of the opening, some of my fraternity brothers came to me and asked me to attend a reception in my honor after the opening performance. I told them that after the opening performance, I might be up in my room hiding under the bed or else floating in the Potomac River. There is no other terror so extreme as that surrounding a "first night." We had about two-thirds of a house. Congress was not in session and the weather was rather warm. The curtain went up and I began to pace up and down the strip of carpet back of the parquette. The first act was supposed to introduce the characters and start the story, but it was not supposed to contain much comedy. My first happy surprise came when the people began to laugh and applaud during the first act. I felt encouraged. The second act went with a bang and was followed by a lot of applause. The third act, if I do say it myself, was a knock-out. It was a very short act dealing with all the thrills of a big football game. There was plenty of action and cheering and people rushing in and out of the main entrance to the playing field, all in a fine frenzy. The climax was the touchdown and the appearance of the players and their friends holding the hero aloft. Well, after that third act, I had to go before the curtain and make a speech. Just at my right, as I stood on the edge of the stage, was a box containing Admiral and Mrs. [George] Dewey and General and Mrs. Fred Grant. I thanked the audience and I said I hoped their applause was sincere. Admiral Dewey stood up in his box and said, "George, it's alright!" I saluted him and said, "Admiral, God bless you for them kind words"! Yes, the play was a hit in Washington and a hit when we opened up the Garden Theater in New York a week later. We didn't have to change any of the lines or do any revising. The play remained at the Garden until the following summer and next year it was being played by three companies. It turned out to be my meal ticket. Just one year after I brought out "The College Widow" at the Garden, another play of mine called "The Bad Samaritan" was produced at the same theater. My newspaper and theatrical friends who attended rehearsals laughed their heads off at the so-called comedy lines and said all of my stuff was great. The play was one of the most dismal flops in history. It lasted one week. Sometimes I think that the wise birds are not always the most dependable prophets.

Well, Everett, I hope this is what you want. It may not be very thrilling, but it is true. You have my best wishes at all times.

GA:JSR Sincerely,
InLP George Ade

Everett Watkins was assigned to the Washington, D.C., office of the Indianapolis Star.

163 TO WILLIAM H. BOLTON

Hazelden
Brook, Indiana
July 17, 1939

My dear Mr. Bolton,

I am interested and amused to have your letter. It seems that an author cannot think up a name without using a name that is already in the directory. When I called the football player in "The College Widow," Billy Bolton, I simply picked the name out of thin air. I thought that Bolton was a good solid American name and that "Billy Bolton" seemed to suggest a young man who might be a football player. I am glad that he did not do anything in the play to discredit you. Some of the Princeton men balled me out for giving the name of Witherspoon to the old Fluff who was President of Atwater College. I had overlooked the fact that the original President of Princeton was a Witherspoon. Many years ago, I wrote a book about a negro bootblack named "Pink Marsh." Later on, I discovered, to my horror, that one of the most popular members of the Chicago Club was named Marshal and his nickname was Pink, because of the high color which he had cultivated through high living. In a play for William H. Crane, I named a gold miner Cal Higbie. That was the name of Mark Twain's old partner at Virginia City. I had the name in the back of my head as a miner but I did not know it. When I fished out the name, I thought I was creating a name. I believe that even Mark Twain discovered, after he had put Mulberry Cellars into the "Gilded Age" that there really was a bird by that name. I used a great many different names and tried not to libel anyone. I am glad that in your case I picked out a hero instead of a villain. Thank you again for your friendly and interesting letter.

GA:JSR Sincerely,
InLP George Ade

John Witherspoon accepted the presidency of the College of New Jersey (Princeton) in 1768. He was the sixth president of the college.

Ade wrote Father and the Boys, *1908, for William H. Crane. Charles Dudley Warner suggested the name of Eschol Sellers to Mark Twain. Twain objected because Warner knew a farmer by that name, but used the name. Another Eschol Sellers objected when the book appeared, and Twain decided that he would change the name to Mulberry Sellers.* The Autobiography of Mark Twain, *ed. Charles Neider (New York: 1959), p. 20.*

164 ☙ TO JOHN EDGAR HOOVER

Hazelden
Brook, Indiana
August 8, 1939

Dear Mr. Hoover,
I am more than glad to have the annual report of your Bureau. It is a model of compactness and tells a lot in a very few pages. You and your associates have certainly made a record of which you may well be proud.

I suppose you operate what might be called a glorified detective agency. You are different from other detective agencies with which I have been familiar because you play no favorites. All criminals look alike to you. It happens that I knew William A. Pinkerton. He managed a very successful detective agency; however, he made no effort to apprehend criminals except those who committed offenses against his clients. He represented the organized bankers. A good many safe blowers made it a rule not to rob any safe or vault which bore the protective label of the organized bankers. Bill Pinkerton got most of his information regarding bank robberies from the safe blowers with whom he was on friendly terms. They were always ready to snitch on the other boys in order to get immunity for themselves. It was a strange situation, this secret partnership between the Pinkerton Agency and a certain group of law breakers who were playing safe. In the old days in Chicago, I came into close contact with the partnership existence between crooks, police, and police court magistrates. Such a partnership still exists in some cities. I am glad to learn that you and your boys are doing your best to break it up. Your personal crusade against crime is sure to bring good results. You are doing a whale of a job and earning the respect and the confidence of all intelligent citizens.

I am, with best wishes.

Sincerely,
George Ade

InLP

J. Edgar Hoover was the head of the Federal Bureau of Investigation, 1929–1972.

165 ☙ TO CYRIL CLEMENS

Miami Beach, Florida
February 1, 1940

Dear Mr. Clemens:

I have your card requesting something about Mark Twain and his antidotes [*sic*]. I wish I could recall some of the things he told me when I visited him along about 1902. He was greatly amused because a woman friend of his was trying to translate some of my "Fables" into French. He did not think she could do it. Robert Underwood Johnson once gave me a sentence from Mark Twain which I never have encountered in his writings. He said that Mark Twain said that "bacon would improve the flavor of an angel." I heard him make an address at the celebration of his 70th birthday anniversary at the big party given by George Harvey. Both were good story tellers but I was much more familiar with [James Whitcomb] Riley and had a tremendous admiration for him. I sat down and talked with Mark Twain only once.

I am, with best wishes

Sincerely,
George Ade

InU

166 ☙ TO DAVID W. HAZEN

Hazelden
Brook, Indiana
March 29, 1940

My dear Mr. Hazen:

I am interested to have your recent letter and I am especially amused to read the comment on me by Hamlin Garland. He said that I looked "pale and grey" in 1916. That was twenty-four years ago. He should see me now. I am possibly a little paler and a little greyer but I am still up and around. When I got out my first book, the publisher, Herbert S. Stone of Chicago, went to Garland, without my knowledge and consent, and asked him to write an introduction to the book. Garland, who took himself very seriously, decided that he had better not sponsor my work because he was not sure that I was sufficiently "lit'ry and realistic". He and I never hit it off. He was simply burdened with a rather gloomy sense of his own importance and I think he was absolutely devoid of a sense of humor. When he founded a Club called the "Cliff Dwellers," I went in and stayed for awhile but I never enjoyed being in the place because Garland was usually there entirely surrounded by solemnity and dignity. He wrote some good stuff but he was never a playmate, if you know what I mean.

I am interested to read your comments on Edgar Lee Masters. I agree with you that he worked overtime on being candid and realistic.

The weather here has been all right for two or three weeks and I rather regret that I will be compelled to depart for the farm on April 15th but I am hoping against hope that the weather, which has been somewhat dreadful in Indiana, will be a little improved by that time. I thank you for your interesting message and I am always glad to hear from you.

Sincerely,
George Ade

InLP

David W. Hazen had visited Hazelden and did an excellent piece on Ade's reminiscences, "George Ade . . . Hoosier Hospitality Personified," Sunday [Portland] Oregonian, *Dec. 13, 1936.*

Hazen had read Hamlin Garland's My Friendly Contemporaries A Literary Log (New York: 1932), *pp. 131–32, and reported Garland's recollection.*

167 TO HENRY W. MARSHALL

Hazelden
Brook, Indiana
April 29, 1940

My dear Henry,

I hope you will not think I am talking out of turn if I venture to write you a friendly letter in behalf of the candidacy of Charley Halleck. I know that you have a high regard for his ability and approve of his record because I was informed some time ago by Jim Rathbun that you favored him for the U. S. Senate. I learned upon good authority that Charley does not think it advisable to come out at this time as a candidate for the Senate. You may be a little disappointed at his decision, but I think you will agree that he should be permitted to make up his own mind. He is in Washington and cannot take any part in the campaign at present, and I learn that he is a little disturbed by certain developments. Young Fred Landis of Logansport came out as a candidate on the assumption that Charley would be a candidate for the Senate. He is remaining in the field largely, I think, because of encouragement he is receiving from advocates of the [Francis E.] Townsend Plan. If you do not know the Landis boy, I may tell you, in strict confidence, that he has none of the dynamic qualities of his Dad. He is rather diffident and timid and has no ability as a speaker. The boy is trying to travel on the family name. I have met him out here at my home two or three times and I am a very good friend of his uncle, Kenesaw and I am reluctant to come out publicly and say anything against him, largely because of the fact that I have always been most friendly with all of the Landis family. But, it would be a calamity if he should defeat Charley Halleck. I don't think he has a chance in the world, but I learn that Charley is somewhat alarmed because Landis is playing ball with the Townsend bunch. You and I know that the Townsend plan is cock-eyed, fantastic, and absolutely unworkable. However, the promise of easy money does appeal to many people of short vision and secondary intelligence. Townsend has many followers in this part of the district and his followers are organized in a great many towns near here. In view of this situation, I think it behooves every loyal Republican to give his active support to Charley Halleck. Perhaps I am wrong, but I suspect that you have been a little lukewarm for him because he has shown no disposition to join in the movement to oust the present

District Chairman, Morrison Rockhill of Warsaw. I suggest that he is not inclined to openly oppose Rockhill because of the fact that a large majority of the County Chairmen in the District are not unfriendly to Rockhill. If you do not approve of Rockhill, I have enough confidence in your judgment to believe that he is not the man for the place, but, at the same time, I can hardly blame Charley Halleck for not wishing to precipitate a battle. What I am leading up to, Henry, is that I hope that you will find it possible to give your very active support to Charley Halleck. He is in Washington and the Townsendites are sneaking up on him. His friends should rally to his support. When I heard that he might be a candidate for the Senate, I felt that I would be glad to support him. Since I learned that he does not wish to enter the senatorial race, I am ready to approve of his decision to remain in Congress. I think it is most important that he should remain in Congress. I am hoping that you will agree with me that, regardless of minor differences of opinion, we should give him our loyal support. You control the two most influential newspapers in the district and I am hoping to goodness that you will decide to whoop it up for Charley Halleck. If the general layout does not suit you that can be changed later. The fact remains that Halleck is our best bet and deserves more than a half-hearted support. I hope you agree with me. Best wishes.

GA:JSR — Sincerely,
InLP — George Ade

Henry W. Marshall was the editor of the Lafayette Journal and Courier.

Frederick Landis, Sr., was a representative from Indiana who was one of the organizers of the Progressive Party, 1912.

Charles Halleck was elected to fill the vacancy caused by the death of Congressman-elect Landis in 1934. Halleck served in Congress, 1935–1968.

Dr. Francis Townsend's remedy for the Depression was to give everyone over sixty federal pensions of $200 a month "on condition that they spend the money as they get it." See Arthur M. Schlesinger, The Age of Roosevelt, *3 (Cambridge: 1960), 29–33.*

Kenesaw Mountain Landis, a former judge, was commissioner of baseball, 1920–1944.

168 TO CYRIL CLEMENS

Hazelden
Brook, Indiana
June 5, 1940

Dear Mr. Clemens,
I will try to answer your questions. I felt sure that [William] McKinley would be nominated in 1896 because he was the logical candidate and had a campaign fund and was taking orders from Mark Hanna and H. H. Kohlsaat, two clever managers.

Regarding the Rotary Clubs, I have spoken before them several times and I am an honorary member. I think the organization is alright and that Sinclair Lewis was all wet when he tried to poke fun at the small town booster. This type of booster has done a lot of good.

You ask about [James Whitcomb] Riley. I knew him very well for several years and appeared on a program with him once but I never introduced him.

Regarding Cordell Hull, I fully endorse his foreign trade treaties and I admire his general conduct of the State Department. I think he is a sincere and honest old bird, not too greatly contaminated by New Deal Fallacies. He is a little old but if we must have a Democratic President I would prefer him to some of the other candidates that are mentioned, including the present incumbent!

I am, with best wishes.
GA:JSR
InU

Sincerely,
George Ade

Ade alludes to Sinclair Lewis' Babbitt, *1922.*
Cordell Hull was secretary of state, 1933–1944.

169 TO CYRIL CLEMENS

Hazelden
Brook, Indiana
September 13, 1940

Dear Mr. Clemens,
I have your postcard of inquiry. I am very strong for Mr. [Wendell]

Willkie but I most certainly am not going to take the stump for him or anyone else. I appeared at Convocation in the vast Music Hall at Purdue night before last and I am quite sure that my act was a flop. I wouldn't get very far as a stump speaker. For one thing, I am a semi-invalid and I must take things easy. That is why I probably will not find it possible to accept your invitation to lunch or supper.

I am not sure regarding the first book I ever read. It may have been by Oliver Optic or it may have been ROUGHING IT by Mark Twain. The latter was certainly one of the first books that I read after I was old enough. I trust you are well and happy.

GA:JSR Sincerely,
InU George Ade

Ade sent the following bulletin to friends endorsing Wendell Willkie's candidacy for president:

Bulletin from George Ade, Brook, Indiana, August 9, 1940.

James W. Carr, head of the Riley Memorial Hospital in Indianapolis, wrote me as follows on July 31, 1940.

"In a conversation with Wendell Willkie a few days ago, he expressed the hope that you were for him. In the light of his conversation, I am sure he would appreciate a letter if you care to write one."

Under the circumstances, I felt justified in sending the following telegram to Wendell Willkie at Colorado Springs, Colo. on August 3:

"James Carr of Indianapolis says you hope I am for you stop I was for you one hundred percent long before Philadelphia Convention stop I was completely converted by your logical analysis of New Deal stop my friend Charley Halleck and I are equally confident of your election. Best wishes."

I was pleased to receive the following response by wire on August 7:

"Thank you for your gracious wire. I appreciate it very much.
Wendell Willkie"

Needless to add that I am more strongly for him now than ever before.

InK George Ade

170 ☙ TO MEREDITH NICHOLSON

Miami Beach, Florida
December 1, 1940

My dear Nicholson:

I am delighted to have your letter and to learn that you approved of my Purdue speech on Mr. [James Whitcomb] Riley. I tried to tell the truth about him but, of course, I had to enthuse a little. I couldn't help it. He was the most interesting human being I ever knew. You knew him much better than I did but I saw a great deal of him in his latter years. I am especially interested to know what you say about his drinking habits. I heard him refer, once in a while, to the fact that he had fought various battles with the Demon Rum but, believe it or not, I never saw him take a drink and I never saw him after he had taken a drink. So as far as my personal observation is concerned, his conduct would have been approved by any member of the W. C. T. U. I am convinced with you that most of the fellows who told about getting drunk with Riley were just plain liars. I am glad you approved of what I said regarding his non-bohemianism. You are right in saying that he had a great sense of personal dignity. I always called him "Mr. Riley" and I never heard anyone call him "Jim." There was only one Riley and I doubt if we shall ever see another.

You will note by the heading that I am in Florida and I plan to remain here until April. The weather just now is lovely. There is every indication that we will have a very busy season here. I am taking the liberty of enclosing to you a little piece concerning Mark Twain in one of his more eruptive moods. Thank you again for your very friendly letter. You have my best wishes at all times.

GA:B Sincerely,
Enclosure George Ade
InLP

Meredith Nicholson pursued a diplomatic career in the 1930s. From 1938–1941 he was an envoy at the legation at Managua, Nicaragua. Nicholson was particularly glad to get news of home from Ade.

171 ❧ TO GEORGE C. SHANKS

Hazelden
Brook, Indiana
April 21, 1941

Dear Mr. Shanks,
I am interested to have your letter. Regarding Mark Twain, I am disposed to pay him the same compliment that he once paid to one of my books in a letter to William Dean Howells. I will quote him and say that my admiration for Mark Twain has overflowed all limits, all frontiers. He is our great master humorist. If I were to name the book I like best I would have to divide my vote between "Life on the Mississippi" and "Huckleberry Finn." I am enclosing a copy of the letter to Mr. Howells.

I am, with best wishes,
Ga;jsr
InLP

Sincerely,
George Ade

Mark Twain's letter to William Dean Howells, July 22, 1908, praising Ade's Pink Marsh *was printed in Ade's* One Afternoon With Mark Twain, *1939.*

172 ❧ TO CLARENCE BUDINGTON KELLAND

Hazelden
Brook, Indiana
May 26, 1941

My dear Bud Kelland,
On Saturday, June 21st, 1941, there will be held here at my home, two miles east of Brook, Indiana a meeting of the friends and admirers of Mark Twain. The purpose of the meeting will be to effect a national organization which will endeavor to be a permanent warehouse of information concerning the life and writings of Mark Twain. Knowing that you are one of the steadfast admirers of Samuel Clemens, I am writing this letter to invite you to attend the meeting. My name is attached to the invitation which has been sent out but the whole plan for the organization has been inspired and created by George H. Brownell and Franklin J. Meine, of Chicago. Mr. Brownell's address is 5830 West Erie St., Chicago. If you

cannot attend the meeting on June 21st, will you be good enough to send to me or to him some comment on the plans we have in mind? We hope that the comment will be favorable. I know that Mr. Brownell and Mr. Meine are prompted by a sincere and somewhat overwhelming admiration for Mark Twain. Come to the meeting if you can. If not, send us your blessing.

GA:JSR Sincerely,
InLP George Ade

Clarence Budington Kelland was a prolific novelist and short story writer. He is best remembered as the creator of Scattergood Baines.

The Mark Twain Society of Chicago was founded in 1939. In 1941 it became the Mark Twain Society of America. Ade was the first president.

173 TO ROBERT EDMUND SHERWOOD

Hazelden
Brook, Indiana
June 7, 1941

Dear Mr. Sherwood,

I am glad to have your letter and I am more than grateful for the copy of your book. I have read it all the way through and enjoyed all of it. It happens that I have been a circus fan all my life. Away back in 1899 I traveled for several weeks with the Ringlings in the South. I have known some of the clowns mentioned in your book including Jules, Turnour, Al Miaco and Bobby Clark. Also, I was very well acquainted with a great clown and a clever pantomimist known as "Slivers." I knew Tony Denier in Chicago after he became a little old and rather fat and retired from the stage. I saw [P. T.] Barnum once and I knew Tody Hamilton. You will understand why I enjoyed your book. Your story in regard to meeting [Booth] "Tark"[ington] and his friends in Chicago is interesting because of the fact that soon after you met him he went on the water wagon and has been the world's champion total abstainer ever since. Permit me to thank you again for your friendly letter and the book.

GA:JSR Sincerely,
InLP George Ade

Ade acknowledges receipt of Robert Edmund Sherwood's Here We Are Again; Recollections of an Old Circus Clown *(Indianapolis: [1926]).*

Ade's travels with the Ringling Brothers Circus resulted in a series of twelve articles entitled "With the Elephant and the Clown in Dixie," which began appearing in his Chicago Record *column, October 25, 1899. See Russo, pp. 225–27. Ade also wrote several publicity pieces at John Ringling's request for local papers. In an interview Ade stated that he was released from this chore when he underestimated the number of elephants in the parade.*

174 ❧ TO ROB WAGNER

Hazelden
Brook, Indiana
Autumn, 1941

My dear Rob Wagner:

The following quip will have no meaning to one who is not familiar with the technique practiced by a rooster preceding a demonstration of gallantry. One evening James Whitcomb Riley and I were sitting in the background at a social affair, watching the antics of a mutual friend who was carrying on, in a very gay manner, with a bevy of attractive gals. I remarked to the beloved Hoosier poet that our friend seemed to be quite a ladies' man.

"Yes, indeed," said Riley. "Whenever he sees a good-looker he drops one wing and begins to run around in a circle."

The Script George Ade

Rob Wagner, editor of The Script, *published the letter November 8, 1941.*

175 ❧ TO AMY H. COOPER

Miami Beach, Fla.
Feb 1st–1942

My Dear Miss Cooper,

Enclosed is my contribution to your paper. I hope it is not too long. It is not very scholarly or instructive or even dignified but I hope it will serve your purpose.

Best wishes,
Sincerely,
George Ade

A Letter to the Foresman Banner
By George Ade

The school at Foresman is nearer my home, known as Hazelden, than any other educational institution and so I feel it is my neighborly privilege and duty to salute the boys and girls who are absorbing knowledge a mile and a half to the east. These youngsters edit a newspaper which is a credit to them and the school. When I was attending school at Kentland, away back yonder in the seventies and eighties, we didnt publish any newspapers. We didnt have any "faculty." We didnt play basket-ball or foot ball and we never had learned to stand up on our hind legs and let out a rah-rah. We specialized on the three R's—readin', writin' and 'rithmetic and we never had heard of the special courses which are provided at every important School, including Foresman. I understand you are no longer subject to corporal punishment. The teacher had a right to do some "licking" when I was young and I had to take a whipping with a hickory gad after I was in grammar school. All I did to deserve the punishment was make too much noise in going to my seat after recess was over. The memory of that humiliation still lingers with me. I dont think I deserved what I got. Many years after the painful incident, when I had become somewhat of a celebrity as the author of books and plays, the man who had licked me wrote from the far west that he was taking credit for starting me on my career. I wrote back and reminded him that he had raised welts on my legs, broken my heart and done his best to ruin me. I am sure that all sensible and humane people agree that sparing the rod no longer spoils the child.

I am hoping that your modern school has not done away with the spelling bees and the Friday afternoon debating sessions. They really helped to educate the juveniles of my generation. I always prided myself on my spelling. Once I attended a "spelling bee" at a country school house south of Kentland. I spelled down all of the contestants except a young School-ma'am and then I flunked out on the word "bruit" meaning "to noise about." The word was a new one on me but I made a feeble stab at it and retired as runner-up, while the School-ma'am was hailed as champion.

At that time Newton County was speckled with country schoolhouses. We didn't have the big centralized school buildings and the pupils didnt ride in buses. They walked. As compared with the country bumpkins of long ago the school children of today, including those at Foresman, are sophisticated, up-to-date and wise beyond their years, thanks somewhat to radio and moving pictures.

The little red school-house is a thing of the past but dont forget that it turned out some of our best people, including possibly your paw and maw and, certainly, your grandparents.
Courtesy Olive Cooper

This letter was published in the Foresman Banner, *February 1942.*

176 ⁂ TO JACK POWERS

Hazelden
Brook, Indiana
April 30, 1942

Dear Mr. Powers,
Perhaps I can give you some information which will enable you to compose a plaque regarding the White Chapel Club. The Club occupied two stories of a building on the alley between your hotel and the old Daily News office. It was made up mostly of newspaper men and it was very active during the nineties and especially along about 1893, the year of the Columbian Exposition. The President was Charlie Perkins, a great wit and a man of undying thirst, who was clerk in Judge Collins' Court. Among the members were Brand Whitlock, later Minister to Belgium; Finley Peter Dunne, who wrote the Dooley articles; Charlie Seymour, one of the great reporters of his day; Charlie Almy, Editor of the Evening Mail; Opie Read, famous as a novelist; Tom Powers and Horace Taylor, well known newspaper artists; Ben King, an expert on the piano and composer of quaint verses; Dr. John Spray, well known physician and veteran of the Civil War; Dr. Frank Rielly, Editor of the Morning News and later Health Commissioner; Judge John Pindiville, who presided over one of the Municipal Courts; Frederick Upham ("Grizzly") Adams, author and inventor; and the author of this letter. The club entertained Rudyard Kipling, Chauncey Depew, the members of the Clover Club of Philadelphia and many other notables. The Club was in session almost every evening and was noted for the witty observation made by some of the members and by some famous songs. It finally went into bankruptcy because it entertained royally and failed to pay the bills. You can get from Charles H. Dennis, still connected with the Daily News, a lot of detailed information regarding the club as he wrote some stories about it a few years ago. It was famous in its day and deserves a

plaque. I am sure that Mr. Dennis can give you the dates and names that you want. I am, with best wishes,

GA:JSR
InLP

Sincerely,
George Ade

Jack Powers was the general manager of the La Salle Hotel, Chicago. The White Chapel Club was founded in 1888. Although noted writers and artists belonged to this organization, the clubroom, decorated with coffin and weapons gathered by journalists on crime beats, was the scene of drinking bouts rather than literary conversation. Alson J. Smith, Chicago's Left Bank *(Chicago: 1953), pp. 6–7.*

177 ➳ TO MILDRED GILMAN

Hazelden
Brook, Indiana
June 16, 1942

My dear Mrs. Gilman,

I know you will forgive me for dictating this letter instead of writing it myself, but I think I have told you many times that I would rather saw a cord of wood than write a letter with a scratchy pen. Also, I know you will forgive me for sending a couple of items for your scrapbook. I just thought that you might want to think of something besides your affliction.

Words are usually inadequate. When I got the sad news over the telephone afterwards I was so upset and grieved and shocked that I could not think of any proper message to send you. I knew that you would understand how I felt and that any stereotyped expression on my part would be superfluous. I was so upset that I even forgot to send in an order for some flowers. Fortunately, Charlie Carson ordered some in my name. I suppose it is up to me to offer consolation and advice. I have the disposition to do so but I hardly know how to go about it. I am wondering if you can compel yourself to be somewhat of a fatalist or stoic. So many friends of mine have passed on in recent years that I have adopted a sort of philosophy in regard to their departure. I have come to recognize the fact that the moment after a friend of mine dies he is just as much in the past tense as he will be ten years from now. I convince myself that grieving over his loss will not do anybody any good. I accept the matter of his going as something that cannot be altered and has already happened and is therefore to be accepted as a fact which does not call for demonstrations of grief. I know you are in a terrible spot but I hope you can use a part of my hard-boiled philosophy. Probably what you need in the present emergency is a "squidge." Years ago Frank Daniels appeared in a comic opera as a king. He had for an attendant a "squidge," whose duty it was to do all the worrying for the king. When Mr. and Mrs. Al Laflin and I traveled in distant countries, we always hired a "squidge" the moment we arrived in a new town. His job was to stay with us and accept all the hardships and worries. It was a lot of fun and saved us a lot of woe and made some money for the "squidge." I think you should pass all of your problems over to some man in whom you have confidence. Perhaps it would be George Trude. Also, Charlie Carson is a good handy-man to have around. Don't worry about anything for a moment. Hand all of your worries over to some convenient "squidge." This may sound foolish but it really works out. Jim Rathbun is my "squidge." He solves all of the problems and I sit back without a wrinkle on my brow. All of which leads up to my saying that I am hoping that you will have your chin up and that you are refusing to be cast down too much by your great bereavement. To which I can only add that you have my best wishes at all times.

Sincerely,
George Ade

InLP

Mildred Evans Gilman, the author of Sob Sister, *1931, and other novels, had recently lost her husband, Dr. William T. Gilman.*

The Gilmans were among Ade's closest friends in later years.

Mrs. Gilman collected nine scrapbooks of Adeana (InLP).

178 ☙ TO JAMES D. RATHBUN

1331 14th Street
Miami Beach, Florida
Wednesday afternoon
Jan 6th—1943

Dear Jim—

Your letter written on New Years Day arrived this morning, which will give you some idea of the delay attending the delivery of nearly all mail. For instance, I have not yet received a copy of the *Brook Reporter* containing my article. I asked George Denham to send me some extra copies. Since writing the piece I have been worried by the fear that I may have become mixed in my dates but I am hoping that when I read the stuff again I will find it O.K. It is all true and I thought it would do no harm to reveal a chapter of unwritten history which I kept under cover for a good many years. xx Did you receive some time ago a box of rubber bands and a box of clips sent from here? Did you get a copy of The Reader's Digest Reader? Also, the book regarding Income Tax? xx I hope you received the picture of the big show in Burdine Stadium. It was something gorgeous and worth remembering xxx Yesterday I attended the weekly luncheon of the *Optimists* at Murray's restaurant on Lincoln Road, Miami Beach, and received a card as Honorary Member. I had already received an Honorary Membership from the Optimists of Hammond, Indiana. I am now a Rotarian, Kiwanian, Optimist and member of Exchange, all honorary memberships involving no initiation fees or dues. At the meeting yesterday I talked for about fifteen minutes, indulging in recollections of famous Hoosiers I had met, and, also, I recited the Microbe's Serenade and it seemed to be well received. Last evening I went to the Committee of 100 to hear a retired army man talk on Mechanized Might. His talk was somewhat technical but fairly interesting. I met many friends including Frank Shutts, formerly of Aurora, Indiana, and late owner of the Miami Herald. He is now the head of the local drive for a Community Chest and I permitted him to talk me into attending an organization meeting next week and making a speech in support of their campaign, which means that I will be hooked for a contribution but I think I will give the very modest sum of $25, the same as last year. I told Frank that I could not give a large amount and he said all he wanted was a speech but I know that any one who sponsors an enterprise is expected to donate something besides a few words of approval. Tomorrow I will probably attend the weekly meeting of Kiwanis. I find it convenient to attend these meetings in Miami Beach and they help to kill time and provide some entertainment and good-fellowship. I am in doubt about going to the Committee of 100 next week to listen to Channing Pollack. While I was in the play-writing game and when I scored my first failure with The Bad Samaritan, Pollack wrote a piece for a pulp magazine and roasted the tar out of me. He said that all of my plays had been punk and that I had been a mere flash-in-the-pan without any real license to write for the stage. In as much as The Sultan of Sulu, The County Chairman and The College Widow had been highly successful it struck me that his violent attack on me was sour grapes on his part because he had failed dismally about the same time with several plays produced in New York. I had never been a show-off and had remained modestly in the background while several plays had scored unmistakable hits and it seemed evident that he hated me because I, an upstart, from the Middle West had been successful while he had been failing. His article about me was so violent and spiteful and unprovoked that I put him down in my books as a stinker for all time to come. I hate his guts, even after all these years and I doubt if I can pretend to be polite to him, even now. After William H. Crane made a success with Father and the Boys, Mrs. Crane collected all the lovely notices we received in New York and mailed them to Pollack just to prove to him that he might be wrong once in a while. She knew a lot about him and despised him and took great joy in calling his attention to the fact that the public and the critics did not agree with him in regard to me. Perhaps I have a little Indian in me. It is hard to forgive any one who knifes you for no reason except that he is over-supplied with spleen. xx At present the weather is just a little cool. The mercury was down to about 50 this morning and the high wind today is just a little nippy but, up to date, we have had no really cold weather, nothing below 40. I have a couple of good letters from Fred [Kurfess] and also one today from George [Ade] Davis. Katie [Krue] and I are well and the new cook continues to give satisfaction.

Best wishes, Sincerely,

InK George Ade

George Ade Davis was Ade's favorite nephew.
Kate Krue was Ade's housekeeper.

179 ❧ TO JAMES D. RATHBUN

1331 14th Street
Miami Beach, Florida
Sunday Afternoon,
Jan 10th–1943

Dear Jim—

I have just been listening to the broadcast from the Tabernacle in Salt Lake City and the sound of the organ recalls the visit paid to the Tabernacle 35 years ago in company with my father, Col.

Roberts and Harry Davis and his wife, the first one. My father was so affected by the kind attentions of the elders and the rendition of his favorite hymns on the marvelous organ that he was almost ready to join the Mormon Church. He said to me, "I have been mistaken all my life. They are the nicest people in the world." He made this remark after he learned that the attractive young woman who held to his arm all day and made a fuss over him was a grand-daughter of Brigham Young! xxx My worst fears were realized when I received copies of the *Brook Reporter* and discovered that I had made the inexcusable blunder of fixing my story in 1910. I wrote the whole thing in a great hurry. If I had taken time to check up I would not have made such a stupid mistake. Every one knows or should know, that [William Howard] Taft was president in 1910 and [Theodore] Roosevelt was in Africa or just returning from there. The correct date must have been 1906. I marked in corrections and sent copies to several friends and relatives including Margaret, [Rathbun Harding] Adah [Randall Plugge] and Lucile [McCray Evans]. But my face is still red. I sent a wire to [George] Denham, apologizing for the error and I hope my explanation got into last week's edition xxx The new gas rationing rules have played hot with the Miami area. The race tracks and two of the dog tracks have gone out of business and I am sure the night clubs are starving to death. The Government has snoopers at the movie theatres and other amusement spots, including all night clubs to take down the license numbers of all cars parked in the immediate neighborhood of the forbidden areas and the owners of these cars are now threatened with a suspension of all ration cards. I have not heard from Mrs. [Mildred] Gilman since the blow fell. She was going high, wide & handsome on an extra allowance of gas secured for her through the influence of friends and she had taken a box at Hialeah for the season. I hope she proceeds cautiously from now on and does not get into trouble. xx Dr. Shaw has prescribed for me some kind of sleeping tablets to reduce blood pressure and improve my general condition. He warned me that they might upset me and make me feel miserable and dopy, and he was right. I am taking three a day as ordered but I feel as if I were about three jumps ahead of an epileptic convulsion. xx I went to the Kiwanis Club luncheon on Thursday and I am booked for the Exchange Club in Miami on Tuesday. I hope that the ban on "fraternal meetings" does not apply to these booster organizations. xxx With the new rationing in effect and because I want to be a law abiding citizen and observe the rules, I can see that I will spend most of my time at home from now on. I wish I had the ambition and the physical energy to take long walks. Walking would help to kill time and get me to near-by places of interest but I am so rickety in the hind legs that a trip to the corner and back is about the limit of my venturing forth and such a brief outing does not provide any excitement or change of scenery. xx I mailed to you yesterday my membership card in the A. A. A. because it goes with the car. I also sent some assorted information regarding Income Tax. All of the same probably being an old story to you. I have just checked up all entries in my check-book and discover, to my horror, that the total receipts from all sources, not counting the loan at Brook, amount to a grand total of $14,591.40. I have included a few doubtful items but they are for small amounts. I sent you figures for the final quarter of 1942 and I am hoping that you can, by some superior method of mathematics, reduce this total or that we may, later on, reduce it by claiming exemptions. By the way, in claiming exemptions this year you had better be cautious and not have too many arguments with Uncle Sam. We don't want to pay any more than we should rightfully pay but we may have to yield a few points even if we are not in the wrong. We are at war and must be prepared to stand the gaff. xx This morning the mercury was down to 50. The sun is shining brightly but the wind from the north west is nippy. We have a fire in the grate. xx I read *all* of the Will Irwin with much interest. Regards to all of the relatives. Best wishes, Sincerely,

InLP George Ade

Col. Roberts was one of Ade's secretaries.

180 ❧ TO WILLIAM J. REDDICK

[Miami Beach, Florida]
January 23, 1943

My dear Mr. Reddick:

I am interested to have your inquiry in regard to Charlie Case. He wrote the book to which you refer and which you must have acquired from the Herbert Jones Library. Charlie Case was a monologue artist of the nineties. He was an octoroon who attend[ed] college and law school and tried to practice law in Lockport, New York, a suburb of Buffalo. Because he was rated as a colored man, he did not succeed as a lawyer so he went on the stage and made a great success. He wrote all of his own stuff. His delivery was not very good but the material was wonderful. For some reason his life was not very happy and I think he was sensitive over the fact that he had failed as a lawyer and he finally committed suicide. I met him several times and admired him very much and did what I could to boost him. I am sure you will find the book out of the ordinary and very amusing. The man who joined with me presenting it to Herb Jones was Joe Reeve, my secretary in 1926.

I am, with best wishes

Sincerely,
George Ade

InLP

The book to which Ade refers is Charley Case, "Charley Case's Father," 1903. There is no record of the publication of the typescript pamphlet which contains Case's monologues.

Newspapers reported Case's death as an accident resulting from cleaning a gun, November 27, 1916.

181 ❧ NEWS LETTER FROM GEORGE ADE

Miami Beach, Florida
January 29th, 1943

I am writing this letter today, Friday, and copies will go out tomorrow. This has been a week of stepping out. On Wednesday evening I put on my dinner coat and attended a dinner of the Book-Fellows at the Urmey Hotel in Miami. A majority of the 150 "fellows" were gals. The dinner had a special interest for me because I met, for the first time, Edison Marshall, author of many novels, who was born in Rensselaer, Indiana, only 12 miles from Hazelden. We had a pleasant visit together. I contributed to the program the freak story by James Whitcomb Riley about the sea captain who wanted to play a game of chess. It made quite a hit. If you don't remember it, I will tell it to you sometime. Yesterday I attended the weekly luncheon of the Kiwanis, having been advertised as one of the attractions, so I repeated the Riley story and it really went over big. Also, I recited "The Microbe's Serenade." My entire offering was recorded by a sound machine and the record will be run off at the next meeting. Last evening I was a guest at the dinner opening a drive for the Community War Chest. No less than 500 people were seated at the tables in the very large and palatial club house of the

Women's Club in Miami. I was one of several speakers. We were entertained by musicians, vocal and instrumental, from the army and navy training camps and they were amazingly high-class. . . . . . My birthday comes on February 9th. I have written some observations regarding my 77th anniversary and they will be released by the North American Newspaper Alliance on Sunday, February 7th. Also, I have sent a contribution to a new magazine, edited by Wythe Williams, entitled "Tough." I think it will be a worthy publication and probably do some good. It is intended to stiffen the morale of our fellow-citizens. . . . . .We continue to have real summer weather. A heavy rain-fall yesterday morning came when it was needed. I am meeting many interesting people these days. Like everyone else, I am surprised and pleased by the recent sensational developments in connection with our effort to put an everlasting Kibosh on the unspeakable Nazis and the ornery Japs.

Best wishes.
George Ade

InLP

Kelly, George Ade, *pp. 259–60, recounts the Riley story of the chess-playing captain.*

Ade's speech for the Miami Community Chest Drive was published in the Miami Herald, *January 29, 1943.*

Ade's birthday article appeared under a variety of titles in syndicated newspapers, cf., "Ade Laughs Off 77 Years: 'Chassis Decrepit but Carburetor Fine,' Says George Ade," the Indianapolis Star, *February 7, 1943; "At 77 I'm Still Trying to Kid Myself," the* Magazine of Sigma Chi, *February–March, 1943.*

182 ☙ TO JAMES D. RATHBUN

1331 14th Street
Miami Beach, Florida
Friday afternoon—
Feb 5th—1943

Dear Jim:

This is my day for dictating but in as much as I had a rather sleepless night and am feeling below par today I have asked Mrs. Boswell to postpone her visit until tomorrow. She lives out near Coral Gables and is employed each day at the Bath Club so she has to do a lot of miscellaneous bus riding in order to keep her appointments with me. I think you met her down here and will remember that she is a very attractive gal. Also she is a rapid shorthander and a good typist. xx I am enclosing a clipping which tells of the death of Charley Atkinson. You may have met him at the farm when he came down with the McCutcheons or possibly you ran into him down here. He was one of my good friends and I knew him for just about 50 years. He married one of the daughters of M. D. Wells, for many years the head of a big wholesale boot and shoe company. It seems to me you once told me that your father handled goods from the M. D. Wells Co. He was a wonderful person—handsome, amiable, highly intelligent, well-mannered and a gifted student of music with a knack for composing songs. In recent years, while spending his winters at Nassau, he organized a choir of Bahaman negroes and taught them singing. One morning in the early nineties he came to the hall bed-room, in the Buelden flat building at Peck Court & Michigan Avenue, where I was living with John McCutcheon. He wanted Mac to draw some pictures to be used as place cards at a dinner he was giving. Mac drew the pictures and Charley paid him $5, which was a lot of money in those days. We became friendly with him and he invited us to dinner at his home on Prairie Avenue. Mr. and Mrs. Howard Shaw lived next door to the Atkinsons and Mrs. Shaw was a sister of Mrs. Atkinson. Charley took us over to call on the Shaws. Evelyn was then a very young girl. When she learned that Mac was an artist she brought him a pad of paper and a pencil and crawled up on his lap and induced him to draw pictures for her. So Mac's future wife sat on his lap at their first meeting and the friendship thus established continued for many years and finally blossomed into romance & matrimony. Both of the Shaws and Mrs. Atkinson died quite a few years ago and now Charley, one of the finest gentlemen I ever knew, has passed on. I am wondering if Mac was at home to attend the funeral. He was planning to be in New Orleans this week to attend the wedding of John, Jr. In the same column of the New York Times with the story of Charley's death was the obituary of Fred Latham. He directed the producer of The Fair Co-Ed and The Old Town and also The Slim Princess, which Henry Blossom adapted from my story. I received a small royalty. Fred was an Englishman of heroic build, King Edward whiskers and the courtly manners of a titled aristocrat. It was a pleasure to work with him because he was considerate and courteous and he knew the technique of the stage and how to deal with the troupers. Please note that he lived to the ripe old age of *90!* xx I have read all parts of your letter with proper interest. You and the other boys certainly did a wholesale job of butchering. You were fortunate in finding a foreman to take John Elestrom's place. I dont know Ty Conn but I have been well acquainted with Tude Conn and thought well of him. xx The not-so-good news in regard to the soy bean crop does not come as a surprise. I have suspected all the time that the unharvested bean crop will have to be marked off as a total loss. Regarding your predictions as to corn I am more than delighted to learn that you may turn over a surplus of about $4000. If you can deliver this amount after taking up the vote and setting aside a reserve to meet emergencies I will be ready to admit that 1942 was a pretty good year. I am hoping that your final computation of the Income Tax may show a total of somewhat less than $4000 but of course, we want to follow directions and observe all of the new rules and if the calculations show that we must pay $4000 or thereabouts the only thing to do is pay it and do so cheerfully. xxx I have a deposit at the Continental Illinois $3212.22—Brook $149.09; Miami Beach, $132.82. If we get $4000 from our corn and the Carbide dividends for April 1st and July 1st remain the same, I will have in sight a grand total of about $9500. That should be enough to carry us until next winter, which may bring with it some problems we cannot solve in advance. I take it for granted that your figures made due allowance for your own compensation. xx Katie [Krue] suggests that our kitchen, the back stairway and the next bath room should be re-painted this spring if possible. Also, she says that the settee in the living room should be cleaned and given a new cover. Katie says that Nellie [Rathbun] can advise you regarding what needs to be done. Also, I understand that you are planning to have the kitchen of the [Timer] Lyons Cottage freshly painted. I hope you can let some one to attend to these jobs. Katie thinks we will have no rugs to be cleaned this spring. I suspect that you have not worked out any plan for shutting off the heat from parts of the house not used every day. I doubt if you can do so. Maybe we can use the fireplace and get along with less fuel oil. We certainly use a lot of it when we try to keep the whole house warm.

Best wishes, Sincerely,

InLP

George Ade

George Ade suffered a stroke, June 1943, which caused temporary paralysis of one arm and leg. James D. Rathbun then answered the author's correspondence. Ade wintered at home for the first time in twenty-five years. He suffered three heart attacks in one week, and on May 16, 1944, George Ade died. Brook storekeepers placed signs in their windows, May 20, which read "Gone to the Funeral." Everyone in the town of 880 went to Hazelden to pay his respects. Eulogies appeared across the nation. *Time* paid tribute succinctly:

"Home Is the Hoosier."

Index

Index

Index

Index

9 781557 531476